ɔn Data Analysis

Become an expert at using Python for advanced statistical
analysis of data using real-world examples

Magnus Vilhelm Persson

Luiz Felipe Martins

BIRMINGHAM - MUMBAI

Mastering Python Data Analysis

Publishing Month: June 2016

Production reference: 1230616

Published by Packt Publishing Ltd.

Livery Place

35 Livery Street

Birmingham

B3 2PB, UK.

ISBN 978-1-78355-329-7

www.packtpub.com

Credits

Authors

Magnus Vilhelm Persson
Luiz Felipe Martins

Reviewers

Hang (Harvey) Yu
Laurie Lugrin
Chris Morgan
Michele Pratusevich

Commissioning Editor

Akram Hussain

Acquisition Editor

Vinay Argekar

Content Development Editor

Arun Nadar

Technical Editors

Bharat Patil
Pranil Pathare

Copy Editor

Tasneem Fatehi

Project Coordinator

Ritika Manoj

Proofreader

Safis Editing

Indexer

Monica Ajmera Mehta

Graphics

Kirk D'Penha
Jason Monteiro

Production Coordinator

Nilesh Mohite

About the Authors

Magnus Vilhelm Persson is a scientist with a passion for Python and open source software usage and development. He obtained his PhD in Physics/Astronomy from Copenhagen University's Centre for Star and Planet Formation (StarPlan) in 2013. Since then, he has continued his research in Astronomy at various academic institutes across Europe. In his research, he uses various types of data and analysis to gain insights into how stars are formed. He has participated in radio shows about Astronomy and also organized workshops and intensive courses about the use of Python for data analysis.

You can check out his web page at `http://vilhelm.nu`.

This book would not have been possible without the great work that all the people at Packt are doing. I would like to highlight Arun, Bharat, Vinay, and Pranil's work. Thank you for your patience during the whole process. Furthermore, I would like to thank Packt for giving me the opportunity to develop and write this book, it was really fun and I learned a lot. There where times when the work was little overwhelming, but at those times, my colleague and friend Alan Heays always had some supporting words to say. Finally, my wife, Mihaela, is the most supportive partner anyone could ever have. For all the late evenings and nights where you pushed me to continue working on this to finish it, thank you. You are the most loving wife and best friend anyone could ever ask for.

Luiz Felipe Martins holds a PhD in applied mathematics from Brown University and has worked as a researcher and educator for more than 20 years. His research is mainly in the field of applied probability. He has been involved in developing code for open source homework system, WeBWorK, where he wrote a library for the visualization of systems of differential equations. He was supported by an NSF grant for this project. Currently, he is an associate professor in the department of mathematics at Cleveland State University, Cleveland, Ohio, where he has developed several courses in applied mathematics and scientific computing. His current duties include coordinating all first-year calculus sessions.

About the Reviewer

Hang (Harvey) Yu is a data scientist in Silicon Valley. He works on search engine development and model optimization. He has ample experience in big data and machine learning. He graduated from the University of Illinois at Urbana-Champaign with a background in data mining and statistics. Besides this book, he has also reviewed multiple other books and papers including *Mastering Python Data Visualization* and *R Data Analysis Cookbook both* by Packt Publishing. When Harvey is not coding, he is playing soccer, reading fiction books, or listening to classical music. You can get in touch with him at hangyu1@illinois.edu or on LinkedIn at http://www.linkedin.com/in/hangyu1.

www.PacktPub.com

For support files and downloads related to your book, please visit www.PacktPub.com.

Did you know that Packt offers eBook versions of every book published, with PDF and ePub files available? You can upgrade to the eBook version at www.PacktPub.com and as a print book customer, you are entitled to a discount on the eBook copy. Get in touch with us at service@packtpub.com for more details.

At www.PacktPub.com, you can also read a collection of free technical articles, sign up for a range of free newsletters and receive exclusive discounts and offers on Packt books and eBooks.

https://www2.packtpub.com/books/subscription/packtlib

Do you need instant solutions to your IT questions? PacktLib is Packt's online digital book library. Here, you can search, access, and read Packt's entire library of books.

Why subscribe?

- Fully searchable across every book published by Packt
- Copy and paste, print, and bookmark content
- On demand and accessible via a web browser

Free access for Packt account holders

If you have an account with Packt at www.PacktPub.com, you can use this to access PacktLib today and view 9 entirely free books. Simply use your login credentials for immediate access.

Table of Contents

Preface

The use of Python for data analysis and visualization has only increased in popularity in the last few years. One reason for this is the availability and continued development of a number of excellent tools for conducting advanced data analysis and visualization. Another reason is the possibility of rapid and easy development, deployment, and sharing of code. For these reasons, Python has become one of the most widely used programming and scripting language for data analysis in many industries.

The aim of this book is to develop skills to effectively approach almost any data analysis problem, and extract all of the available information. This is done by introducing a range of varying techniques and methods such as uni- and multi-variate linear regression, cluster finding, Bayesian analysis, machine learning, and time series analysis. Exploratory data analysis is a key aspect to get a sense of what can be done and to maximize the insights that are gained from the data. Additionally, emphasis is put on presentation-ready figures that are clear and easy to interpret.

Knowing how to explore data and present results and conclusions from data analysis in a meaningful way is an important skill. While the theory behind statistical analysis is important to know, to be able to quickly and accurately perform hands-on sorting, reduction, analysis, and subsequently present the insights gained, is a make or break for today's quickly evolving business and academic sector.

What this book covers

Chapter 1, *Tools of the Trade*, provides an overview of the tools available for data analysis in Python and details the packages and libraries that will be used in the book with some installation tips. A quick example highlights the common data structure used in the Pandas package.

Chapter 2, *Exploring Data*, introduces methods for initial exploration of data, including numeric summaries and distributions, and various ways of displaying data, such as histograms, Kernel Density Estimation (KDE) plots, and box plots.

Chapter 3, *Learning About Models*, covers the concept of models in data analysis and how using the cumulative distribution function and probability density function can help characterize a variable. Furthermore, it shows how to make point estimates and generate random numbers with a given distribution.

Chapter 4, *Regression*, introduces linear, multiple, and logistic regression with in-depth examples of using SciPy and statsmodels packages to test various hypotheses of relationships between variables.

Chapter 5, *Clustering*, explains some of the theory behind cluster finding analysis and goes through some more complex examples using the K-means and hierarchical clustering algorithms available in SciPy.

Chapter 6, *Bayesian Methods*, explains how to construct and test a model using Bayesian analysis in Python using the PyMC package. It covers setting up stochastic and deterministic variables with prior information, constructing the model, running the Markov Chain Monte Carlo (MCMC) sampler, and interpreting the results. In addition, a short bonus section covers how to plot coordinates on maps using both the basemap and cartopy packages, which are important for presenting and analyzing data with geographical coordinate information.

Chapter 7, *Supervised and Unsupervised Learning*, looks at linear regression, clustering, and classification with two machine learning analysis techniques available in the Scikit-learn package.

Chapter 8, *Time Series Analysis*, examines various aspects of time series modeling using Pandas and statsmodels. Initially, the important concepts of smoothing, resampling, rolling estimates, and stationarity are covered. Later, autoregressive (AR), moving average (MA), and combined ARIMA models are explained and applied to one of the data sets, including making shorter forecasts using the constructed models.

Appendix, *More on Jupyter Notebook and matplotlib Styles*, shows some convenient extensions of Jupyter Notebook and some useful keyboard shortcuts to make the Jupyter workflow more efficient. The matplotlib style files are explained and how to customize plots even further to make beautiful figures ready for inclusion in reports. Lastly, various useful online resources are listed and described.

What you need for this book

All you need to follow through the examples in this book is a computer running any recent version of Python. While the examples use Python 3, they can easily be adapted to work with Python 2, with only minor changes. The packages used in the examples are NumPy, SciPy, matplotlib, Pandas, statsmodels, PyMC, Scikit-learn. Optionally, the packages basemap and cartopy are used to plot coordinate points on maps. The easiest way to obtain and maintain a Python environment that meets all the requirements of this book is to download a prepackaged Python distribution. In this book, we have checked all the code against Continuum Analytics' Anaconda Python distribution and Ubuntu Xenial Xerus (16.04) running Python 3.

To download the example data and code, an Internet connection is needed.

Who this book is for

This book is intended for professionals with a beginner to intermediate level of Python programming knowledge who want to move in the direction of solving more sophisticated problems and gain deeper insights through advanced data analysis. Some experience with the math behind basic statistics is assumed, but quick introductions are given where required. If you want to learn the breadth of statistical analysis techniques in Python and get an overview of the methods and tools available, you will find this book helpful. Each chapter consists of a number of examples using mostly real-world data to highlight various aspects of the topic and teach how to conduct data analysis from start to finish.

Conventions

In this book, you will find a number of text styles that distinguish between different kinds of information. Here are some examples of these styles and an explanation of their meaning. Code words in text, database table names, folder names, filenames, file extensions, pathnames, dummy URLs, user input, and Twitter handles are shown as follows: "This code has the effect of selecting matplotlib stylesheet `mystyle.mplstyle`."

A block of code is set as follows:

```
gss_data = pd.read_stata('data/GSS2012merged_R5.dta',
                        convert_categoricals=False)
gss_data.head()
```

Any command-line input or output is written as follows:

```
python -c 'import numpy'
```

New terms and important words are shown in bold. Words that you see on the screen, for example, in menus or dialog boxes, appear in the text like this: "Here, you can check the box for **add a toolbar button to open the shortcuts dialog/panel**."

Warnings or important notes appear in a box like this.

Tips and tricks appear like this.

Reader feedback

Feedback from our readers is always welcome. Let us know what you think about this book-what you liked or disliked. Reader feedback is important for us as it helps us develop titles that you will really get the most out of.

To send us general feedback, simply e-mail feedback@packtpub.com, and mention the book's title in the subject of your message.

If there is a topic that you have expertise in and you are interested in either writing or contributing to a book, see our author guide at www.packtpub.com/authors.

Customer support

Now that you are the proud owner of a Packt book, we have a number of things to help you to get the most from your purchase.

Downloading the example code

You can download the example code files for this book from your account at `http://www.packtpub.com`. If you purchased this book elsewhere, you can visit `http://www.packtpub.com/support` and register to have the files e-mailed directly to you.

You can download the code files by following these steps:

1. Log in or register to our website using your e-mail address and password.
2. Hover the mouse pointer on the **SUPPORT** tab at the top.
3. Click on **Code Downloads & Errata**.
4. Enter the name of the book in the **Search** box.
5. Select the book for which you're looking to download the code files.
6. Choose from the drop-down menu where you purchased this book from.
7. Click on **Code Download**.

You can also download the code files by clicking on the **Code Files** button on the book's webpage at the Packt Publishing website. This page can be accessed by entering the book's name in the **Search** box. Please note that you need to be logged in to your Packt account.

Once the file is downloaded, please make sure that you unzip or extract the folder using the latest version of:

- WinRAR / 7-Zip for Windows
- Zipeg / iZip / UnRarX for Mac
- 7-Zip / PeaZip for Linux

The code bundle for the book is also hosted on GitHub at `https://github.com/PacktPublishing/Mastering-Python-Data-Analysis`. We also have other code bundles from our rich catalog of books and videos available at `https://github.com/PacktPublishing/`. Check them out!

Downloading the color images of this book

We also provide you with a PDF file that has color images of the screenshots/diagrams used in this book. The color images will help you better understand the changes in the output. You can download this file from `https://www.packtpub.com/sites/default/files/downloads/masteringpythondataanalysis_ColorImages.pdf`.

Errata

Although we have taken every care to ensure the accuracy of our content, mistakes do happen. If you find a mistake in one of our books-maybe a mistake in the text or the code-we would be grateful if you could report this to us. By doing so, you can save other readers from frustration and help us improve subsequent versions of this book. If you find any errata, please report them by visiting http://www.packtpub.com/submit-errata, selecting your book, clicking on the **Errata Submission Form** link, and entering the details of your errata. Once your errata are verified, your submission will be accepted and the errata will be uploaded to our website or added to any list of existing errata under the Errata section of that title.

To view the previously submitted errata, go to https://www.packtpub.com/books/content/support and enter the name of the book in the search field. The required information will appear under the Errata section.

Piracy

Piracy of copyrighted material on the Internet is an ongoing problem across all media. At Packt, we take the protection of our copyright and licenses very seriously. If you come across any illegal copies of our works in any form on the Internet, please provide us with the location address or website name immediately so that we can pursue a remedy.

Please contact us at copyright@packtpub.com with a link to the suspected pirated material.

We appreciate your help in protecting our authors and our ability to bring you valuable content.

Questions

If you have a problem with any aspect of this book, you can contact us at questions@packtpub.com, and we will do our best to address the problem.

1
Tools of the Trade

This chapter gives you an overview of the tools available for data analysis in Python, with details concerning the Python packages and libraries that will be used in this book. A few installation tips are given, and the chapter concludes with a brief example. We will concentrate on how to read data files, select data, and produce simple plots, instead of delving into numerical data analysis.

Before you start

We assume that you have familiarity with Python and have already developed and run some scripts or used Python interactively, either in the shell or on another interface, such as the Jupyter Notebook (formerly known as the **IPython notebook**). Hence, we also assume that you have a working installation of Python. In this book, we assume that you have installed Python 3.4 or later.

We also assume that you have developed your own workflow with Python, based on needs and available environment. To follow the examples in this book, you are expected to have access to a working installation of Python 3.4 or later. There are two alternatives to get started, as outlined in the following list:

- Use a Python installation from scratch. This can be downloaded from `https://www.python.org`. This will require a separate installation for each of the required libraries.
- Install a prepackaged distribution containing libraries for scientific and data computing. Two popular distributions are Anaconda Scientific Python (`https://store.continuum.io/cshop/anaconda`) and Enthought distribution (`https://www.enthought.com`).

Even if you have a working Python installation, you might want to try one of the prepackaged distributions. They contain a well-rounded collection of packages and modules suitable for data analysis and scientific computing. If you choose this path, all the libraries in the next list are included by default.

We also assume that you have the libraries in the following list:

- `numpy` and `scipy`: These are available at `http://www.scipy.org`. These are the essential Python libraries for computational work. NumPy defines a fast and flexible array data structure, and SciPy has a large collection of functions for numerical computing. They are required by some of the libraries mentioned in the list.
- `matplotlib`: This is available at `http://matplotlib.org`. It is a library for interactive graphics built on top of NumPy. I recommend versions above 1.5, which is what is included in Anaconda Python by default.
- `pandas`: This is available at `http://pandas.pydata.org`. It is a Python data analysis library. It will be used extensively throughout the book.
- `pymc`: This is a library to make Bayesian models and fitting in Python accessible and straightforward. It is available at `http://pymc-devs.github.io/pymc/`. This package will mainly be used in `Chapter 6`, *Bayesian Methods*, of this book.
- `scikit-learn`: This is available at `http://scikit-learn.org`. It is a library for machine learning in Python. This package is used in `Chapter 7`, *Supervised and Unsupervised Learning*.
- `IPython`: This is available at `http://ipython.org`. It is a library providing enhanced tools for interactive computations in Python from the command line.
- `Jupyter`: This is available at `https://jupyter.org/`. It is the notebook interface working on top of IPython (and other programming languages). Originally part of the IPython project, the notebook interface is a web-based platform for computational and data science that allows easy integration of the tools that are used in this book.

Notice that each of the libraries in the preceding list may have several dependencies, which must also be separately installed. To test the availability of any of the packages, start a Python shell and run the corresponding `import` statement. For example, to test the availability of NumPy, run the following command:

```
import numpy
```

If NumPy is not installed in your system, this will produce an error message. An alternative approach that does not require starting a Python shell is to run the command line:

```
python -c 'import numpy'
```

We also assume that you have either a programmer's editor or Python IDE. There are several options, but at the basic level, any editor capable of working with unformatted text files will do.

Using the notebook interface

Most examples in this book will use the Jupyter Notebook interface. This is a browser-based interface that integrates computations, graphics, and other forms of media. Notebooks can be easily shared and published, for example, http://nbviewer.ipython.org/ provides a simple publication path.

It is not, however, absolutely necessary to use the Jupyter interface to run the examples in this book. We strongly encourage, however, that you at least experiment with the notebook and its many features. The Jupyter Notebook interface makes it possible to mix formatted, descriptive text with code cells that evaluate at the same time. This feature makes it suitable for educational purposes, but it is also useful for personal use as it makes it easier to add comments and share partial progress before writing a full report. We will sometimes refer to a Jupyter Notebook as just *a notebook*.

To start the notebook interface, run the following command line from the shell or Anaconda command prompt:

```
jupyter notebook
```

The notebook server will be started in the directory where the command is issued. After a while, the notebook interface will appear in your default browser. Make sure that you are using a standards-compliant browser, such as Chrome, Firefox, Opera, or Safari. Once the Jupyter dashboard shows on the browser, click on the **New** button on the upper-right side of the page and select **Python 3**. After a few seconds, a new notebook will open in the browser. A useful place to learn about the notebook interface is http://jupyter.org.

Imports

There are some modules that we will need to load at the start of every project. Assuming that you are running a Jupyter Notebook, the required imports are as follows:

```
%matplotlib inline
import matplotlib.pyplot as plt
import numpy as np
import pandas as pd
```

Enter all the preceding commands in a single notebook cell and press *Shift + Enter* to run the whole cell. A new cell will be created when there is none after the one you are running; however, if you want to create one yourself, the menu or keyboard shortcut *Ctrl +M +A/B* is handy (*A* for above, *B* for below the current cell). In Appendix, *More on Jupyter Notebook and matplotlib Styles*, we cover some of the keyboard shortcuts available and installable extensions (that is, plugins) for Jupyter Notebook.

The statement `%matplotlib inline` is an example of Jupyter Notebook magic and sets up the interface to display plots inline, that is, embedded in the notebook. This line is not needed (and causes an error) in scripts. Next, optionally, enter the following commands:

```
import os
plt.style.use(os.path.join(os.getcwd(), 'mystyle.mplstyle') )
```

As before, run the cell by pressing *Shift +Enter*. This code has the effect of selecting matplotlib stylesheet `mystyle.mplstyle`. This is a custom style sheet that I created, which resides in the same folder as the notebook. It is a rather simple example of what can be done; you can modify it to your liking. As we gain experience in drawing figures throughout the book, I encourage you to play around with the settings in the file. There are also built-in styles that you can by typing `plt.style.available` in a new cell.

This is it! We are all set to start the fun part!

An example using the Pandas library

The purpose of this example is to check whether everything is working in your installation and give a flavor of what is to come. We concentrate on the Pandas library, which is the main tool used in Python data analysis.

We will use the MovieTweetings 50K movie ratings dataset, which can be downloaded from `https://github.com/sidooms/MovieTweetings`. The data is from the study MovieTweetings: a Movie Rating Dataset Collected From Twitter – by Dooms, De Pessemier and Martens presented during Workshop on Crowdsourcing and Human Computation for Recommender Systems, CrowdRec at RecSys (2013). The dataset is spread in several text files, but we will only use the following two files:

- `ratings.dat`: This is a double colon-separated file containing the ratings for each user and movie
- `movies.dat`: This file contains information about the movies

To see the contents of these files, you can open them with a standard text editor. The data is organized in columns, with one data item per line. The meanings of the columns are described in the `README.md` file, distributed with the dataset. The data has a peculiar aspect: some of the columns use a double colon (::) character as a separator, while others use a vertical bar (|). This emphasizes a common occurrence with real-world data: we have no control on how the data is collected and formatted. For data stored in text files, such as this one, it is always a good strategy to open the file in a text editor or spreadsheet software to take a look at the data and identify inconsistencies and irregularities.

To read the ratings file, run the following command:

```
cols = ['user id', 'item id', 'rating', 'timestamp']
ratings = pd.read_csv('data/ratings.dat', sep='::',
                        index_col=False, names=cols,
                        encoding="UTF-8")
```

The first line of code creates a Python list with the column names in the dataset. The next command reads the file, using the `read_csv()` function, which is part of Pandas. This is a generic function to read column-oriented data from text files. The arguments used in the call are as follows:

- `data/ratings.dat`: This is the path to file containing the data (this argument is required).
- `sep='::'`: This is the separator, a double colon character in this case.
- `index_col=False`: We don't want any column to be used as an index. This will cause the data to be indexed by successive integers, starting with 1.
- `names=cols`: These are the names to be associated with the columns.

The `read_csv()` function returns a DataFrame object, which is the Pandas data structure that represents tabular data. We can view the first rows of the data with the following command:

```
ratings[:5]
```

This will output a table, as shown in the following image:

	user id	item id	rating	timestamp
0	1	1074638	7	1365029107
1	1	1853728	8	1366576639
2	2	104257	8	1364690142
3	2	1259521	8	1364118447
4	2	1991245	7	1364117717

To start working with the data, let us find out how many times each rating appears in the table. This can be done with the following commands:

```
rating_counts = ratings['rating'].value_counts()
rating_counts
```

The first line of code computes the counts and stores them in the `rating_counts` variable. To obtain the count, we first use the `ratings['rating']` expression to select the `rating` column from the table ratings. Then, the `value_counts()` method is called to compute the counts. Notice that we retype the variable name, `rating_counts`, at the end of the cell. This is a common notebook (and Python) idiom to print the value of a variable in the output area that follows each cell. In a script, it has no effect; we could have printed it with the print command, (`print(rating_counts)`), as well. The output is displayed in the following image:

```
8          12012
7          11063
9           7119
6           6373
10          6281
5           3399
4           1696
3            924
1            595
2            533
0              5
Name:  rating,  dtype:  int64
```

Notice that the output is sorted according to the count values in descending order. The object returned by `value_counts` is of the Series type, which is the Pandas data structure used to represent one-dimensional, indexed, data. The Series objects are used extensively in Pandas. For example, the columns of a DataFrame object can be thought as Series objects that share a common index.

In our case, it makes more sense to sort the rows according to the ratings. This can be achieved with the following commands:

```
sorted_counts = rating_counts.sort_index()
sorted_counts
```

This works by calling the `sort_index()` method of the Series object, `rating_counts`. The result is stored in the `sorted_counts` variable. We can now get a quick visualization of the ratings distribution using the following commands:

```
sorted_counts.plot(kind='bar', color='SteelBlue')
plt.title('Movie ratings')
plt.xlabel('Rating')
plt.ylabel('Count')
```

The first line produces the plot by calling the `plot()` method for the `sorted_counts` object. We specify the `kind='bar'` option to produce a bar chart. Notice that we added the `color='SteelBlue'` option to select the color of the bars in the histogram. `SteelBlue` is one of the HTML5 color names (for example, `http://matplotlib.org/examples/col or/named_colors.html`) available in matplotlib. The next three statements set the title, horizontal axis label, and vertical axis label respectively. This will produce the following plot:

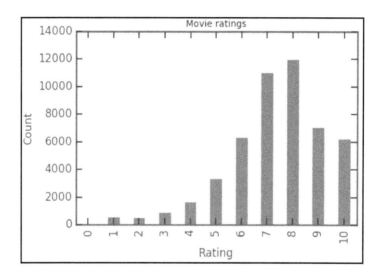

The vertical bars show how many voters that have given a certain rating, covering all the movies in the database. The distribution of the ratings is not very surprising: the counts increase up to a rating of 8, and the count of 9-10 ratings is smaller as most people are reluctant to give the highest rating. If you check the values of the bar for each rating, you can see that it corresponds to what we had previously when printing the `rating_counts` object. To see what happens if you do not sort the ratings first, plot the `rating_counts` object, that is, run `rating_counts.plot(kind='bar', color='SteelBlue')` in a cell.

Let's say that we would like to know if the ratings distribution for a particular movie genre, say `Crime Drama`, is similar to the overall distribution. We need to cross-reference the ratings information with the movie information, contained in the `movies.dat` file. To read this file and store it in a Pandas DataFrame object, use the following command:

```
cols = ['movie id','movie title','genre']
movies = pd.read_csv('data/movies.dat', sep='::',
                     index_col=False, names=cols,
                     encoding="UTF-8")
```

Downloading the example code
Detailed steps to download the code bundle are mentioned in the Preface of this book. Please have a look.
The code bundle for the book is also hosted on GitHub at `https://githu b.com/PacktPublishing/Mastering-Python-Data-Analysis`. We also have other code bundles from our rich catalog of books and videos available at `https://github.com/PacktPublishing/`. Check them out!

We are again using the `read_csv()` function to read the data. The column names were obtained from the `README.md` file distributed with the data. Notice that the separator used in this file is also a double colon, `::`. The first few lines of the table can be displayed with the command:

```
movies[:5]
```

Notice how the genres are indicated, clumped together with a vertical bar, `|`, as separator. This is due to the fact that a movie can belong to more than one genre. We can now select only the movies that are crime dramas using the following lines:

```
drama = movies[movies['genre']=='Crime|Drama']
```

Notice that this uses the standard indexing notation with square brackets, `movies[...]`. Instead of specifying a numeric or string index, however, we are using the Boolean `movies['genre']=='Crime|Drama'` expression as an index. To understand how this works, run the following code in a cell:

```
is_drama = movies['genre']=='Crime|Drama'
is_drama[:5]
```

This displays the following output:

```
0       True
1       False
2       False
3       False
4       False
Name: genre, dtype: bool
```

The `movies['genre']=='Crime|Drama'` expression returns a Series object, where each entry is either `True` or `False`, indicating whether the corresponding movie is a crime drama or not, respectively.

Thus, the net effect of the `drama = movies[movies['genre']=='Crime|Drama']` assignment is to select all the rows in the movies table for which the entry in the `genre` column is equal to `Crime|Drama` and store the result in the `drama` variable, which is an object of the DataFrame type.

All that we need is the `movie id` column of this table, which can be selected with the following statement:

```
drama_ids = drama['movie id']
```

This, again, uses standard indexing with a string to select a column from a table.

The next step is to extract those entries that correspond to dramas from the `ratings` table. This requires yet another indexing trick. The code is contained in the following lines:

```
criterion = ratings['item id'].map(lambda x:(drama_ids==x).any())
drama_ratings = ratings[criterion]
```

The key to how this code works is the definition of the variable `criterion`. We want to look up each row of the `ratings` table and check whether the `item id` entry is in the `drama_ids` table. This can be conveniently done by the `map()` method. This method applies a function to all the entries of a Series object. In our example, the function is as follows:

```
lambda x:(drama_ids==x).any()
```

This function simply checks whether an item appears in `drama_ids`, and if it does, it returns `True`. The resulting object `criterion` will be a Series that contains the `True` value only in the rows that correspond to dramas. You can view the first rows with the following code:

```
criterion[:10]
```

We then use the `criterion` object as an index to select the rows from the `ratings` table.

We are now done with selecting the data that we need. To produce a rate count and bar chart, we use the same commands as before. The details are in the following code, which can be run in a single execution cell:

```
rating_counts = drama_ratings['rating'].value_counts()
sorted_counts = rating_counts.sort_index()
sorted_counts.plot(kind='bar', color='SteelBlue')
plt.title('Movie ratings for dramas')
plt.xlabel('Rating')
plt.ylabel('Count')
```

As before, this code first computes the counts, indexes them according to the ratings, and then produces a bar chart. This produces a graph that seems to be similar to the overall ratings distribution, as shown in the following figure:

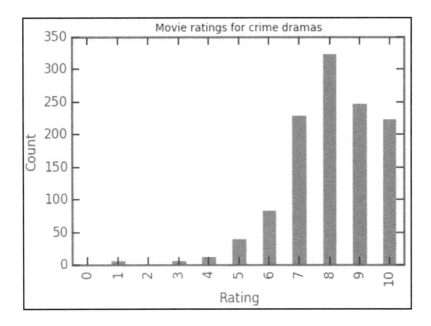

Summary

In this chapter, we have seen what tools are available for data analysis in Python, reviewed issues related to installation and workflow, and considered a simple example that requires reading and manipulating data files.

In the next chapter, we will cover techniques to explore data graphically and numerically using some of the main tools provided by the Pandas module.

2
Exploring Data

When starting to work on a new dataset, it is essential to first get an idea of what conclusions can be drawn from the data. Before we can do things such as inference and hypothesis testing, we need to develop an understanding of what questions the data at hand can answer. This is the key to exploratory data analysis, which is the skill and science of developing intuition and identifying statistical patterns in the data. In this chapter, we will present graphical and numerical methods that help in this task. You will notice that there are no hard and fast rules of how to proceed at each step, but instead, we give recommendations on what techniques tend to be suitable in each case. The best way to develop the set of skills necessary to be an expert data explorer is to see lots of examples and, perhaps more importantly, work on our own datasets. More specifically, this chapter will cover the following topics:

- Performing the initial exploration and cleaning of data
- Drawing a histogram, kernel density estimate, probability, and box plot for univariate distributions
- Drawing scatterplots for bivariate relationships and giving an initial overview of various point estimates of the data, such as mean, standard deviation, and so on

Before starting through the examples in this chapter, start the Jupyter Notebook and run the same initial commands as mentioned in the previous chapter. Remember the directory where the notebook resides. The data folder for the examples needs to be stored in the same directory.

The General Social Survey

To present concrete data examples in this chapter, we will use the **General Social Survey** (**GSS**). The GSS is a large survey of societal trends conducted by the **National Opinion Research Center** (**NORC**–http://www3.norc.org) at the University of Chicago. As this is a very complex dataset, we will work with a subset of the data, the compilation from the 2012 survey. With a size 5.5 MB, this is a small data size by the current standards, but still well-suited for the kind of exploration being illustrated in this chapter. (Smith, Tom W, Peter Marsden, Michael Hout, and Jibum Kim. General Social Surveys, 1972-2014 [machine-readable data file] /Principal Investigator, Tom W. Smith; Co-Principal Investigator, Peter V. Marsden; Co-Principal Investigator, Michael Hout; Sponsored by National Science Foundation. –NORC ed.– Chicago: NORC at the University of Chiago [producer]; Storrs, CT: The Roper Center for Public Opinion Research, University of Connecticut [distributor], 2015.)

Obtaining the data

The subset of the GSS used in the examples is available at the book's website, but can also be downloaded directly from the NORC website. Notice that, besides the data itself, it is necessary to obtain files with the metadata, which contains the list of abbreviations for the variables considered in the survey.

To download the data, proceed as indicated in the following steps:

1. Go to http://www3.norc.org.
2. In the search field, type GSS 2012 merged with all cases and variables.
3. Click on the link titled **SPSS | NORC**.
4. Scroll down to the **Merged Single-Year Data Sets** section. Click on the link named **GSS 2012 merged with all cases and variables**. If there is more than one release, choose the latest one.
5. Follow the procedure to download the file to the computer. The file will be named gss2012merged_stata.zip. Uncompressing the file will create the GSS2012merged_R5.dta data file. (The filename may be slightly different for a different release.)
6. If necessary, move the data file to the directory where your notebooks are.

We also need the file that describes the variable abbreviations in the data. This can be done in the following steps:

1. Go to `http://gss.norc.org/Get-Documentation`.
2. Click on the link named **Index to Data Set**. This will download a PDF file with a list of the variable abbreviations and their corresponding meanings. Browsing this file gives you an idea of the scope of questions asked in this survey.

You can feel free to browse the information available on the GSS website. A researcher using the GSS will probably have to familiarize themselves with all the details related to the dataset.

Reading the data

Our next step is to make sure that we can read the data into our notebook. The data is in STATA format. STATA is a well-known package for statistical analysis, and the use of its format for data files is widespread. Fortunately, Pandas allows us to read STATA files in a straightforward way.

If you have not done so yet, start a new notebook and run the default commands to import the libraries that we will need. (Refer to `Chapter 1`, *Tools of the Trade.*)

Next, execute these commands:

```
gss_data = pd.read_stata('data/GSS2012merged_R5.dta',
                         convert_categoricals=False)
gss_data.head()
```

Reading the data may take a few seconds, so we ask you to be a little patient. The first code line calls Pandas' `read_stata()` function to read the data, and then stores the result, which is an object of the DataFrame type in the `gss_data` variable.
The `convert_categoricals=False` option instructs Pandas to not attempt to convert the column data to categorical, sometimes called factor data. As the columns in the dataset are only numbers, where the supporting documents are needed to interpret many of them (for example, gender, 1=male, 2=female), converting to categorical variables does not make sense because numbers are ordered but the translated variable may not be. Categorical data is data that comes in two or more, usually limited, number of possible values. It comes in two types: ordered (for example, size) and unordered (for example, color or gender).

It is important to point out here that categorical data is a Pandas data type, which differs from a statistical categorical variable. A statistical categorical variable is only for unordered variables (as described previously); ordered variables are called statistical ordinal variable. Two examples of this are education and income level. Note that the distance (interval) between the levels need not be fixed. A third related statistical variable is the statistical interval variable, which is the same as an ordinal variable, just with a fixed interval between the levels; an example of this is income levels with a fixed interval.

Before moving on, let's make a little improvement in the way that the data is imported. By default, the `read_stata()` function will index the data records with integers starting at 0. The GSS data contains its own index in the column labelled `id`. To change the index of a DataFrame object, we simply assign a new value to the index field, as indicated in the following lines of code (input in a separate Notebook cell):

```
gss_data.set_index('id')
gss_data.drop('id', 1, inplace=True)
gss_data.head()
```

The first line of the preceding code sets the index of `gss_data` field to the column labelled `id`. As we don't need this column in the data any longer, we remove it from the table using the `drop()` method. The `inplace=True` option causes `gss_data` to be modified itself. (The default is to return a new DataFrame object with the changes.)

Let's now save our table to a file in the CSV format. This step is not strictly necessary, but simplifies the process of reloading the data, in case it is necessary. To save the file, run the following code:

```
gss_data.to_csv('GSS2012merged.csv')
```

This code uses the `to_csv()` method to output the table to a file named `GSS2012merged.csv`, using the default options. The CSV format does not actually have an official standard, but because of the simple rules, a file where the entries in each row are separated by some delimiter (for example, a comma), it works rather well. However, as always when reading in data, we need to inspect it to make sure that we have read it correctly. The file containing the data can now be opened with standard spreadsheet software as the dataset is not really large.

Univariate data

We are now ready to start playing with the data. A good way to get an initial feeling of the data is to create graphical representations with the aim of getting an understanding of the shape of its distribution. The word distribution has a technical meaning in data analysis, but we are not concerned with this kind of detail now. We are using this word in the informal sense of *how the set of values in our data is distributed.*

To start with the simplest case, we look at the variables in the data individually without, at first, worrying about relationships between variables. When we look at a single variable, we say that we are dealing with univariate data. So, this is the case that we will consider in this section.

Histograms

A histogram is a standard way of displaying the distribution of quantitative data, that is, data that can be represented in terms of real numbers or integers. (Notice that integers can also be used to indicate some types of categorical data.) A histogram separates the data in a number of bins, which are simply intervals of values, and counts how many of the data points lie in each of the bins.

Let's concentrate on the column labelled age, which records the respondent's age. To display a histogram of the data, run the following line of code:

```
gss_data['age'].hist()
plt.grid()
plt.locator_params(nbins=5);
```

In this code, we use `gss_data['age']` to refer to the column named age, and then call the `hist()` method to draw the histogram. Unfortunately, the plot contains some superfluous elements, such as a grid. Therefore, we remove it by calling the `plt.grid()` trigger function, and after this, we redefine how many tick locators to place with the `plt.locator_params(nbins=5)` call. Running the code will produce the following figure, where the *y* axis is the number of elements in the bin and the *x* axis is the age:

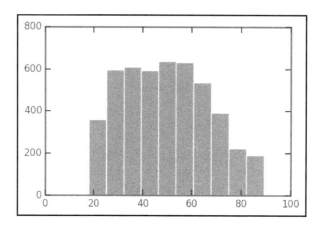

The key feature of a histogram is the number of bins in which the data is placed. If there are too few bins, important features of the distribution may be hidden. On the other hand, too many bins cause the histogram to visually emphasize the random discrepancies in the sample, making it hard to identify general patterns. The histogram in the preceding figure seems to be too *smooth*, and we suspect that it may hide details of the distribution. We can increase the number of bins to 25 by adding the option bins to the call of `hist()`, as shown in the code that follows:

```
gss_data['age'].hist(bins=25)
plt.grid()
plt.locator_params(nbins=5);
```

The plot in the following screenshot is displayed:

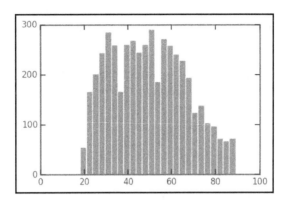

Notice that now the histogram looks different; we see more structure in the data. However, the resolution is still good enough to show the main features of the plot:

- The distribution is approximately *unimodal*, that is, there is only one significant *hump*. Notice that in making this assessment, we do not take into account small gaps and peaks that are most likely due to sample randomness.
- The distribution is *asymmetrical*, being somewhat skewed to the right, that is, it has a longer tail extending toward the high values.
- The distribution ranges, approximately, from 20 to 90 years, and is centered somewhere near 50 years. It is not clear what is the mode, or highest point, of the distribution.
- There are no unusual features, such as outliers, gaps, or clusters.

Notice that, from these observations, we can already say something about the data collection: it is likely that there is a minimum age requirement for respondents. This may be the cause of the asymmetry in the distribution. Requiring a lower bound in the sampling usually makes the upper tail of the distribution stand out.

It is useful to compare this distribution with a distribution of the income of the respondent, contained in the realrinc column. There is a little trap lying there, however. Let's start by creating a DataFrame that contains only the two columns of interest and display the first few lines of the result, by running the following commands:

```
inc_age = gss_data[['realrinc','age']]
inc_age.head(10)
```

Notice the *double brackets* in the first line of the preceding code. We are using one of the many sophisticated indexing capabilities provided by Pandas and passing a Python list, `['realinc','age']`, as the index to the `gss_data` DataFrame. This has the expected effect of selecting the two columns specified in the Python list.

Looking at the output of the previous command, we can see that the `realinc` column has many missing values, indicated by the `NaN` value, which is the default that Pandas uses for missing data. This may happen due to several reasons, but some respondents simply opt not to reveal their incomes. Thus, to compare the distribution of the two columns, we can omit these rows, as shown in the following code:

```
inc_age = gss_data[['realrinc','age']].dropna()
inc_age.head(10)
```

We use the same indexing to select the two columns, but now we call the `dropna()` method to exclude the rows with missing data. Examining the output, notice that Pandas smartly keeps the row indexing, ID, from the original DataFrame from where the values were extracted. This way, if needed, we can cross-reference the data with the original table.

It is now pretty straightforward to produce side-by-side histograms of the two variables, using the following lines of code:

```
ax_list = inc_age.hist(bins=40, figsize=(8,3), xrot=45)
for ax in ax_list[0]:
    ax.locator_params(axis='x', nbins=6)
    ax.locator_params(axis='y', nbins=3)
```

Notice the options that we used in the `hist()` method. Besides setting the number of bins, we use the `figsize=(8,3)` option, setting the figure size to 8 inches by 3 inches and the `xrot=45` option, causing the *x* axis labels to be rotated by 45 degrees, improving readability. The command returns a list of the axes' objects of the figure. We save this to the `ax_list` variable. Next, we iterate over this list to make modifications of the axes' objects (that is, the plots we are drawing). As before, we change the number of tick marks, this time with a different function, using the object-oriented interface of matplotlib. Play around with the nbins setting and see what happens.

Examining the resulting histograms, we can see that they are significantly different: the distribution of incomes is heavily skewed and, more importantly, there is a large gap with an isolated bar in the region above 300,000 dollars. Let's count how many values are in this region, as in the following code:

```
inc_age[inc_age['realrinc'] > 3.0E5].count()
```

In this code, we are using a Boolean index, `inc_age['realrinc'] > 3.0E5`, in the DataFrame. This selects all the rows for which the value in the `realinc` column is larger than 300,000 dollars (`3.0E5` is equivalent to `3.0 * 10`^{5}). The `count()` method simply counts how many values are there that satisfy the condition.

Looking at the output, we can see that there are 80 rows with an income above 300,000 dollars. As always, when there is something that looks unusual, we should look at the data more carefully. Let's display the data for the corresponding values by running the following code:

```
inc_age[inc_age['realrinc'] >3.0E5].head(10)
```

This is very similar to the command line in the previous example, but now we take a slice of the data corresponding to the first ten rows. The output contains a surprise: all data values are equal!
To understand what is happening, we have to dig deeper into the assumptions made in the GSS survey. The survey does not ask respondents for a number value for their incomes. Instead, the respondent is presented with income categories, which imposes an upper bound on the incomes in the questionnaire. That is, all respondents with an income above a certain value are lumped together. By the way, the problem of estimating the real incomes from the categories is nontrivial, and there is quite a body of research on the subject.

Anyway, for our purposes, it is legitimate to simply exclude the values above 300,000 dollars. To produce histograms with this assumption, run the code indicated in the following lines:

```
inc_age = gss_data[['realrinc','age']].dropna()
lowinc_age = inc_age[inc_age['realrinc'] <3.0E5]
ax_list = lowinc_age.hist(bins=20, figsize=(8,3), xrot=45)
for ax in ax_list[0]:
    ax.grid()
    ax.locator_params(axis='x' ,nbins=6)
    ax.locator_params(axis='y' ,nbins=3)
```

Notice the second line in the preceding code, which selects the rows in the `inc_age` DataFrame corresponding to entries where the value in the `realrinc` column is less than 300,000 and stores this in a new `lowinc_age` object. This produces the histograms displayed in the following picture:

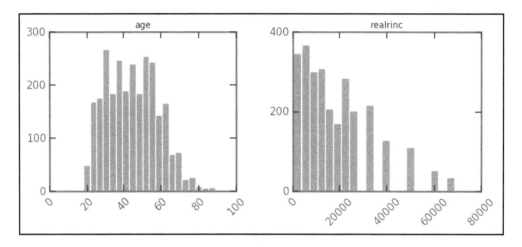

By looking at the output, we can see that the distributions are quite distinct. The income distribution is markedly skewed toward large values and appears to have several gaps. Note that the gaps may be due to the survey construction, especially with what concerns the way the real income is computed from the income ranges.

Making things pretty

The histograms shown in the examples so far are adequate for data exploration but are not quite visually appealing. Pandas uses matplotlib for graphs. Matplotlib is an extensive library for technical plotting, capable of producing high-quality, presentation-ready graphs (http://matplotlib.org). To illustrate the possibilities, run the following code (`lowinc_age` stored in the previous code):

```
ax_list = lowinc_age.hist(bins=20, figsize=(8,3),
                          xrot=45, color='SteelBlue')
ax1, ax2 = ax_list[0]
ax1.set_title('Age (years)')
ax2.set_title('Real Income ($)')
for ax in ax_list[0]:
    ax.grid()
    ax.locator_params(axis='x' ,nbins=6)
    ax.locator_params(axis='y' ,nbins=4)
```

Let's start by analyzing the call to the `hist()` method in the third line of the preceding code. When using matplotlib for plotting, there are several approaches to each command. Here, we show the object-oriented way, where `ax1, ax2 = ax_list[0]` fetches and stores the two axes. Then, we set the title and turn off the background grid of each axis using these objects.

Characterization

We now consider the question of trying to fit the data into one of the standard models in classical statistics. This may be a complicated problem as real data may not conform to any predefined model. The first step may be to try to approximate the density of the distribution, that is, a fraction of the people at a certain age in this case (assuming that it is continuous). A frequently used method is **Kernel Density Estimation** (**KDE**), which can be thought of as a *smoothed histogram*. Pandas can easily produce KDE plots, as shown in the following code:

```
age = gss_data['age'].dropna()
age.plot(kind='kde', lw=2, color='green')
plt.title('KDE plot for Age')
plt.xlabel('Age (years)')
```

In this code, we first select the age column from the data, dropping the missing values. We then call the `plot()` method with the `kind='kde'` option (with kde as an option, the SciPy package is a dependency). Notice that this is a slightly different interface from what we used for histograms. Also notice that we use options to set the line width and color of the plot. The last two lines set the title and label of the *x* axis, although with the direct function approach this time as opposed to the object-oriented approach as shown previously. How would you plot this with an object-oriented approach?

An important factor to notice is that Pandas does not support setting parameters for the KDE plot, in particular, bandwidth used in the smoothing procedure. The bandwidth is somewhat analogous to the bin width in a histogram, and different bandwidth can produce significantly different approximations. Pandas uses a heuristic approximation that produces a nearly optimal fit in most cases, but this may not produce the best results in some cases. We expect that future versions of Pandas will be more flexible here.

Running the preceding code, we get the following display:

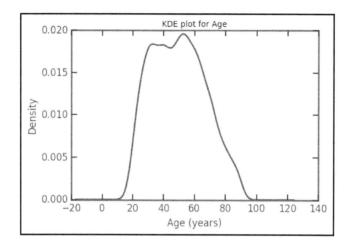

While this is all good, we might want to plot the KDE over the histogram. This can be done with the following code:

```
ax = age.hist(bins=30, color='LightSteelBlue', normed=True)
age.plot(kind='kde', lw=2, color='Green', ax=ax)
plt.title('Histogram and KDE for Age')
plt.xlabel('Age (years)');
```

This will produce a figure with the histogram, normalized just like the KDE plot, and the KDE curve on top of it. The figure will look as follows:

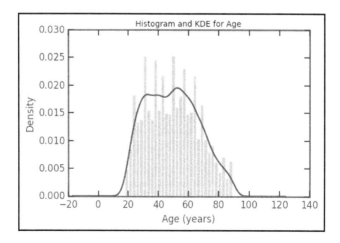

The KDE curve is somewhat bell-shaped, but if you are familiar with the normal distribution, you will notice that the plot seems to drop too quickly to zero at the tails. To visually access how much the data deviates from a normal distribution, we can use a **Normal Distribution Plot**. In a normal distribution plot, the data is plotted alongside values of a normal distribution with similar characteristics as the data would have. This kind of plot is not supported in the current version of Pandas, but we can use SciPy to create the plot, as indicated in the following lines of code:

```
import scipy.stats as stats
stats.probplot(age, dist='norm', plot=plt)
```

The first parameter, `age`, is the data to be plotted. We then use the `dist='norm'` option to compare the data with a normal distribution. The final option, `plot=plt`, specifies that the `plt` module should be used for the plotting. This can be an existing axis instance (object) or a plotting module; in this case, we just send it the `plt`, which is the `matplotlib.pyplot` module. The resulting plot is shown in the following figure:

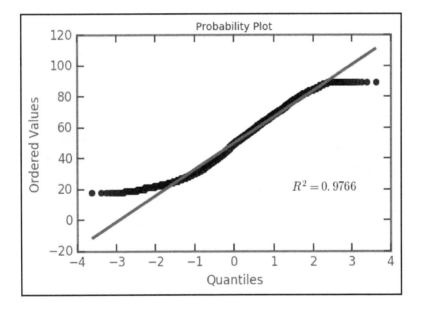

Notice that the data deviates significantly from the straight line at the ends of the plot: it is above the line on the left and below the line on the right. The more similarities with a normal distribution, the more the data values will follow the straight line. The age data presented here is consistent with data that has tails that are shorter than those of a normal distribution, which is consistent with our earlier observations. We would thus conclude that a normal distribution would not be adequate for this data.

Concept of statistical inference

At this point of the analysis, we have figured out something about the sample. It is not normally distributed. Further on in the exploration, we will find out even more about the sample. With adequately sampled data from the full population, we can draw conclusions about the population by conducting analysis on the data sample. This is the basis of statistical inference, and the following image illustrates this concept. The concept is mentioned in the following steps:

1. We draw a hopefully unbiased sample from the population.
2. Through data analysis, we characterize the sample data.
3. With statistical tests, parameter estimation, and similar tools, we draw conclusions about the sample.
4. Through inference, we can now draw conclusions on the whole population.

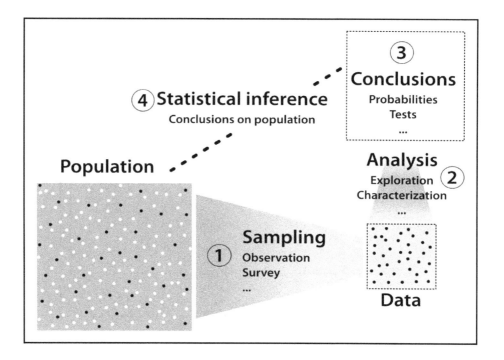

Numeric summaries and boxplots

We now move in the direction of describing the data numerically. Before we start, we need a word of caution. It is not good practice to simply use a set of numbers from the data to draw conclusions from it. It is very tempting to rely on the feeling that definite numbers provide a level of *certainty*. However, numerical values without context and no further analysis are not very useful and may be misleading. In this chapter, we are only considering methods for initial study, trying to familiarize ourselves with the data in order to get a feeling for how it behaves.

When considering numerical data, we may ask the following questions:

- What is the range of the data? That is, what are the smallest and largest values?
- Where is the center of the data values located? We will consider two measures of centrality, the *mean* and *median*.
- How much does the data spread from its center? We will consider the *standard deviation* as well as the notions of *quartiles* and *percentiles* as measures of spread.

All these quantities are easily computed in Pandas with the `describe()` method, available for objects of the Series and DataFrame types. Going back to the distribution of income, we can plot a data summary as follows:

```
inc = gss_data['realrinc'].dropna()
lowinc = inc[inc <3.0E5]
lowinc.describe()
```

In the first line, we select the `realrinc` column from the table using the `dropna()` method to discard missing data. We then select only incomes less than 300,000 dollars as the income reported in that column may not reliably reflect the distribution of high incomes, which we have discussed before. Finally, we use the `describe()` method to generate a summary of the data. Running this code, we obtain the output shown in the following lines:

```
count      2751.000000
mean       18582.194656
std        14841.581333
min          245.000000
25%         6737.500000
50%        15925.000000
75%        26950.000000
max        68600.000000
Name: realrinc, dtype: float64
```

The information provided in this output is described as follows:

- The `count` is the number of data points. So, there are 2,751 people that reported incomes less than 300,000 dollars in the survey.
- The `mean` is the average of the data. So, the average income of respondents is approximately $18,582.
- The `standard deviation` (`std`) is a measure of how the data spreads around the mean. The formula for the standard deviation is somewhat technical and will be introduced in a later chapter.
- The `minimum` (`min`) and `maximum` (`max`) are the smallest and largest values in the data. Together, they specify the range of the data. In our example, income goes from the lowest value of $245 to the highest value of $68,600.
- The `median` (50%) is the value that corresponds to the middle point of the dataset, in the sense that half of the values are below the median and half of the values are above the median. For example, for our data, half of the reported incomes are below $15,925 and half are above this value.

The single values derived here represent certain characteristics of our data referred to as **point estimates**. The most common and widely used point estimate is the sample mean, which gives a point estimate of the population mean through statistical inference. Point estimates are compliments to *interval estimates*. These are defined by two or more numbers, for example, if the sample mean is indicated to lie in a certain interval, this indicates that the population mean lies in this certain interval as well.

- The `quartiles` (25% and 75%) together with the median give a more specific view of how the data is distributed. In our data, they can be interpreted as follows:
  - 25% of the incomes are below $6,737
  - 25% of the incomes are between $6,737 and $15,925
  - 25% of the incomes are between $15,925 and $26,950
  - 25% of the incomes are between $26,950 and $15,925

If a more detailed view of the distribution is desired, we can request the output of a larger number of `percentiles`, as shown in the following code:

```
lowinc.describe(percentiles=np.arange(0, 1.0, 0.1))
```

In this code, we use the percentiles option of the `describe()` method. The `np.arange(0, 1.0, 0.1)` expression represents a NumPy array with the numbers `0.0, 0.1, 0.2, ..., 0.9`. The output of the previous example will provide values that split the data into 10 intervals, each containing 10% of the reported incomes.

Numerical summaries can be, admittedly, hard to visualize. A very old, but still useful, graphical tool is the **boxplot**. Although somewhat out of fashion, boxplots can still be used to display the center and spread of the data. We can display a boxplot of incomes with the following code:

```
lowinc.plot(kind='box');
```

Alternatively, it is possible to run the following:

```
lowinc.plot.box();
```

Running either of these commands produces the following plot:

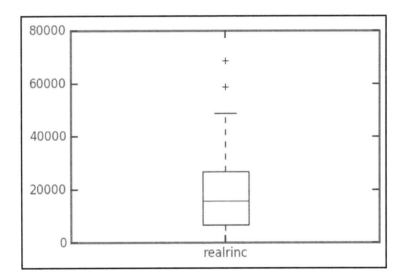

This boxplot can be interpreted as follows:

- The points marked with a cross symbol are outliers. Outliers are values that are far removed from the center of the distribution. There is no clear universally accepted definition of what an outlier is, so Pandas determines them heuristically (http://matplotlib.org/api/pyplot_api.html#matplotlib.pyplot.boxplot).

- The horizontal bars at the bottom and top (the *whiskers* of the boxplot) represent the minimum and maximum, respectively.
- The bottom and top of the box represent the 25% and 75% quartiles, respectively.
- The line inside the box represents the median or 50% quartile.

A quick way to interpret a boxplot is to remember that, excluding outliers, 50% of the data values are inside the box, 25% are below the box, and 25% are above the box. Notice that, in our example, the asymmetry of the data is evident with the boxplot being skewed toward high values.

Boxplots are also useful to compare data for different subpopulations. Let's say, for example, that we want to compare the incomes of males and females. This can be accomplished with the following code:

```
inc_gen = gss_data[['realrinc','sex']]
inc_gen = inc_gen[inc_gen['realrinc'] < 3.0E5]
inc_gen.boxplot(column='realrinc', by='sex');
```

The first two lines select the data to be plotted, excluding incomes above 300,000. Then, the `boxplot()` method of the DataFrame object is called. We specify the data to be plotted with the `column='realrinc'` option and the groups with the `by='sex'` option. When executed, the following plot will be displayed:

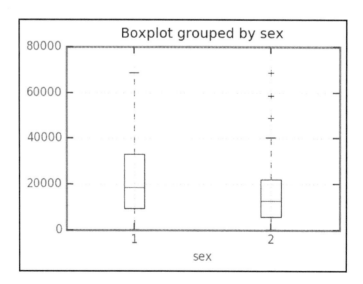

These boxplots tell an interesting story about how incomes are distributed. The incomes for males (**1**) are more spread than the values for females (**2**), with the incomes for males being markedly above the female incomes. For example, the top quartile of the female's distribution is just a little above the median male income. That is, almost 75% of the females have an income corresponding to the bottom half of male incomes. The upper level of the distribution tells a similar story. The portion of the boxplot above the upper quartile is much longer for the male distribution than that of the female distribution. Notice, in particular, the outliers in the female distribution. There definitely seems to be a *glass ceiling* effect, with very few women being able to command the top salaries that men achieve.

Relationships between variables – scatterplots

The real power in data analysis is realized when we study how different variables relate. At the end of the previous section, we related income and gender, that is, a quantitative variable with a categorical one. In this section, we will investigate scatterplots, which are a graphical representation of the relationship between two quantitative variables.

To illustrate how Pandas can be used to explore the relationship between two variables, we will use an important example from the history of astronomy. Astronomer Edwin Hubble, in 1929, published a very important paper where he discovered that there is an approximately linear relationship between the distance and velocity of extragalactic nebulae. This was the foundation that would come to be the big bang theory.

A reprint of the article is available at `http://apod.nasa.gov/diamond_jubilee/d_1996/hub_1929.html`, where the data was obtained from. Notice that the dataset is very small and simply printed in the article itself! Some minor formatting and cleanup was done to the data to make it easier to use. In particular, the velocity values were manually changed to be all positive as only the magnitude of the velocity matters. To plot a scatterplot of the data, enter and run the following code:

```
hubble_data = pd.read_csv('data/hubble-data.csv')
hubble_data.plot(kind='scatter', x='r', y='v');
```

In this code, after reading the data using the `read_csv()` function, we plot the data using the `plot()` method with the `kind='scatter'` option. The `x='r'` and `y='v'` option tell Pandas which columns to plot in the *x* and *y* axes, respectively.

Observing the plot, it is clearly seen that there is a relationship between distance and velocity, contradicting the view, prevalent at the time, that the Universe is stationary. To make the relationship clearer, we can add a trend line to the plot.

A central part of statistical inference is hypothesis testing, where one dataset/sample is tested against another or tested against a model-generated dataset. Statistical hypothesis testing is then used to investigate a proposed relationship between the two datasets. The proposed relationship is compared to an idealized null hypothesis, that is, that no relationship exists between the two datasets. The null hypothesis is rejected only if the probability of it being true is below a certain significant level. That is, hypothesis testing can only give the significance of the null hypothesis, not the proposed model. This is a very odd and usually hard concept to grasp. We will touch on hypothesis testing in this chapter, and take a deeper dive in `Chapter 4`, *Regression*.

We first need to compute the linear regression line for the relationship. We do this using SciPy with the following code:

```
from scipy.stats import linregress
rv = hubble_data.as_matrix(columns=['r','v'])
a, b, r, p, stderr = linregress(rv)
print(a, b, r, p, stderr)
```

We start by importing the `linregress` function from the `scipy.stats` module. This module is not Pandas-aware, so we first convert the data to a NumPy array using the `as_matrix()` method. Next, we call the `linregress` function, which returns the following:

- `a`: This is the slope of the regression line
- `b`: This is the intercept of the regression line
- `r`: This is the correlation coefficient
- `p`: This is the two-sided p-value for the hypotheses test-for the null hypothesis that assumes the slope is zero
- `stderr`: This is the standard error of the estimate

For our example, we get, rounding to two decimals, `a=454.16`, `b=-40.78`, `r=0.79`, `p=4.48E-6`, and `stderr=75.24`.

Linear regression is covered in `Chapter 4`, *Regression*, but we will interpret the results here. The correlation coefficient of 0.79 indicates a strong relationship, and the very small p-value indicates that the null hypothesis should be rejected, giving support to the existence of a relationship between the variables. The square of r is 0.62, so 62% of the variability in the data is explained by the linear model as opposed to random variation.

All this indicates that a linear model can describe the increase in velocity as a function of distance for galaxies in the Universe. To display this visually, we can plot the regression line together with the data using the following code:

```
hubble_data.plot(kind='scatter', x='r', y='v')
rdata = hubble_data['r']
rmin, rmax = min(rdata), max(rdata)
rvalues = np.linspace(rmin, rmax, 200)
yvalues = a * rvalues + b
plt.plot(rvalues, yvalues, color='red', lw=1.5)
plt.locator_params(nbins=5);
```

As Pandas does not currently support the option of drawing regression lines on scatterplots, we take advantage of the fact that matplotlib is used by Pandas in the background to construct plots. After graphing the scatterplot, we compute the maximum and minimum values of the data and generate a NumPy array with equally spaced values of the distance with a call to the `linspace()` function. Then, the *yvalues = a* rvalues + b* statement computes the points in the line. Finally, we call matplotlib's `plot()` function to plot the line. The resulting graph is displayed in the following image:

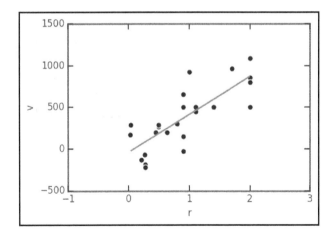

From this model, Hubble went on to hypothesize that the Universe is expanding, an idea that eventually yielded the model for the Universe currently accepted in cosmology.

Summary

In this chapter, you learned how to use Pandas to perform an initial exploration of the data. You learned about displays of data, including histograms, KDE plots and boxplots for univariate distributions, and scatterplots for bivariate relationships. We also discussed summaries of data, including mean, standard deviation, range, median, quartiles, and percentiles.

In the next chapter, you will learn about statistical models for data.

3
Learning About Models

In the most generic sense, a **model** is an approximate description of a portion of reality. Models are essential to science and, in fact, any area of knowledge: it is only possible to comprehend the world by concentrating on a small part of it at a time and making suitable simplifications.

In this chapter, we will discuss the following topics:

- Using basic models in data analysis
- Using the cumulative distribution function and probability density function to characterize a variable
- Using the preceding functions and various tools to make point estimates and generating random numbers with a certain distribution
- Discussing examples of discrete and continuous random variables and an overview of multivariate distributions

Models and experiments

Models can take many forms: a verbal description, set of mathematical equations, or segment of computer code. In this book, we are interested in a specific kind of model, *probabilistic* or *statistical* model, which represents the variability that occurs in a nondeterministic experiment.

We use the term **experiment** in this book in a somewhat non-technical sense. For us, an experiment is any observation of an event of interest. Examples of experiments are observing the number of visitors to a website or conducting an opinion poll or clinical trial. The main characteristic of experiments, for us, is that they can be repeated and that there is randomness, that is, each repetition of the same experiment may result in different outcomes.

The models that we will consider take the form of random variables. A random variable is an idealized representation of a probabilistic outcome that has numerical results. It is important to realize that a random variable is an abstraction: it does not represent the outcome of a particular experiment, it just models what results we expect to get once the experiment is actually performed.

In the remainder of this chapter, we will discuss how statistical models are formulated and describe the most important models used in data analysis.

Before running the examples in this chapter, start the Jupyter Notebook. After the default imports, run the following commands in a cell:

```
from pandas import Series, DataFrame
import numpy.random as rnd
import scipy.stats as st
```

You are now ready to start running the code for this chapter.

The cumulative distribution function

In the previous chapter, when discussing visual representations of numerical data, we introduced histograms, which represent the way the data is distributed across a number of intervals. One of the drawbacks of histograms is that the number of bins is always chosen somewhat arbitrarily, and incorrect choices may give useless or misleading information about the distribution of the data.

We say that histograms abstract some of the characteristics of the data. That is, a histogram allows us to ignore some of the fine-grained variability in the data so that general patterns are more apparent.

Abstraction is, in general, a good thing when analyzing a dataset but we would like to have an accurate representation of *all* data points that is visually compelling and computationally useful. This is provided by the *cumulative distribution function*. This function has always been important for statistical computations, and cumulative distribution tables were in fact an essential tool before the advent of the computer. However, as a graphical tool, the cumulative distribution function is not usually emphasized in introductory statistics texts. In my opinion, this is partly due to a historical bias as it is unwieldy to draw a cumulative distribution function without the aid of a computer.

To give a concrete example, let's first generate a set of random values following a Normal distribution with the following code segment:

```
mean = 0
sdev = 1
nvalues = 10
norm_variate = mean + sdev * rnd.randn(nvalues)
print(norm_variate)
```

In this code, we use the NumPy `numpy.random` module (abbreviated as `rnd`) to generate the randomized values. The documentation for the random module can be found at `http://docs.scipy.org`. Specifically, we use the `randn()` function, which generates normally distributed pseudorandom numbers with mean 0 and variance 1, then we move the distribution to the mean through addition and widen the distribution by `sdev` through multiplication. This function takes the number of values that we want as an argument, which we stored in the `nvalues` variable.

Notice that we use the term **pseudorandom**. When generating the random numbers, the computer actually uses a formula that produces values that are distributed, approximately, according to a given distribution. These values cannot be truly random as they are generated by a deterministic formula. It is possible to use sources of *true randomness*, as provided, for instance, by the site `https://www.random.org/`. However, pseudorandom numbers are usually sufficient for computer simulations and most data analysis problems.

The result is stored in the `norm_variates` variable, which is a NumPy array. We can pretend that the numbers represent the offset in grams from the target weight for a 10 gram package of saffron, perhaps to make more sense of the numbers. This would mean that `-0.1` means that the package contains `0.1` gram less saffron than it should and `+0.2` means that it contains more saffron than it should.

Running this cell will produce an array containing 10 numbers. Running the code with more values, say 100 (that is, `nvalues=100`), would produce a distribution that follows a normal distribution more closely. This array should follow, approximately, a Normal distribution with a mean 0 and standard deviation of 1. Values that result from the sampling from a random variable, for example, the values in the `norm_variate` array, are called **random variates**. The cumulative distribution function of a dataset is, by definition, a function that, given a value of x, returns the number of data points that do not exceed x, normalized to the range from 0 to 1. To give a concrete example, let's sort the values we generated previously and print them using the following code:

```
for i, v in enumerate(sorted(norm_variates), start=1):
    print('{0:2d} {1:+.4f}'.format(i, v))
```

This code uses a `for` loop structure to iterate over the sorted list of random variates. We use `enumerate()`, which provides a Python iterator that returns both the index `i` and corresponding value `v` from the list in each iteration. The `start=1` parameter causes the iteration number to start at 1. Then, for each pair, `i` and `v` are printed. In the print statement, we use format specifiers, which are the expressions enclosed by curly brackets, `{...}`. In this example, `{0:2d}` specifies that `i` is printed as a *2-digit decimal value* and `{1:+.4f}` specifies that `v` is printed as *assigned float value with four digits of precision*. As a result, we obtain a sorted list of the data, numbered from `1`.

The values obtained by me are as follows:

```
 1  -0.1412
 2  +0.6152
 3  +0.6852
 4  +2.2946
 5  +3.2791
 6  +3.4699
 7  +3.6961
 8  +4.2375
 9  +4.4977
10  +5.3756
```

As we are sampling from a (pseudo) random variable, you will obtain a different set of values.

From this list, it is easy to compute values of the cumulative distribution function. Consider the value 2.2946, for example. There are four data points that are less than or equal to the given value: `-0.1412`, `0.6152`, `0.6852`, and `2.2946` itself. We now divide the number of values, 4, by the number of points so that the result is between 0 and 1. So, the value of the cumulative distribution function is *4/10=0.4* for these 10 values. In terms of a mathematical expression, we write the following:

$$\boxed{F(2.2946) = 0.4}$$

It is common practice to abbreviate *cumulative distribution function* by *cdf*, and we will do so from now on.

An important point to notice is that the cdf is not defined only at values in the dataset. In fact, it is defined for any numeric value whatsoever! Let's suppose, for example, that we want to find the value of the cdf at `x=2.5`. Notice that the number `2.5` is between the fourth and fifth values in the dataset, so there are still four data values less than or equal to 2.5. As a consequence, the value of the function at 2.5 is also `4/10=0.4`. In fact, it can be seen that, for all numbers between `2.2946` and `3.2791`, the cdf will have the value `0.4`.

Thinking a little bit about this process, we can infer the following behavior for a cdf: it remains constant (that is, *flat*) between values in the dataset. At each data value, the function will *jump*, the size of the jump being the reciprocal of the number of data points. This is illustrated in the following figure:

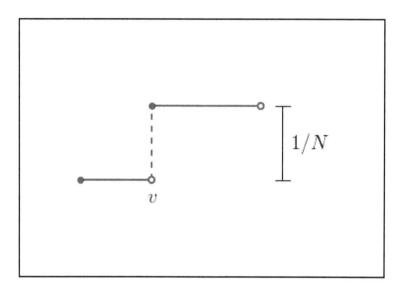

In the preceding figure, **v** is a point in the dataset and the graph displays the cdf in the neighborhood of **v**. Notice the flat intervals between the data points and the jump exactly at the data point **v**. The filled circle at the discontinuity indicates the value of the function at that point. These are characteristics of any cumulative distribution function for a discrete dataset.

Let's now define a Python function that can be used to plot the graph of a cdf. This is done with the following code:

```
def plot_cdf(data, plot_range=None, scale_to=None, **kwargs):
num_bins = len(data)
sorted_data = np.array(sorted(data), dtype=np.float64)
    data_range = sorted_data[-1] - sorted_data[0]
    coutns, bin_edges = np.histogram(sorted_data, bins=num_bins)
xvalues = bin_edges[:1]
yvalues = np.cumsum(counts)
if plot_range is None:
        xmin = sorted_data[0]
        xmax = sorted_data[-1]
    else:
        xmin, xmax = plot_range
```

```
#pad the arrays
xvalues = np.concatenate([[xmin, xvalues[0]], xvalues, [xmax]])
yvalues = np.concatenate([[0.0, 0.0], yvalues, [yvalues.max()]])
   if scale_to is not None:
       yvalues = yvalues / len(data) * scale_to
plt.axis([xmin, xmax, 0, yvalues.max()])
   return plt.plot(xvalues, yvalues, **kwargs)
```

Notice that running this code will not produce any output as we are simply defining the
`plot_cdf()` function. The code is somewhat complex, but all we are doing is defining lists
of points stored in the `xvalues` and `yvalues` arrays. These values are the leading edge of
the staircase and the height of the specific step. The `plt.step()` function plots these in a
step plot. We use NumPy's `concatenate()` function to pad the array, in the start with
zeroes, and in the end with the maximum (or last) value of the array. To plot the cdf for a
dataset, we can run the following code:

```
nvalues = 20
norm_variates = rnd.randn(nvalues)
plot_cdf(norm_variates, plot_range=[-3,3], scale_to=1.0,
         lw=2.5, color='Brown')
for v in [0.25, 0.5, 0.75]:
    plt.axhline(v, lw=1, ls='--', color='black')
```

In this code, we first generate a new set of data values. Then, we call the `plot_cdf()`
function to generate the graph. The arguments of the function call are `plot_range`,
specifying the range in the *x* axis, and `scale_to`, which specifies that we want the values (*y*
axis) to be normalized from 0 to 1. The remaining arguments to the `plot_cdf()` function
are passed to the Pyplot function, `plot()`. In this example, we set the line width with
the `lw=2.5` option and line color with the `color="Brown"` option.

The purpose of the `scale_to` option is to allow setting a different range
for `yvalues` in the plot. With `scale_to=100.0`, the *y* axis is scaled in
percentages and `scale_to=None` represents the count of data points
without any scaling.

Running this code will produce an image similar to the following one:

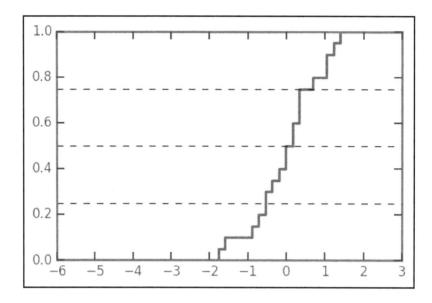

The graph obtained by you will be somewhat different as the data is randomly generated. In the preceding figure, we also draw horizontal lines at `yvalues` `0.25`,`0.5`, and `0.75`. These correspond, respectively, to the first quartile, median, and third quartile in the data. Looking at the corresponding values in the *x* axis, we see that these values correspond approximately to -0.5, 0, and 0.5. This makes sense as the actual values for a theoretical Normal distribution are `-0.68`, `0.0`, and `0.68`. Notice that we do not expect to recover these values exactly due to randomness and the small size of the sample.

Now, I invite you to perform the following experiment. Increase the number of values in the dataset by changing the value of the `nvalues` variable in the preceding code, and run the cell again. It will be noticed that, as the number of data values increases, the curve becomes smoother and converges toward an S-shaped curve, symmetric about its center. Also notice that the quartiles and median will tend to approach the theoretical values for the Normal distribution, `-0.68`, `0.0`, and `0.68`. As we will see in the next section, these are some of the characteristics of the standard Normal distribution.

Let's investigate the cdf for a realistic dataset. The `housefly-wing-lengths.txt` file contains wing lengths in tenths of a millimeter for a small sample of houseflies. The data is from a 1968 paper by *Sokal, R. R.,* and *Rohlf, J. R.* in the journal *Biometry* (page 109) and a 1955 paper by *Sokal, R. R.* and *P.E. Hunter* in the journal *Annual Entomol. Soc. America* (Volume 48, page 499). The data is also available online at `http://www.seattlecentral .edu/qelp/sets/057/057.html`.

To read the data, make sure that the `housefly-wing-lengths.txt` file is in the same directory as the Jupyter Notebook, and then run the following code segment:

```
wing_lengths = np.fromfile('data/housefly-wing-lengths.txt',
                           sep='\n', dtype=np.int64)
print(wing_lengths)
```

This dataset is in a plain text file with one value per line, so we simply use NumPy's `fromfile()` function to load the data into an array, which we name `wing_lengths`. The `sep='\n'` option tells NumPy that this is a text file, with values separated by the new line character, `\n`. Finally, the `dtype=np.int64` option specifies that we want to treat the values as integers. The dataset is so small that we can print all the points, which we do by repeating the `wing_lengths` array name at the end of the cell.

Let's now generate a plot of the cdf for this data by running the following code in a cell:

```
plot_cdf(wing_lengths, plot_range=[30, 60],
         scale_to=100, lw=2)
plt.grid(lw=1)
plt.xlabel('Housefly wing length (x.1mm)', fontsize=18)
plt.ylabel('Percent', fontsize=18);
```

We, again, use the `plot_cdf()` function that was previously defined. Notice that now we use `scale_to=100` so that, instead of proportions, we can read a percentage in the vertical axis. We also add a grid and axis labels to the plot. We obtain the following plot:

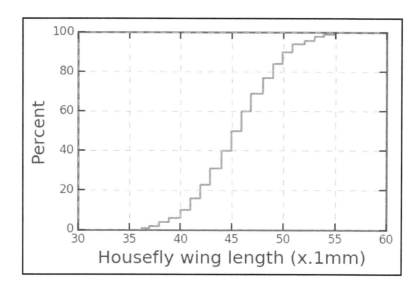

Notice that the cdf has, roughly, the same symmetric S-shaped pattern that we observed before. This indicates that a Normal distribution might be an adequate model for this data. It is, indeed, the case that this data fits a Normal distribution quite closely.

Just as an example of the kind of information that can be extracted from this plot, let's suppose that we want to design a net that will catch 80% of the flies. That is, the mesh should allow only flies with a wing length in the bottom 20% to pass. From the preceding graph, we can see that the 20th percentile corresponds to a wing length of about 42 tenths of a millimeter. This is not intended to be a realistic application and if we were really building this net, we would probably want to do a more careful analysis, but it shows how we can get information about the data quickly from a cumulative distribution plot.

Working with distributions

The main reason that we emphasize the cumulative distribution function is because, once we have access to it, we can compute any probabilities associated with the model. This is because the cdf is a universal way to specify a random variable. In particular, there is no distinction between the descriptions for **continuous** or discrete data. The density function of a random variable is also an important concept so we will present it in the next section. In this section, we will see how to use the cdf to do computations related to a random variable.

The functions that we will use with distributions are part of SciPy and contained in the `scipy.stats` module, which we import with the following code:

```
import scipy.stats as st
```

After this, we can refer to functions in the package with the abbreviation `st`.

This module contains a large number of predefined distributions, and we encourage you to visit the official documentation at `http://docs.scipy.org/doc/scipy/reference/stats.html` to see what is available. Fortunately for us, the module is organized in such a way that all distributions are handled in a uniform way, as shown in the following line:

```
st.<rv_name>.<function>(<arguments>)
```

The components of this expression are as follows:

- `st` is the abbreviation that we chose for the stats package.
- `<rv_name>` is the name of the distribution (`rv` stands for random variable).
- `<function>` is the specific function that we want to calculate.
- `<arguments>` are the values that need to be passed to each function. These might include the shape parameters for each distribution as well as other required parameters that depend on the function being called.

The following table lists some of the functions that are available for each random variable:

Function	Description
`rvs()`	Random variates, that is, pseudorandom number generation
`cdf()`	Cumulative distribution function
`pdf()` or `pmf()`	Probability density function (for continuous variables) and probability mass function (for discrete variables)

`ppf()`	Percent point function, the inverse of the cumulative distribution function
`stats()`	Compute statistics (moments) for distribution
`mean()`, `std()`, or `var()`	Compute mean, standard deviation, and variance, respectively
`fit()`	Fit data to the distribution and return the parameters for the shape, location, and scale parameters from the data

Whenever we specify a distribution, we need to set the parameters that characterize the random variable of interest. Most models have, at least, a *location* and *scale*, which are commonly referred to as the `shape` parameters of the random variable. The location specifies a shift in the distribution and the scale represents a rescaling of the values (such as when units are changed).

In the following example, we will concentrate on Normal distribution as this is certainly an important case. However, you should be aware that the computation patterns we present can be used with *any* distribution. So, if one needs, for example, to work with a Log-Laplace distribution, all they have to do is replace `norm` in the following examples with `loglaplace`. Of course, it is necessary to consult the documentation to make sure that the correct parameters are being used for the distribution of interest.

An invaluable resource for statistical techniques is the NIST Engineering Statistics Handbook, available at `http://www.itl.nist.gov/div898/h andbook/index.htm`. Section *1.3.6, Probability Distributions*, contains an excellent introduction to random variables and distributions. Another quick reference is the Wikipedia list of probability distributions, located at `http://en.wikipedia.org/wiki/List_of_probability_distrib utions`.

For a Normal distribution, the location parameter gives the *mean* of the distribution and the scale represents the *standard deviation* of the distribution. These terms will be defined later in the chapter, but they are numbers that measure the center and spread of the distribution. To give a concrete example of a normally distributed random variable, let's consider the height of women over 20 years of age, as in National Health Statistics Reports, Number 10, October 2008, available online at `http://www.cdc.gov/nchs/data/nhsr/nhsr010.pdf`. This report contains anthropometric reference data for the U.S. population, according to age group. On page 14, the height of women over 20 is reported as having a mean of 63.8 inches with a standard error of 0.06. The sample size is 4,857.

We will assume that heights are normally distributed (which, as it happens, is a reasonable assumption). To characterize the distribution, we need the mean and standard deviation. The mean is given directly in the report. The standard deviation is not reported directly but can be computed from the standard error and sample size, according to the following formula:

$$\text{standard error} = \frac{\text{standard deviation}}{\sqrt{N}}$$

The standard error is a measure of sample variability that will be introduced in Chapter 4, *Regression*. We are also ignoring the issue that we are using the *sample standard deviation* instead of the population standard deviation, but the sample is large enough to justify this approach, as will be seen in Chapter 4, *Regression*. We start by defining the distribution to be used as the model for this situation, using the following code:

```
N = 4857
mean = 63.8
serror = 0.06
sdev = serror * np.sqrt(N)
rvnorm = st.norm(loc=mean, scale=sdev)
```

In this code, we first define variables to represent the sample size, mean, and standard error. Then, the standard deviation is computed according to the preceding formula. In the last line of code, we call the norm() function, passing the mean and standard deviation as parameters. The object returned by the function is assigned to the rvnorm variable, and it is through this variable that we access the functionality of the package.

 It is possible to do all calculations without constructing an object first, but this is the recommended approach if we want to do several computations related to the same random variable.

A good place to start with any distribution is to make graphs so that we can have an idea of the shape of the distribution. This can be accomplished with the following code:

```
xmin = mean-3*sdev
xmax = mean+3*sdev
xx = np.linspace(xmin,xmax,200)
plt.figure(figsize=(8,3))
plt.subplot(1,2,1)
plt.plot(xx, rvnorm.cdf(xx))
```

```
plt.title('Cumulative distribution function')
plt.xlabel('Height (in)')
plt.ylabel('Proportion of women')
plt.axis([xmin, xmax, 0.0, 1.0])
plt.subplot(1,2,2)
plt.plot(xx, rvnorm.pdf(xx))
plt.title('Probability density function')
plt.xlabel('Height (in)')
plt.axis([xmin, xmax, 0.0, 0.1]);
```

Most of the lines of the preceding code deal with setting up and formatting the plot. The two most important pieces of code are the two calls to the plot() function. The first call is as follows:

```
plt.plot(xx, rvnorm.cdf(xx))
```

The xx array was previously defined to contain the *x* coordinates to be plotted. The rvnorm.cdf(xx) function call computes the value of the cdf. The second call is analogous as follows:

```
plt.plot(xx, rvnorm.pdf(xx))
```

The only difference is that now we call rvnorm.pdf(xx) to compute the probability density function. The overall effect of the code is to generate side-by-side plots of the cdf and density function. These are the familiar S-shaped and bell-shaped curves, which are characteristic of a Normal distribution:

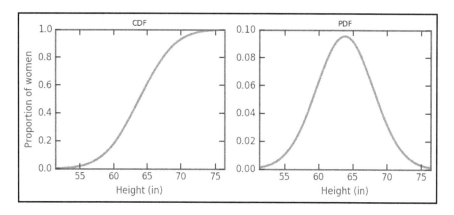

Let's now see how we can use the cdf to compute quantities related to the distribution. Suppose that a garment factory uses a classification of women's heights, as indicated in the following table:

Size	Height
Petite	59 inches to 63 inches
Average	63 inches to 68 inches
Tall	68 inches to 71 inches

What percentage of women are in the *Average* category? We can get this information directly from the cdf. Recall that this function gives the proportion of data values up to a given value. So, the proportion of women with heights up to 68 inches is computed by the following expression:

```
rvnorm.cdf(68)
```

Likewise, the proportion of women with heights up to 63 inches is computed with the following expression:

```
rvnorm.cdf(63)
```

The proportion of women with heights between 63 inches and 68 inches is the difference between these values. As we want a percentage, we have to multiply the result by 100, as shown in the following line of code:

```
100 * (rvnorm.cdf(68) - rvnorm.cdf(63))
```

The result of this computation shows that approximately 42.8% of women are *Average* according to this classification. To compute the percentages for the three categories and display them in a nice format, we can use the following code:

```
categories = [
    ('Petite', 59, 63),
    ('Average', 63, 68),
    ('Tall', 68, 71),
    ]
for cat, vmin, vmax in categories:
    percent = 100 * (rvnorm.cdf(vmax) - rvnorm.cdf(vmin))
    print('{:>8s}: {:.2f}'.format(cat, percent))
```

In this code segment, we start by creating a Python list that describes the categories. Each category is represented by a three-element tuple, containing the category name, minimum height, and maximum height. We then use a `for` loop to iterate over the categories. For each category, we first compute the percentage of women in the category using the cdf, and then print the result.

A somewhat unexpected feature of this classification is that it imposes the lowest and highest values on women's heights. We can compute the percentage of women that are too short or too tall to fit in any of the categories with the following code:

```
too_short = 100 * rvnorm.cdf(59)
too_tall = 100 * (1 - rvnorm.cdf(71))
unclassified = too_short + too_tall
print(too_short, too_tall, unclassified)
```

Running this code, we conclude that almost 17% of the women are unclassified! This may not seem too much, but any sector of industry that neglects such a portion of its customer base will be losing profits. Suppose that we have been hired to come up with a more effective classification. Let's say that we agree that 50% of women at the center of the distribution should be classified as *Average*, the top 25% should be considered *Tall*, and the lower 25% should be considered *Petite*. In other words, we want to use the quartiles of the distribution to define height categories. Notice that this is an arbitrary decision and may not be realistic.

We can find the threshold values between the categories using the inverse of the cdf. This is computed by the ppf() method, which stands for **percent point function**. This is shown in the following code:

```
a = rvnorm.ppf(0.25)
b = rvnorm.ppf(0.75)
print(a, b)
```

This computation shows you how to compute the first and third quartiles of any distribution. In general, to find the percentile c of the distribution, we can use the rvnorm.ppf(c/100.) expression.

From the preceding computation, it follows that, according to our criterion, women should be considered *Average* if their heights are between approximately 61 inches and 67 inches. It seems that the original classification is skewed toward taller women (there is a large proportion of short women that do not fit the classification). We can only speculate why this is the case. Industry standards are sometimes inherited from tradition and may have been set without regard to actual data.

It is worthy to notice that, in all the computations we did, we used the *cumulative distribution function* and not the probability density function, which we will present in the next section. Indeed, this will be the case with most computations that are needed in inference. The fact that most people prefer to use probability densities when defining distributions may simply be due to historical bias. In fact, *both* views of a random variable are important and find a place in theory and applications.

To finish this example, let's compute some relevant parameters (that is, point estimates) for the distribution of heights using the following code:

```
mean, variance, skew, kurtosis = rvnorm.stats(moments='mvks')
print(mean, variance, skew, kurtosis)
```

This will print values of `63.8` for the mean, `17.4852` for the variance, and 0 for both skew and kurtosis. These values are interpreted as follows:

- The `mean` is the average value of the distribution. As the distribution is symmetric, it coincides with the median.
- The `variance` is the square of the standard deviation. It is defined as the average value of the square of the deviation from the mean.
- The `skew` measures the asymmetry of the distribution. As the Normal distribution is symmetric, the skew is zero.
- The `kurtosis` indicates how the distribution peaks: does it have a sharp peak or a flatter bump? The value of kurtosis for the Normal distribution is zero because it is used as a reference distribution.

For our next example, let's suppose that we need to build a simulation for the time-to-failure of some equipment. A frequently used model for this situation is the Weibull distribution, named after Waloddi Weibull, who carefully studied the distribution in 1951. This distribution is described in terms of two numbers called the `scale` parameter, denoted by η (`eta`) and the `shape` parameter, denoted by β (`beta`). Both parameters must be positive numbers.

 There is a three-parameter version of the Weibull distribution that introduces a location parameter. We assume that the equipment can fail from the start of its operation, so the location parameter is zero and can be ignored.

The `shape` parameter is related to how the failure rate of the equipment depends on its age (or operation time) as follows:

- If the shape parameter is smaller than `1`, then the failure rate decreases as time passes. This occurs, for example, if there is a significant number of items that are defective and tend to fail early when put in use.
- If the shape parameter is equal to `1`, the failure rate is constant in time. This is the well-known **exponential distribution**. In this model, the chance that the equipment fails in a given interval does not depend on how long it has been operating. This is an unrealistic assumption in most cases.

- If the shape parameter is larger than 1, then the failure rate of the equipment increases as time passes. This is reflective of an aging process, in which older equipment is more prone to failure.

The scale parameter, on the other hand, determines how much the distribution spreads. Put in an intuitive way, a larger value of the scale parameter corresponds to more uncertainty regarding predictions for the failure time. Notice that, in this case, the scale parameter cannot be interpreted as the standard deviation of the model.

Let's say that we want to simulate a Weibull distribution with the shape parameter βpara and scale parameter ηand. You are encouraged, at this point, to generate plots of the cumulative distribution and probability density functions for the Weibull distribution by modifying the code that we previously used for the Normal distribution. To create the distribution, the following code can be used:

```
eta = 1.0
beta = 1.5
rvweib = st.weibull_min(beta, scale=eta)
```

After defining the eta and beta parameters, we call the weibull_min() function, which generates the appropriate object. After producing the graphs, you will notice that the Weibull distribution is markedly asymmetric, having a long right tail after peaking.

Let's now get back to the problem of simulating the distribution. To produce a sample of size 500 following a Weibull distribution, we use the following code:

```
weib_variates = rvweib.rvs(size=500)
print(weib_variates[:10])
```

In this code, we simply call the rvs() method, passing the desired sample size as an argument. The abbreviation **rvs** stands for **random variates**. As the generated sample is quite large, we simply print the first 10 values. We can use a histogram to visualize the sample, as shown in the following code:

```
weib_df = DataFrame(weib_variates,columns=['weibull_variate'])
weib_df.hist(bins=30);
```

In this code, we first convert the data to a Pandas DataFrame object as we want to use Pandas' plotting capabilities. Then, we simply call the hist() method, passing the number of bins as an argument. This results in the following histogram:

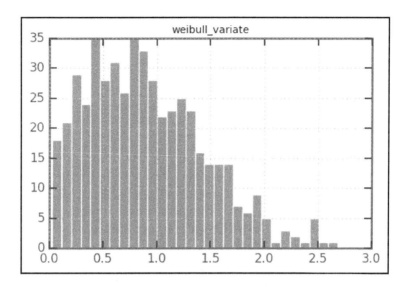

Notice the peak around **0.5** followed by a decaying tail toward the right. Also notice the few values at the extreme right of the histogram. These represent survival times that are large compared with the bulk of the data.

Finally, we want to assess how good the simulation is. To this end, we can plot the cumulative distribution function of the sample, compared with that of the theoretical distribution. This is achieved with the following code:

```
xmin = 0
xmax = 3.5
xx = np.linspace(xmin,xmax,200)
plt.plot(xx, rvweib.cdf(xx), color='orange', lw=5)
plot_cdf(weib_variates, plot_range=[xmin, xmax], scale_to=1, lw=2,
color='green')
plt.axis([xmin, xmax, 0, 1])
plt.title('Weibul distribution simulation', fontsize=14)
plt.xlabel('Failure Time', fontsize=12);
```

This code is essentially a combination of code segments that we have seen before. We call the `plot()` function with appropriate arguments to generate a plot of the theoretical cdf, and then use the `plot_cdf()` function, previously defined in this chapter, to plot the cdf of the data. It is seen that the two curves show pretty good agreement.

As a final example in this section, let's explore the `fit()` method, which attempts to fit a distribution to the data. Let's go back to the dataset with wing lengths of houseflies. As previously stated, we suspect that the data is normally distributed. We can find the Normal distribution that *best fits* the data with the following code:

```
wing_lengths = np.fromfile('data/housefly-wing-lengths.txt',
                           sep='\n', dtype=np.int64)
mean, std = st.norm.fit(wing_lengths)
print(mean, std)
```

Just to be on the safe side, we read the data again using the `fromfile()` function. We then use the `st.norm.fit()` function to fit a Normal distribution to the dataset. The `fit()` function returns the mean and standard deviation of the fitted Normal distribution. This is an example of parameter estimation (point estimate). The next question is: *how good is the fit?* We can evaluate this graphically by generating a quantile plot, as shown in Chapter 2, *Exploring Data*. The following is the code:

```
st.probplot(wing_lengths, dist='norm', plot=plt)
plt.grid(lw=1.5, lw='dashed');
```

This code will produce the following plot:

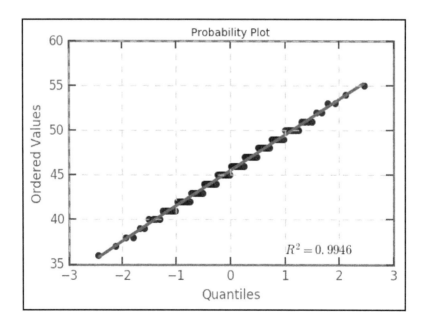

Notice that the sample falls very close to a straight line, indicating that a Normal distribution is a good fit for this data. Notice, however, that there is some clustering in the data, which is a consequence of repeated values (measurement imprecision and rounding).

 Fitting a model to a sample is a complex topic and should be approached with care. In this section, we concentrated on learning how to use the tools provided by NumPy and SciPy, without going deeply into the question of how adequate are the methods that we used. A more careful discussion of some of the topics appears in the remaining chapters of the book.

We finalize this section by encouraging you to visit the SciPy documentation for the `stats` module. This is an extensive module that encompasses a great deal of functionality. The documentation is very well-organized and comprehensive and includes a discussion of the methods used and relevant links to the theory where adequate.

The probability density function

So far, we have considered the cumulative distribution function as the main way to describe a random variable. However, for a large class of important models, the **probability density function (pdf)** is an important alternative characterization.

To understand the distinction between the cdf and pdf, we need the notion of probability. In the context of random variables, probability simply means the likelihood that the random outcome falls within a certain range of values, normalized to a number between 0 and 1. For example, let's consider the example of women's heights discussed in the previous section. We concluded that 42.8% of women have a height between 63 inches and 68 inches. An alternative way to express this is to say that, for the random variable that represents women's heights, *the probability that the outcome is between 63 and 68 is .428*.

The main distinction between the cdf and pdf is the way probabilities are represented by each of them:

- For a cdf, the probability that the outcome is in a range is computed as the *difference* between the values of the cdf at the endpoints of the range
- For a pdf, the probability that the outcome is in a range is computed as the *area* under the curve determined by the range

To clarify these concepts, let's consider the following figure:

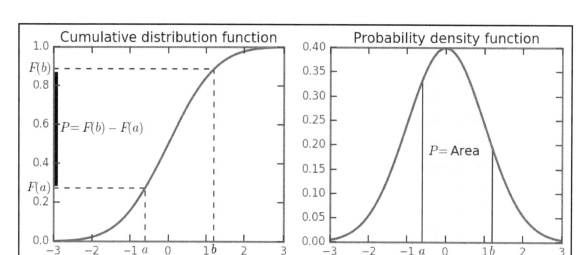

This figure displays both the cdf and pdf for a standard Normal distribution. In both figures, we have a range of values on the horizontal axis defined by the values **a** and **b**. The figure graphically illustrates the probability that the outcome falls in this range in each case:

- In the case of the cdf, the probability is given by $F(b)-F(a)$, which corresponds to the length of the highlighted segment on the y axis
- In the case of the cdf, the probability is given by the *area* bound by the curve between the values **a** and **b**

This observation actually explains why the cdf is more useful computationally. To compute the probability using the cdf, all we need is the difference between two values, while to do the same calculation using the pdf, it is necessary to find the value of an area. As this is not a simple shape, we need calculus to compute the area. In fact, in the case of the Normal distribution, this is an area that cannot be computed even by the methods usually seen in calculus courses! Of course, this complexity still exists when we do computations in Python, but the details are fortunately hidden from us.

This is a good time to mention briefly how the pdf is related to significant characteristics of a distribution such as mean and standard deviation. When talking about a random variable, the notion of *average* is technically called the **expected value** or **mean** of the random variable. Intuitively, this is the average of the values that we expect to see if a large number of trials with the same distribution is observed. Likewise, the variance of the random variable is the average squared deviation from the mean.

Finally, the *standard deviation* is the square root of the variance. Unfortunately, to give a mathematical definition of these notions for a continuous random variable, we again need calculus. As this book concentrates on the practical application of Python to data analysis, we will be content with the intuitive meaning of these concepts and let the computer do the dirty computational work under the hood.

We finalize by pointing out that we have, in this section, concentrated on a continuous distribution characterized by a smooth cdf. On the other extreme are *discrete distributions*, which have a cdf that looks like a *staircase*, much like the examples seen in the previous section. Discrete random variables cannot be represented by a pdf. Instead, they are defined in terms of a **probability mass function (pmf)**. An example of a discrete random variable is considered in the next section.

Where do models come from?

In this section, we will consider what is perhaps the most important practical point about models. How are models conceived and how do we know what is the right model to use in a given situation?

These are not simple questions, and the process of designing and choosing appropriate models is as much an art as a science. At the risk of oversimplifying, we could say that probabilistic models can come from two sources:

- In *priori models*, the researcher considers the relevant factors, identifies important quantities and relationships, and creates a description that fits the problem being considered
- In *limit models*, the researcher attempts to find an approximation to a model that is too complex, either conceptually or computationally

In both cases, the resulting model may take several different forms. It can be, for example, a mathematical formula, simulation, or algorithm. Always, the model must be validated against real data after the experiments or observations are carried out.

The most important point to emphasize is that all models have *assumptions*. These establish the boundaries within which the model is valid. Identifying the assumptions that are made is probably the first important step in successful model selection.

As examples, we will consider two models with both historical and practical importance: the *Binomial distribution* and *de Moivre approximation*.

The Binomial distribution is an example of a discrete random variable that was originally conceived in the context of gambling but has wide applicability to many situations. Here are the assumptions that underlie the model:

- A series of *N* trials is conducted, where each trial can only have one of two results. We will call the two possible outcomes 0 and 1 (failure and success).
- Each trial has a known probability *p* of having the outcome 1 and a corresponding probability *1-p* of having the outcome .
- The trials are independent, in the sense that the result of each trial is not affected by the results of the other trials.
- The variable being observed is the number of outcomes equal to 1 in the *N* trials.

It is easy to see why this model appeals to gamblers: in a game of chance, one can either win, represented by 1 or lose, represented by 0. The probability of each outcome is known. The gambler plays the game repeatedly and is interested in knowing how much money will be made, which is determined by the number of wins.

In a more practical application, we can think of a quality control system. In this case, 1 represents a good item and 0 represents a defective item. We know the probability *p* of an item being good or defective and want to know the variability of the number of good items when *N* items are produced.

To be concrete, let's say that we are playing a *fair* game in which the probability of winning and losing are both 0.5. We assume that 20 games are played. The Binomial distribution is also part of the `scipy.stats` module, and we can create an object representing the distribution with the following code:

```
N = 20
p = 0.5
rv_binom = st.binom(N, p)
```

As the game is played 20 times, the number of wins in the series is an integer between 0 and 20. To compute the probability that we win 12 out of 20 games, for example, we use the probability mass function, as indicated by the following expression:

```
rv_binom.pmf(12)
```

Evaluating this code, we conclude that the probability of winning exactly 12 out of 20 games is about 0.12 or 12%.

In many cases, we are not interested in the probability of an exact number of wins but on the probability of a range. For example, let's suppose that on a particular day, we win only 7 out of 20 games and wonder if we have been cheated. One way to assess this is to compute the probability of winning seven or fewer games. If this probability is small, it is likely that the assumption that the game is fair is not valid. To compute this probability, we need the cumulative distribution function, which can be computed with the following line of code:

```
rv_binom.cdf(7)
```

The result shows that this event happens with a probability of approximately 0.13, that is, 13% of the time. This is not such a small number, so we would expect that, from time to time, we would actually win only 7 of the 20 games, even in a fair game. So, there does not seem to be reason to suspect cheating, at least in this isolated case.

To get an idea of how the distribution behaves, let's make plots of the cdf and pmf. This can be done with the following code:

```
xx = np.arange(N+1)
cdf = rv_binom.cdf(xx)
pmf = rv_binom.pmf(xx)
xvalues = np.arange(N+1)
plt.figure(figsize=(9,3.5))
plt.subplot(1,2,1)
plt.step(xvalues, cdf, lw=2, color='brown')
plt.grid(lw=1, ls='dashed')
plt.title('Binomial cdf, $N=20$, $p=0.5$', fontsize=16)
plt.subplot(1,2,2)
left = xx - 0.5
plt.bar(left, pmf, 1.0, color='CornflowerBlue')
plt.title('Binomial pmf, $N=20$, $p=0.5$', fontsize=16)
plt.axis([0, 20, 0, .18]);
```

This code is similar to the methods that we used in the graphs previously displayed in this chapter, but we repeat it here as you might find it useful to have a model to make plots of discrete distributions. For the cdf, we simply plot the xvalues and yvalues arrays, which contain the stairs of the cdf taken from the cdf method of the rv_binom object. As we want it to be displayed as such (that is, a staircase), we use the step function to plot it. For the pmf, we use a slightly different approach, the bar() function, which is a matplotlib function that draws a generic bar chart. The arguments for this function are two arrays containing the left coordinate and height of each bar and a number specifying the width of the bars. The plots are displayed in the following figure:

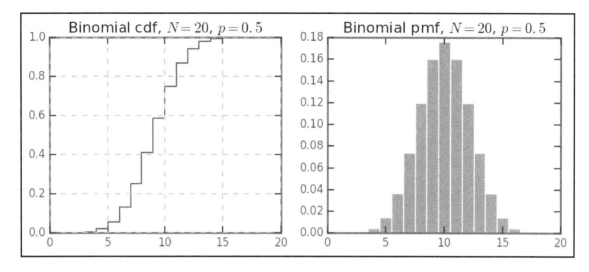

There is an important point to notice here: the pmf is a function that is defined only for the integer values from 1 to 20. However, for visualization purposes, instead of just plotting the discrete points, we plot bars with width one since the data is discrete. Each bar is centered at the integer value that corresponds to the number of *wins*. With these choices, the probabilities in the pmf correspond to the areas of the bars, which is the same interpretation for the pdf of a continuous distribution.

You probably noticed that there is a striking similarity between the preceding plots and Normal distribution. The French mathematician, de Moivre, was the first one to notice that the plot of the pmf for the Binomial distribution approximates a smooth curve if the number of trials N is large. He realized that, if he were able to find a formula for this curve, he would have a simpler way to calculate binomial probabilities for a large number of trials. He was able to find the formula for the curve and, using this formula, he computed binomial probabilities for 3,600 trials, a remarkable feat at the time. This was the birth of the Normal distribution.

To understand the de Moivre approximation, we must first compute the mean and standard deviation of the Binomial distribution. We will do this in two ways. First, let's use the functions provided in `scipy.stats`, as indicated in the following code:

```
mean = rv_binom.mean()
std = rv_binom.std()
print(mean, std)
```

Here, we are simply calling the `mean()` and `std()` methods to compute the mean and standard deviation. An alternative approach is to use the theoretical formulas, as shown in the following code:

```
mean = N * p
std = np.sqrt(N * p * (1 - p))
print(mean, std)
```

Either way, we get 10.0 for the mean and approximately 2.236 for the standard deviation. The de Moivre approximation theorem can be informally stated as follows:

For large N, a Binomial distribution is approximated by a Normal distribution with the same mean and standard deviation.

The following figure shows the pmf of the Binomial distribution superimposed with a plot of the Normal distribution with the same mean and standard deviation. It can be seen that the agreement is remarkable:

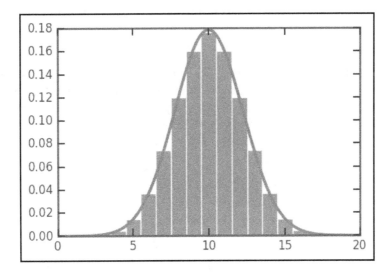

Multivariate distributions

So far in this chapter, we considered only the case of a random experiment that has a single numeric outcome. Within this framework, we can model only a single variable. In most data analysis problems, we may be interested in relationships between variables. For example, we might want to understand the relation between the height and weight of a person or between income and educational levels. In another situation, we may be observing a variable repeatedly. As an example, we might be interested in the daily snowfall in a region during the winter months.

To handle these situations, we need models described by *multivariate distributions*. We have the analogous of the cdf and pdf (or pmf for discrete distributions), but now we have to use functions depending on several variables. The univariate distributions that we discussed in the previous sections are used as building blocks, but we have the extra complication of having to specify how the different variables interact with each other.

A typical example is the bivariate Normal distribution. In this model, we observe two random variables that, individually, are normally distributed. Each of the two variables is characterized by its own mean and standard deviation. However, we must also say how the two variables interact.

In the simplest case, the outcome of one of the variables has no influence whatsoever on the outcome of the other. Consider, for example, the relationship between the snowfall in London and the score of a soccer match in Sidney. Unless we believe in some kind of supernatural connection, we don't expect there to be any connection between these variables. In this case, we say that the variables are *independent*.

On the other hand, and more interestingly, the variables may be *correlated*; in the sense that the result of one of the observations will affect the probabilities for the other. For example, we expect the weight and height of a person to be correlated. In this case, we will be interested in knowing how strong the correlation is and perhaps use one of the variables to make predictions about the other.

The multivariate Normal distribution is also part of the `scipy.stats` package. For now, we will just see how to generate random variates according to a bivariate Normal distribution. We will look at multivariate distributions in detail later in the book. Let's run the following code to generate random variables:

```
binorm_variates = st.multivariate_normal.rvs(mean=[0,0], size=300)
df = DataFrame(binorm_variates, columns=['Z1', 'Z2'])
df.head(10)
```

In this code, we are using the `multivariate_normal.rvs()` function to generate a sample of size 300 from a bivariate normal with the mean zero and default covariance 1. We then convert the NumPy array to a Pandas DataFrame and print the first 10 components of the DataFrame. We can now create a scatterplot of the variates using the following lines of code:

```
df.plot(kind='scatter', x='Z1', y='Z2')
plt.title('Bivariate Normal Distribution')
plt.axis([-4,4,-4,4]);
```

Here, we are using the `plot()` method of the `df` object. The `kind=scatter` option is used to produce a scatterplot. We have to specify the x and y components for the scatterplot with the corresponding options. After that, we set the title of the plot and adjust the axis ranges:

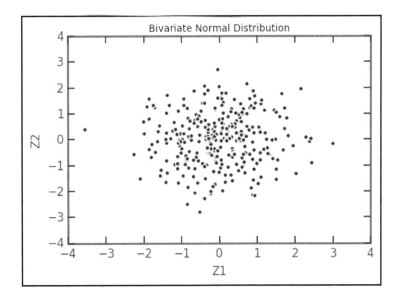

Summary

In this chapter, you learned about the basic models used in data analysis. We studied how the cumulative distribution function and probability density function can be used to characterize a random variable and how to do computations using these tools, including calculating means, standard deviation, and variance and generating random variates.

We have seen examples of continuous and discrete random variables and studied two important cases: the Binomial distribution and its approximation by a Normal distribution. The chapter concludes with an overview of multivariate distributions.

In the next chapter, we will take a closer look at various ways of doing regression.

4
Regression

Linear regression is part of the general introduction to experimental techniques; it forms the base for many of the scientific breakthroughs for the last few centuries. We made some short dives into linear regression before, looking at Hubble's law among other things. The previous chapter consisted of looking at distributions, which is an integral part of exploratory data analysis and indeed one of the first steps in gaining insights into the data. All of the things that we have gone through so far are, as you will see, useful in this chapter as well. You are strongly encouraged to experiment and try out these new things in combination with what was learned in the previous chapters. In this chapter, we will cover the following forms of regression:

- Linear regression
- Multiple regression
- Logistic regression

In the simplest formulation, linear regression deals with estimating a variable from another variable. In multiple regression, a variable is estimated from two or more others. This, of course, only works when the variables have some kind of correlation between them. It's important to point out at this point is that correlation does not imply causation; just because two or more variables show a dependence on one another, it does not mean that they actually affect/depend each other in real life. Logistic regression fits models to one or more discrete variables, which are sometimes binary (that is, can only take the values 0 or 1).

In this chapter, we will start with a quick introduction to linear regression, then we dive directly into getting the data and testing a hypothesis of a simple relationship between two variables. After this, the extension to multiple variables is covered, where we simply add data to what we have from the previous section. Logistic regression is covered in the last part of the chapter.

Curiosity is strongly encouraged, and use what we have learned in the previous chapters to explore the data. Before running the examples in this chapter, start the Jupyter Notebook and run the default imports.

Introducing linear regression

The simplest form of linear regression is given by the relation $y = k_x + k_0$, where k_0 is called **intercept**, that is, the value of y when x=0 and k is the slope. A general expression for this could be found by thinking of each point as the preceding relation plus an error ε. This would then look, for N points, as follows:

$$y_1 = kx_1 + k_0 + \varepsilon_1$$

$$y_2 = kx_2 + k_0 + \varepsilon_2$$

$$y_{N-1} = kx_{N-1} + k_0 + \varepsilon_{N-1}$$

$$y_N = kx_N + k_0 + \varepsilon_N$$

We can express this in matrix form:

$$Y = Xk + \varepsilon$$

Here, the various matrices/vectors are represented as follows:

$$Y = \begin{bmatrix} y_1 \\ \vdots \\ y_N \end{bmatrix} \quad X = \begin{bmatrix} 1 & x_1 \\ 1 & \vdots \\ 1 & x_N \end{bmatrix} \quad k = \begin{bmatrix} k_0 \\ k \end{bmatrix} \quad \varepsilon = \begin{bmatrix} \varepsilon_1 \\ \vdots \\ \varepsilon_N \end{bmatrix}$$

Performing the multiplication and addition of the matrix and vectors should yield the same set of equations that are defined here. The goal of the regression is to estimate the parameters, k, in this case. There are many types of parameter estimation methods—ordinary least squares being one of the most common—but there are also maximum likelihood, Bayesian, mixed model, and several others. In ordinary least-squares minimization, the square of the residuals are minimized, that is, $r^T r$ is minimized (T denotes the transpose and r denotes the residuals, that is Y_{data}-Y_{fit}). It is nontrivial to solve the matrix equation; however, it is instructive to at least do this once if time permits. In the following example, we will use the least-squares minimization method. Most of the time, underlying computations use matrices to calculate the estimates of the parameters and uncertainty in the determination. What also comes out of the analysis is how correlated the variables are, that is, how likely it is that a linear relation exists between them.

Getting the dataset

Before we start estimating parameters of linear relationships, we need a dataset. In this first example, we will look at the suicide rate data from the **World Health Organization** (**WHO**) at http://www.who.int. One very important and complex part of data analysis is getting the data into manageable data structures appropriate for our analysis. Therefore, we will see how to get the data and map it to our desired data structures. The first part of the dataset is age-standardized suicide rates (per 100,000 inhabitants) per country and gender.

Age-standardization (also called age-adjustment) is a technique used to allow populations to be compared when the age profiles of the populations are different.

The following code downloads the data and stores it in a file:

```
importurllib.request
payload='target=GHO/MH_12&profile=crosstable&filter=COUNTRY:*;REGION:*&x-
sideaxis=COUNTRY&x-topaxis=GHO;YEAR;SEX'
suicide_rate_url='http://apps.who.int/gho/athena/data/xmart.csv?'

local_filename, headers =
urllib.request.urlretrieve(suicide_rate_url+payload,
filename='data/who_suicide_rates.csv')
```

The `urllib` module is part of the Python standard library (`https://docs.python.org/3/library`). If the filename input is not given, the file is stored in a temporary location on the disk. If problems arise, it is possible to also go directly to the URL and download the file. Alternatively, the OECD database contains suicide rates that also go back in time to 1960 (`http://stats.oecd.org`).

As before, we use Pandas' `read_csv` function from the Pandas data reader. Here, we give names to the columns; it is possible to send only the `header=2` parameter. This would tell you that the column names are given in the header; however, this might not always be what we want:

```
LOCAL_FILENAME = 'data/who_suicide_rates.csv_backup'
rates = pandas.read_csv(LOCAL_FILENAME, names=['Country','Both', 'Female',
'Male'], skiprows=3)
rates.head(10)
```

	Country	Both	Female	Male
0	Afghanistan	5.7	5.3	6.2
1	Albania	5.9	5.2	6.6
2	Algeria	1.9	1.5	2.3
3	Angola	13.8	7.3	20.7
4	Argentina	10.3	4.1	17.2
5	Armenia	2.9	0.9	5.0
6	Australia	10.6	5.2	16.1
7	Austria	11.5	5.4	18.2
8	Azerbaijan	1.7	1.0	2.4
9	Bahamas	2.3	1.3	3.6

To make it easier for you, we tell it to skip the first three rows, where the metadata of the file is stored. As covered before, the CSV file format lacks a proper standard, hence it can be difficult to interpret everything correctly, so skipping the header makes it more robust in this case. However, experimenting with different input parameters is encouraged and can be very instructive. As shown in previous chapters, we start out by exploring this dataset:

```
rates.plot.hist(stacked=True, y=['Male', 'Female'],
                bins=30, color=['Coral', 'Green'])
plt.xlabel('Rate');
```

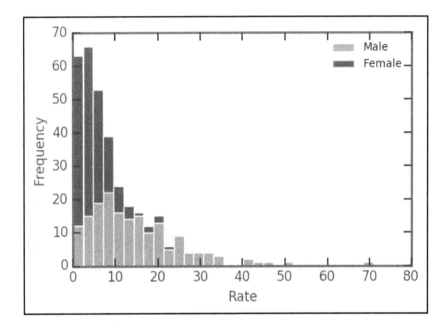

The histogram now plots the columns with names matching **Male** and **Female**, stacked on top of each other. It shows that the suicide rates are a bit different for males and females. Printing out the mean suicide rates for the genders shows that males have a significantly higher rate of suicide:

```
print(rates['Male'].mean(), rates['Female'].mean())
14.69590643274854 5.070602339181275
```

To look closer at some of the basic statistics of the rates, we use the boxplot command:

```
rates.boxplot();
```

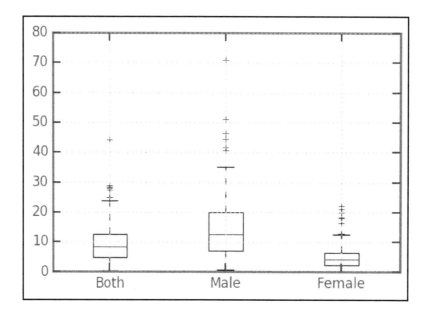

As it's clear, the suicide rate is higher for men in comparison with women. Looking at the boxplot and also the combined distribution (that is, the **Both** key), we can see that there is one outlier (that is, crosses) with a really high rate. It has over 40 suicides per 100,000; which country/countries is/are this? Let's have a look:

```
print(rates[rates['Both']>40])
    Country Both Female Male
66  Guyana 44.2  22.1 70.8
```

Here, we filter by saying that we want only the indices where the rates in the Both column are higher than 40. Apparently, the suicide rate in Guyana is very high. There are some interesting and, obviously, troublesome facts surrounding this. A quick web search reveals that while theories to explain the high rate have been put forth, studies are yet to reveal the underlying reason(s) for the significantly higher than average rate.

As seen in the preceding histograms, the suicide rates all have a similar distribution (shape). Let's first use the CDF plotting function defined in the examples in previous chapters:

```
def plot_cdf(data, plot_range=None, scale_to=None, nbins=False, **kwargs):
    if not nbins:
        nbins = len(data)
    sorted_data = np.array(sorted(data), dtype=np.float64)
    data_range = sorted_data[-1] - sorted_data[0]
    counts, bin_edges = np.histogram(sorted_data, bins=nbins)
    xvalues = bin_edges[1:]
    yvalues = np.cumsum(counts)
    if plot_range is None:
        xmin = xvalues[0]
        xmax = xvalues[-1]
    else:
        xmin, xmax = plot_range
    # pad the arrays
    xvalues = np.concatenate([[xmin, xvalues[0]], xvalues, [xmax]])
    yvalues = np.concatenate([[0.0, 0.0], yvalues, [yvalues.max()]])
    if scale_to:
        yvalues = yvalues / len(data) * scale_to
    plt.axis([xmin, xmax, 0, yvalues.max()])
    return plt.step(xvalues, yvalues, **kwargs)
```

With this, we can again study the distribution of suicide rates. Run the function on the combined rates, that is, the Both column:

```
plot_cdf(rates['Both'], nbins=50, plot_range=[-5, 70])
```

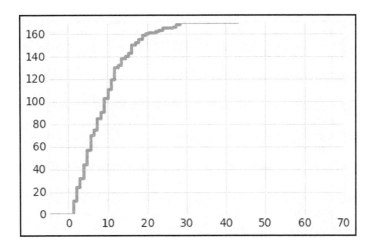

We can first test the normal distribution as it is the most common distribution:

```
st.probplot(rates['Both'], dist='norm', plot=plt);
```

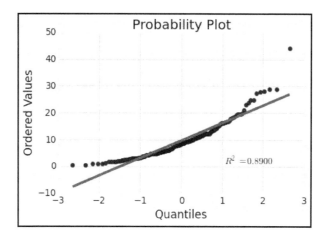

Comparing what we saw previously when creating plots like this, the fit is not good at all. Recall the Weibull distribution from the previous chapter; it might fit better with its skew toward lower values. So let's try it:

```
beta = 1.5
eta = 1.
rvweib = st.weibull_min(beta, scale=eta)
st.probplot(rates['Both'], dist=rvweib, plot=plt);
```

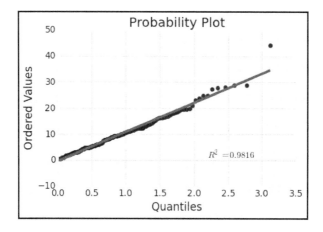

The Weibull distribution seems to reproduce the data quite well. The r-value, or the **Pearson correlation coefficient**, is a measure of how well a linear model represents the relationship between two variables. Furthermore, the r-square value given by `st.probplot` is the square of the r-value, in this case. It is possible to fit the distributions to the data. Here, we fix the location parameter to 0 with `floc=0`:

```
beta, loc, eta = st.weibull_min.fit(rates['Both'],
                     floc=0, scale = 12)
```

This gives `beta` of `1.49`, `loc` of 0, and `scale` of `10.76`. With the fitted parameters, we can plot the histogram of the data and overplot the distribution. I have included a fixed random seed value so that it should reproduce the results in the same way for you:

```
rates['Both'].hist(bins=30)
np.random.seed(1100)
rvweib = st.weibull_min(beta, scale=eta)
plt.hist(rvweib.rvs(size=len(rates.Both)),bins=30, alpha=0.5);
```

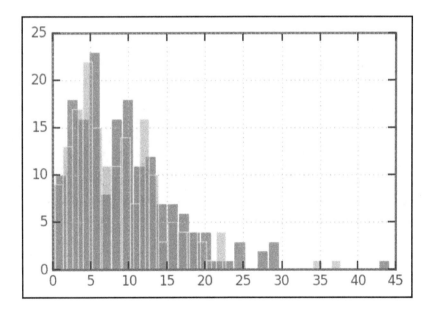

Then, comparing the CDFs of the Weibull and our data, it is obvious that they are similar. Being able to fit the parameters of a distribution is very useful:

```
plot_cdf(rates['Both'], nbins=50,scale_to=1)
np.random.seed(1100)
plot_cdf(rvweib.rvs(size=50),scale_to=1)
plt.xlim((-2,50));
```

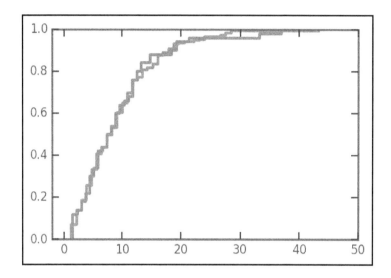

Now that we have the first part of the dataset, we can start to try to understand this. What are some possible parameters that go into suicide rates? Perhaps economic indicators or depression-related variables, such as the amount of sunlight in a year? In the coming section, we will test if the smaller amount of sunlight that one gets, the further away from the equator you go, will show any correlation with the suicide rate. However, as shown in the case of Guyana, some outliers might not fall into any general interpretation of any discovered trend.

Testing with linear regression

With linear regression, it is possible to test a proposed correlation between two variables. In the previous section, we ended up with a dataset of the suicide rates per country. We have a Pandas DataFrame with three columns: the country name, suicide rates for males and females, and mean of both genders. To test the hypothesis that suicide rate depends on how much sunlight the country gets, we are going to use the country coordinate centroid, that is, latitude (and longitude) for each country. We assume that the amount of sunlight in each country is directly proportional to the latitude. Getting centroids of each country in the world is more difficult than what one might imagine. Some of the resources for this are as follows:

- A simple countries centroid can be found on the Gothos web page: `http://gothos.info/2009/02/centroids-for-countries/`
- A more complex table, which would demand more processing before the analysis, is at OpenGeocode: `http://www.opengeocode.org/download.php#cow`
- OpenGeocode has geolocation databases that are free public domain

We are using the Gothos version, so you should make sure that you have the data file (CSV format):

```
coords=pandas.read_csv('data/country_centroids/
                        country_centroids_primary.csv', sep='\t')
coords.keys()
```

```
Index(['LAT', 'LONG', 'DMS_LAT', 'DMS_LONG', 'MGRS', 'JOG', 'DSG', 'AFFIL',
       'FIPS10', 'SHORT_NAME', 'FULL_NAME', 'MOD_DATE', 'ISO3136'],
      dtype='object')
```

A lot of column names to work with! First, we take a peek at the table:

```
coords.head()
```

	LAT	LONG	DMS_LAT	DMS_LONG	MGRS	JOG	DSG	AFFIL	FIPS10	SHORT_NAME	FULL_NAME	MOD_DATE	ISO3136
0	33.000000	66.0	330000	660000	42STB1970055286	NI42-09	PCLI	NaN	AF	Afghanistan	Islamic Republic of Afghanistan	2009-04-10	AF
1	41.000000	20.0	410000	200000	34TDL1589839239	NK34-08	PCLI	NaN	AL	Albania	Republic of Albania	2007-02-28	AL
2	28.000000	3.0	280000	30000	31REL0000097202	NH31-15	PCLI	NaN	AG	Algeria	People's Democratic Republic of Algeria	2011-03-03	DZ
3	-14.333333	-170.0	-142000	-1700000	1802701	NaN	PCLD	US	AS	American Samoa	Territory of American Samoa	1998-10-06	AS
4	42.500000	1.5	423000	13000	31TCH7675006383	NK31-04	PCLI	NaN	AN	Andorra	Principality of Andorra	2007-02-28	AD

The interesting columns are SHORT_NAME and LAT. We shall now match the SHORT_NAME in the coords DataFrame with Country in the rates DataFrame and store the Lat and Lon value when the country name matches. In theory, it would be best if the WHO tables also had the ISO country code, which is a standard created by the **International Organization for Standardization (ISO)**:

```
rates['Lat'] = ''
rates['Lon'] = ''
for i in coords.index:
    ind = rates.Country.isin([coords.SHORT_NAME[i]])
val = coords.loc[i, ['LAT', 'LONG']].values.astype('float')
rates.loc[ind,['Lat','Lon']] = list(val)
```

Here, we loop over the index in the coords DataFrame, and rates.Country.isin([coords.SHORT_NAME[i]]) finds the country that we have taken from the coords object in the rates object. Thus, we are at the row of the country that we have found. We then take the LAT and LONG values found in the coords object and put it into the rates object in the Lat and Lon column. To check whether everything worked, we print out the first few rows:

```
rates.head()
```

	Country	Both	Female	Male	Lat	Lon
0	Afghanistan	5.7	5.3	6.2	33	66
1	Albania	5.9	5.2	6.6	41	20
2	Algeria	1.9	1.5	2.3	28	3
3	Angola	13.8	7.3	20.7	-12.5	18.5
4	Argentina	10.3	4.1	17.2	-34	-64

Some of the values are still empty, and Pandas, matplotlib, and many other modules do not handle empty values in a great way. So we find them and set the empty values to NaN (Not A Number). These are empty because we did not have the Country centroid or the names did not match:

```
rates.loc[rates.Lat.isin(['']), ['Lat']] = np.nan
rates.loc[rates.Lon.isin(['']), ['Lon']] = np.nan
rates[['Lat', 'Lon']] = rates[['Lat', 'Lon']].astype('float')
```

At the same time, we converted the values to floats (the last line of code) instead of strings; this makes it easier to plot and perform other routines. Otherwise, the routine has to convert to float and might run into problems that we have to fix. Converting it manually makes certain that we know what we have. In our simple approximation, the amount of sunlight is directly proportional to the distance from the equator, but we have Latitude. Therefore, we create a new column and calculate the **distance from equator** (**DFE**), which is just the absolute value of the Latitude:

```
rates['DFE'] = ''
rates['DFE'] = abs(rates.Lat)
rates['DFE'] = rates['DFE'].astype('float')
```

Furthermore, countries within +/-23.5 degrees away from the equator get an equal amount of sunlight throughout the year, so they should be considered to have the same suicide rate according to our hypothesis. To first illustrate our new dataset, we plot the rates versus DFE:

```
import matplotlib.patches as patches
import matplotlib.transforms as transforms
fig = plt.figure()
ax = fig.add_subplot(111)
ax.plot(rates.DFE, rates.Both, '.')
trans = transforms.blended_transform_factory(
```

```
        ax.transData, ax.transAxes)
rect = patches.Rectangle((0,0), width=23.5, height=1,
        transform=trans, color='yellow', alpha=0.5)
ax.add_patch(rect)
ax.set_xlabel('DFE')
ax.set_ylabel('Both');
```

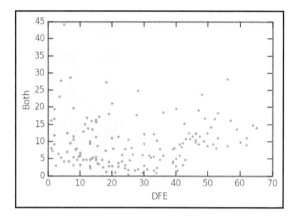

First, we plot the rates versus DFE, then we add a rectangle, for which we do a blended transform on the coordinates. With the blended transform, we can define the x coordinates to follow the data coordinates and the y coordinates to follow the axes (0 being the lower edge and 1 the upper edge). The region with DFE equal to or smaller than 23.5 degrees are marked with the yellow rectangle. It seems that there is some trend toward higher DFE and higher suicide rates. Although tragic and a sad outlook for people living further away from the equator, it lends support to our hypothesis.

To check whether we are sampling roughly even over the DFE, we draw a histogram over the DFE. A uniform coverage ensures that we run a lower risk of sample bias:

```
rates.DFE.hist(bins=13)
plt.xlabel('DFE')
plt.ylabel('Counts');
```

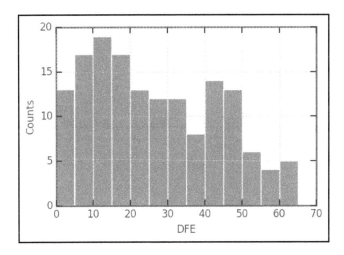

There are fewer countries with DFE > 50 degrees; however, there still seem to be enough for a comparison and regression. Eyeballing the values, it seems that we have about as many countries with DFE > 50 as one of the bins with DFE < 50. One possibility at this stage is to bin the data. Basically, this is taking the histogram bins and the mean of all the rates inside that bin, and letting the center of the bin represent the position and the mean, the value. To bin the data, we use the `groupby` method in Pandas together with the digitize function of NumPy:

```
bins = np.arange(23.5, 65+1,10, dtype='float')
groups_rates = rates.groupby(np.digitize(rates.DFE, bins))
```

Digitize finds the indices for the input array of each bin. The `groupby` method then takes the list of indices, takes those positions from the input array, and puts them in a separate data group. Now we are ready to plot both the unbinned and binned data:

```
import matplotlib.patches as patches
import matplotlib.transforms as transforms
fig = plt.figure()
ax = fig.add_subplot(111)
ax.errorbar(groups_rates.mean().DFE,
        groups_rates.mean().Both,
        yerr=np.array(groups_rates.std().Both),
        marker='.',
        ls='None',
        lw=1.5,
        color='g',
        ms=1)
ax.plot(rates.DFE, rates.Both, '.', color='SteelBlue', ms=6)
```

```
trans = transforms.blended_transform_factory(
    ax.transData, ax.transAxes)
rect = patches.Rectangle((0,0), width=23.5, height=1,
    transform=trans, color='yellow', alpha=0.5)
ax.add_patch(rect)
ax.set_xlabel('DFE')
ax.set_ylabel('Both');
```

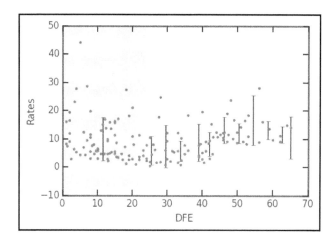

We now perform linear regression and test our hypothesis that less sunlight means a higher suicide rate. As before, we are using `linregress` from SciPy:

```
From scipy.stats import linregress
mindfe = 30
selection = ~rates.DFE.isnull() * rates.DFE>mindfe
rv = rates[selection].as_matrix(columns=['DFE','Both'])
a, b, r, p, stderr = linregress(rv.T)
print('slope:{0:.4f}\nintercept:{1:.4f}\nrvalue:{2:.4f}\npvalue:{3:.4f}\nst
derr:{4:.4f}'.format(a, b, r, p, stderr))
```

```
slope:0.3204
intercept:-4.2373
rvalue:0.5102
pvalue:0.0000
stderr:0.0715
```

Here, the `mindfe` parameter was introduced only to fit a line where DFE is higher than this; you can experiment with the value. Logically, we will start this where DFE is `23.5`; you will get slightly different results for different values. In our example, we use 30 degrees. If you want, you can plot the results just as in the previous chapter with the output of `linregress`.

As an alternative fitting method to `linregress`, we can use the powerful `statsmodels` package. It is installed by default in the Anaconda 3 Python distribution. The `statsmodels` package has a simple way of putting in the assumed relationship between the variables; it is the same as the R-style formulas and was included in `statsmodels` as of version 0.5.0. We want to test a linear relationship between `rates.DFE` and `rates.Both`, so we just tell this to `statsmodels` with `DFE ~ Both`. We are simply giving it the relationship between the keys/column names of the DataFrame.

> The formula framework makes it very easy and clear to express the relationship that you want to fit. Except for relationships such as `Y ~ X + Z`, it is also possible to add functions to the formula, such as `Y ~ X + np.log10(Z)`, to investigate more complex relationships.

The function is fitted with the **Ordinary Least Squares** (**OLS**) method, which basically minimizes the square of the difference between the fit and data (also known as the `loss` function):

```
import statsmodels.formula.api as smf
mod = smf.ols("DFE ~ Both", rates[selection]).fit()
print(mod.summary())
```

```
                        OLS Regression Results
==============================================================================
Dep. Variable:                    Both   R-squared:                       0.260
Model:                             OLS   Adj. R-squared:                  0.247
Method:                  Least Squares   F-statistic:                     20.06
Date:                 Mon, 21 Dec 2015   Prob (F-statistic):           3.65e-05
Time:                         03:40:19   Log-Likelihood:                 -175.72
No. Observations:                   59   AIC:                             355.4
Df Residuals:                       57   BIC:                             359.6
Df Model:                            1
Covariance Type:             nonrobust
==============================================================================
                 coef    std err          t      P>|t|      [95.0% Conf. Int.]
------------------------------------------------------------------------------
Intercept     -4.2373      3.272     -1.295      0.201     -10.789      2.315
DFE            0.3204      0.072      4.479      0.000       0.177      0.464
==============================================================================
Omnibus:                        13.615   Durbin-Watson:                   2.424
Prob(Omnibus):                   0.001   Jarque-Bera (JB):               14.566
Skew:                            1.099   Prob(JB):                     0.000687
Kurtosis:                        4.047   Cond. No.                         238.
==============================================================================

Warnings:
[1] Standard Errors assume that the covariance matrix of the errors is correctly specified.
```

The first part, that is, the left side of the top table gives general information. The dependent variable (**Dep. Variable**) states the name of the variable that is fitted. **Model** states what model we used in the fit; except OLS, there are several other models such as **weighted least squares** (**WLS**). The number of observations (**No. Observations**) are listed and the degrees of freedom of the residuals (**Df Residuals**), that is, the number of observations (59) minus the parameters determined through the fitting 2 (*k* and *k*). **Df Model** shows how many parameters were determined (except the constant, that is, intercept). The table to the right of the top table shows you information on how well the model fits the data. R-squared was covered before; here, the adjusted R-square value (**Adj. R-squared**) is also listed and this is the R-square value corrected for the number of data points and degrees of freedom. The **F-statistic** number gives you an estimate of how significant the fit is. Practically, it is the mean squared error of the model divided by the mean squared error of the residuals. The next value, Prob (F-statistic), gives you the probability to get the F-statistic value if the null hypothesis is true, that is, the variables are not related. After this, three sets of `log-likelihood` function values follow: the value of the log-likelihood value of the fit, the **Akaike Information Criterion** (**AIC**), and **Bayes Information Criterion** (**BIC**). The AIC and BIC are various ways of adjusting the log-likelihood function for the number of observations and model type.

After this, there is a table of the determined parameters, where, for each parameter, the estimated value (`coeff`), standard error of the estimate (`std err`), t-statistic value (`t`), P-value (P>|t|), and 95% confidence interval is shown. A P-value lower than a fixed confidence level, here 0.05 (that is, 5%), shows that there is a statistically significant relationship between the `data` and `model` parameter.

The last section shows the outcome of several statistical tests, which relates to the distribution of the fit residuals. Information about these can be found in the literature and the statsmodels documentation (`http://statsmodels.sourceforge.net/`). In general, the first few test for the shape (skewness) of the errors (residuals): Skewness, Kurtosis, Omnibus, and Jarque-Bera. The rest test if the errors are independent (that is, autocorrelation)—Durbin-Watson—or how the fitted parameters might be correlated with each other (for multiple regression)—**Conditional Number** (**Cond. No**).

From this, we can now say that the suicide rate increases roughly by 0.32+/-0.07 per increasing degree of absolute latitude above 30 degrees per 100,000 inhabitants. There is a weak correlation with absolute Latitude (DFE). The very low Prob (F-statistic) value shows that we can reject the null hypothesis that the two variables are unrelated with quite a high certainty, and the low *P*>|*t*| value shows that there is a relationship between DFE and suicide rate.

We can now plot the fit together with the data. To get the uncertainty of the fit drawn in the figure as well, we use the built-in `wls_prediction_std` function that calculates the lower and upper bounds with 1 standard deviation uncertainty. The WLS here stands for Weighted Least Squares, a method like OLS, but where the uncertainty in the input variables is known and taken into account. It is a more general case of OLS; for the purpose of calculating the bounds of the uncertainty, it is the same:

```
from statsmodels.sandbox.regression.predstd import wls_prediction_std
prstd, iv_l, iv_u = wls_prediction_std(mod)
fig = plt.figure()
ax = fig.add_subplot(111)
rates.plot(kind='scatter', x='DFE', y='Both', ax=ax)
xmin, xmax = min(rates['DFE']), max(rates['DFE'])
ax.plot([mindfe, xmax],
        [mod.fittedvalues.min(), mod.fittedvalues.max()],
        'IndianRed', lw=1.5)
ax.plot([mindfe, xmax], [iv_u.min(), iv_u.max()], 'r--', lw=1.5)
ax.plot([mindfe, xmax], [iv_l.min(), iv_l.max()], 'r--', lw=1.5)
ax.errorbar(groups_rates.mean().DFE,
            groups_rates.mean().Both,
            yerr=np.array(groups_rates.std().Both),
            ls='None',
            lw=1.5,
```

```
              color='Green')
trans = transforms.blended_transform_factory(
    ax.transData, ax.transAxes)

rect = patches.Rectangle((0,0), width=mindfe, height=1,
                         transform=trans, color='Yellow',
                         alpha=0.5)
ax.add_patch(rect)
ax.grid(lw=1, ls='dashed')
ax.set_xlim((xmin,xmax+3));
```

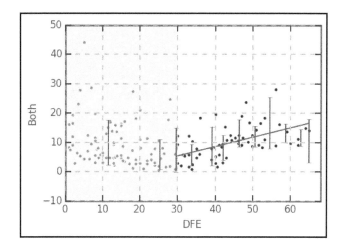

There are a quite a few studies showing the dependency of suicide rates and Latitude (for example, *Davis GE* and *Lowell WE, Can J Psychiatry. 2002 Aug; 47(6):572-4. Evidence that latitude is directly related to variation in suicide rates.*). However, some studies used fewer countries (20), so they could suffer from selection bias, that is, accidentally choosing those countries that favor a strong correlation. What's interesting from this data though is that there seems to be a minimum suicide rate at a higher latitude, which speaks in favor of some relationship.

A few things to remember here are as follows:

- There is a significant spread around the trend. This indicates that this is not one of the major causes for the spread in suicide rates over the world. However, it does show that it is one of the things that might affect it.
- In the beginning, we took the coordinate centroids; some countries span long ranges of latitude. Thus, the rates might vary within that country.

- Although we assume that a direct correlation with the amount of sunlight per year one receives is directly proportional to the latitude, weather of course also plays a role in how much sunlight we see and get.
- It is difficult interpreting the gender data; perhaps women try suicide just as much as men but fail more often, then getting proper help. This would bias the data so that we believe men are more suicidal.

In the long run, the amount of exposure to sunlight affects the production of vitamin D in the body. Many studies are trying to figure out how all of these factors affect the human body. One indication of the complex nature of this comes from studies that show seasonal variations in the suicide rates closer to the equator (Cantor, Hickey, and De Leo, Psychopathology 2000; 33:303-306), indicating that increased and sudden changes in sun exposure increase the suicide risk. The body's reaction to changes in sun exposure is to release or inhibit the release various hormones (melatonin, serotonin, L-tryptophan, among others); a sudden change in the levels of the hormones seems to increase the risk of suicide.

Another potential influence on suicide rates is economic indicators. Thus, we will now try to see if there is a correlation between these three variables through multivariate regression.

Multivariate regression

In this section, we are adding a second variable to the linear model constructed previously. The function that we use to express the correlation now basically becomes a plane, $y = k_2x_2 + k_1x_1 + k$. Just keep in mind that x_1 and x_2 are different axes/dimensions. To clarify a bit, we can also write it as $z = k_2y + k_1x + k$. Just as described in the beginning of the chapter, we can write this as a matrix multiplication. The variable that we choose to include is an economic variable, the **gross domestic product (GDP)**. As hypothesized before, the economy of the country could affect the suicide rate, as suicide prevention needs a developed medical system that isolates people in need and provides help, which is expensive.

Adding economic indicators

Luckily in this case, Pandas has a built-in remote data module that can be used to get certain indicators (`http://pandas.pydata.org/pandas-docs/stable/remote_data.html`). Currently, the services possible to query from Pandas directly are as follows:

- Yahoo! Finance
- Google Finance
- St.Louis FED (FRED)

- Kenneth French's data library
- World Bank
- Google Analytics

To query the World Bank for GDP per capita indicators, we simply do a search for it:

```
from pandas.io import wb
wb.search('gdp.*capita.*').iloc[:,:2]
```

	id	name
680	6.0.GDPpc_constant	GDP per capita, PPP (constant 2011 internation...
4611	GDPPCKD	GDP per Capita, constant US$, millions
4612	GDPPCKN	Real GDP per Capita (real local currency units...
6390	NE.GDI.FTOT.CR	GDP expenditure on gross fixed capital formati...
6478	NV.AGR.PCAP.KD.ZG	Real agricultural GDP per capita growth rate (%)
6600	NY.GDP.PCAP.CD	GDP per capita (current US$)
6601	NY.GDP.PCAP.CN	GDP per capita (current LCU)
6602	NY.GDP.PCAP.KD	GDP per capita (constant 2005 US$)
6603	NY.GDP.PCAP.KD.ZG	GDP per capita growth (annual %)
6604	NY.GDP.PCAP.KN	GDP per capita (constant LCU)

In upcoming versions of Pandas, the `pandas.io.data` module will be a separate package called `pandas-datareader`. If you happen to read this when this update has occured, please install `pandas-datareader` (`conda install pandas-datareader`) and replace the import `from pandas.io import wb` with `from pandas_datareader import wb`.

The indicator that we are looking for is the GDP per capita (current U.S. $). Now we can download this dataset in a very easy way by asking for its ID, `NY.GDP.PCAP.PP.CD`, directly:

```
dat = wb.download(indicator='NY.GDP.PCAP.PP.CD', country='all', start=2014,
end=2014)
dat.head()
```

		NY.GDP.PCAP.PP.CD
country	year	
Arab World	2014	15975.039211
Caribbean small states	2014	15231.111124
Central Europe and the Baltics	2014	23884.797208
East Asia & Pacific (all income levels)	2014	14853.204148
East Asia & Pacific (developing only)	2014	11922.720831

The data structure is a bit complex, so we need to make it more easily accessible for us. We do this by getting the data out into arrays and creating a new Pandas DataFrame called *data*:

```
country = np.array(dat.index.tolist())[:,0]
gdp = np.array(np.array(dat['NY.GDP.PCAP.PP.CD']))
data = pd.DataFrame(data=np.array([country,gdp]).T, columns=['country',
'gdp'])
print(dat['NY.GDP.PCAP.PP.CD'].head())
print(data.head())
```

```
country                                  year
Arab World                               2014    15975.039211
Caribbean small states                   2014    15231.111124
Central Europe and the Baltics           2014    23884.797208
East Asia & Pacific (all income levels)  2014    14853.204148
East Asia & Pacific (developing only)    2014    11922.720831
Name: NY.GDP.PCAP.PP.CD, dtype: float64
                                     country                 gdp
0                                 Arab World   15975.039210528601
1                     Caribbean small states   15231.111124481498
2             Central Europe and the Baltics   23884.797208032996
3    East Asia & Pacific (all income levels)   14853.204148331899
4      East Asia & Pacific (developing only)     11922.7208309251
```

The data is now much more accessible for us and in the same format as the previous dataset. Just as with the coordinate centroid, we need to match the country names and put the relevant data into the rates object. We do this in exactly the same way as before:

```
rates['GDP_CD'] = ''
for i in np.arange(len(data)):
    ind = rates.Country.isin([data.country[i]
    val = data.loc[i, ['gdp']].values.astype('float')
    rates.loc[ind]), ['GDP_CD'] ] = val
    rates.loc[rates.GDP_CD.isin(['']), ['GDP_CD']] = np.nan
```

To check whether everything worked, we can print one of the items. In this example, we look at Sweden:

```
print(rates[rates.Country=='Sweden'])
print(data[data.country=='Sweden'])
print(data.loc[218, ['gdp']].values.astype('float'))
rates.loc[rates.Country.isin(['Sweden'])]
```

	Country	Both	Female	Male	Lat	Lon	DFE	GDP_CD
146	Sweden	11.1	6.1	16.2	62	15	62	45183

```
        country              gdp
218     Sweden   45183.0196872713
[ 45183.01968727]
```

	Country	Both	Female	Male	Lat	Lon	DFE	GDP_CD
146	Sweden	11.1	6.1	16.2	62	15	62	45183

This looks like we got it right. When we were working with **DFE**, we defined a `mindfe` variable. We use that here to select only those countries that satisfy being above the minimum latitude that we set previously and should have values for DFE as well. Then we add the rows where we have GDP to the selection:

```
selection = ~rates.DFE.isnull() * rates.DFE>mindfe
selection *= ~rates.GDP_CD.isnull()
```

Check first whether there is any obvious correlation between the GDP and suicide rate:

```
plt.plot(rates[selection].GDP_CD.values,rates[selection].Both.values, '.',
ms=10)
plt.xlabel('GDP')
plt.ylabel('Suicide rate');
```

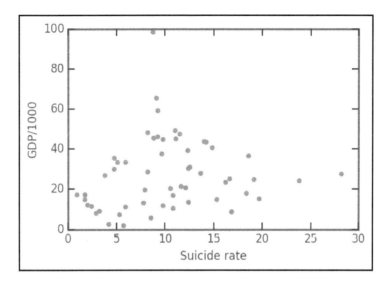

It seems like a very broad relationship. We add the DFE variable and plot the size of the markers as the suicide rate:

```
plt.scatter(rates[selection].GDP_CD.values/1000,
            rates[selection].DFE.values,
      s=rates[selection].Both.values**1.5)
plt.xlabel('GDP/1000')
plt.ylabel('DFE')
```

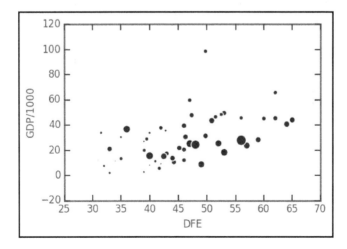

It seems that high GDP countries have high DFE but also high suicide rates. Now, of course, we want to fit a linear model to this. Basically, the model will be a plane fitted to the points. To do this, we can use `statsmodels` again, and for the plotting, we import matplotlib 3D axes:

```
import statsmodels.api as sm

A = rates[selection][['DFE', 'GDP_CD']].astype('float')
A['GDP_CD'] = A['GDP_CD']/1000
b = rates[selection]['Both'].astype('float')
A = sm.add_constant(A)
est = sm.OLS(b, A).fit()
```

First, we select the data that we need for the fit, DFE and GDP_CD for the A matrix. Then, we run the fitting assuming that the suicide rates are dependent on A (that is, both DFE and GDP). For it to work, we have to add a column with a constant value (1); the `statsmodels` developers have provided such a function that we can use. Note that we show how to use another way of defining a fitting function in `statsmodels`, which is not the R-formula method but uses NumPy arrays instead. The linear function being fitted is exactly what we covered in the beginning of this section, which is the following relationship:

$$z = k_0 + k_1 x + k_2 y$$

Here, we express the relationship between the variables with a matrix multiplication (that is, k_0, k_1, k_2 are found by the fitting routine). Note the different import here; the method is called **OLS** (capital letters) instead of **ols**, which was used with the formula in the previous example. We can now plot the fit together with the data:

```
from mpl_toolkits.mplot3d import Axes3D
X, Y = np.meshgrid(np.linspace(A.DFE.min(), A.DFE.max(), 100),
np.linspace(A.GDP_CD.min(), A.GDP_CD.max(), 100))
Z = est.params[0] + est.params[1] * X + est.params[2] * Y
fig = plt.figure(figsize=(12, 8))
ax = Axes3D(fig, azim=-135, elev=15)
surf = ax.plot_surface(X, Y, Z, cmap=plt.cm.RdBu, alpha=0.6,
linewidth=0)
ax.scatter(A.DFE, A.GDP_CD, y, alpha=1.0)
ax.set_xlabel('DFE')
ax.set_ylabel('GDP_CD/1000')
ax.set_zlabel('Both');
```

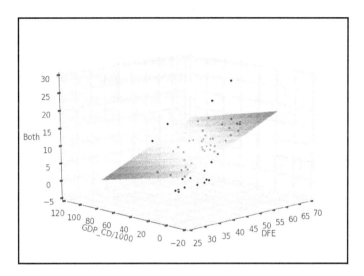

The viewing direction can be controlled with the `azim` and `evel` keywords during the Axes3D object creation. To plot the plane, we use the `meshgrid` function from NumPy to create a coordinate grid and then use the parameters determined from the fitting routine to get the values of the plane. Once again, to get the fitting summary, we print it:

```
print(est.summary())
```

```
                            OLS Regression Results
==============================================================================
Dep. Variable:                   Both   R-squared:                       0.288
Model:                            OLS   Adj. R-squared:                  0.260
Method:                 Least Squares   F-statistic:                     10.33
Date:                Mon, 21 Dec 2015   Prob (F-statistic):           0.000171
Time:                        03:40:42   Log-Likelihood:                -161.90
No. Observations:                  54   AIC:                             329.8
Df Residuals:                      51   BIC:                             335.8
Df Model:                           2
Covariance Type:            nonrobust
==============================================================================
                 coef    std err          t      P>|t|      [95.0% Conf. Int.]
------------------------------------------------------------------------------
const         -5.9298      3.626     -1.635      0.108     -13.210      1.350
DFE            0.3942      0.090      4.397      0.000       0.214      0.574
GDP_CD     -6.238e-05   4.55e-05     -1.371      0.176      -0.000     2.9e-05
==============================================================================
Omnibus:                       11.836   Durbin-Watson:                   2.272
Prob(Omnibus):                  0.003   Jarque-Bera (JB):               11.958
Skew:                           1.062   Prob(JB):                      0.00253
Kurtosis:                       3.899   Cond. No.                     1.72e+05
==============================================================================

Warnings:
[1] Standard Errors assume that the covariance matrix of the errors is correctly specified.
[2] The condition number is large, 1.72e+05. This might indicate that there are
strong multicollinearity or other numerical problems.
```

The resulting r-squared is similar to the one obtained when only using DFE. The hypothesis is not completely wrong; however, the situation is much more complex than these two variables. This is reflected in the fitting results. The coefficient for the GDP is small, very close to zero (-6.238×10^{-5}), that is, the dependence on GDP is less pronounced than for Latitude. What about the $P > |t|$ values—what conclusion can you draw from it? Furthermore, there is a warning about multicollinearity because of the high conditional number. Thus, some of the fitted variables may be interdependent.

Taking a step back

Remember that we cut out everything with a low value of DFE; let's check what the full dataset looks like. In this plot, you also see that we use another magic command (starts with %); instead of the matplotlib inline, we use the notbook plotting interface. This gives you interactive controls to pan, zoom, and save the data directly in the Jupyter Notebook:

```
%matplotlib notebook
selection2 = ~rates.DFE.isnull()
plt.scatter(rates[selection2].GDP_CD.values/1000,
rates[selection2].DFE.values, s=rates[selection2].Both.values**1.5)
plt.xlabel('GDP/1000')
plt.ylabel('DFE');
```

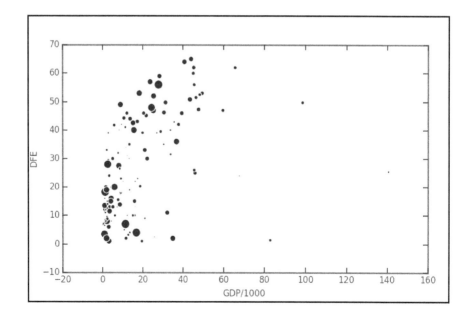

Introducing the size of the markers depending on the suicide rates, we can see that there seems to be at least two main clusters in the data with higher suicide rates—one with low GDP and absolute Latitude and one with high. We will use this in the next chapter to continue our analysis and attempt to identify the clusters. Thus, we should save this data, but we first create a new DataFrame with only the columns needed:

```
data=pd.DataFrame(data=rates[['Country','Both','Male','Female','GDP_CD',
'DFE']][~rates.DFE.isnull()])
data.head()
```

	Country	Both	Male	Female	GDP_CD	DFE
0	Afghanistan	5.7	6.2	5.3	1932.89	33.0
1	Albania	5.9	6.6	5.2	10304.7	41.0
2	Algeria	1.9	2.3	1.5	14193.4	28.0
3	Angola	13.8	20.7	7.3	NaN	12.5
4	Argentina	10.3	17.2	4.1	NaN	34.0

We only include data where we have DFE; some rows will still lack GDP though. Now that we have created a new DataFrame, it is very easy to save it. This time, we save it in a more standardized format, the HDF format:

```
TABLE_FILE = 'data_ch4.h5'
data.to_hdf(TABLE_FILE, 'ch4data', mode='w', table=True)
```

This code will save the data to the `data_ch4.h5` file in the current directory.

HDF stands for **Hierarchical Data Format**; it is a scientific data format developed by the **National Center for Supercomputing Applications** (**NCSA**), specifically for large datasets. It is very fast at reading and writing large data from/to disk. Most major programming languages have libraries to interact with HDF files. The current legacy format version is HDF version 5.

To read the HDF data, we simply use the `read_hdf` function of Pandas:

```
d2 = pd.read_hdf(TABLE_FILE)
```

You can now run `d2.head()` for a sanity check, whether it is the same as what we wrote to the file. Remember to have this file handy for the next chapter.

Logistic regression

The examples so far have been of continuous variables. However, other variables are discrete and can be of a binary type. Some common examples of discrete binary variables are if it is snowing in a city on a given day or not, if a patient is carrying a virus or not, and so on. One of the main differences between binary logistic and linear regression is that in binary logistic regression, we are fitting the probability of an outcome given a measured (discrete or continuous) variable, while linear regression models deal with characterizing the dependency of two or more continuous variables on each other. Logistic regression gives the probability of an occurrence given some observed variable(s). Probability is sometimes expressed as *P(Y|X)* and read as *Probability that the value is Y given the variable X.*

Algorithms that guess the discrete outcome are called classification algorithms and are a part of machine learning techniques, which will be covered later in the book.

The logistic regression model can be expressed as follows:

$$\ln\left(\frac{P}{1-P}\right) = m + kx$$

Solving this equation for *P*, we get the logistic probability:

$$\frac{P}{1-P} = e^{m+kx}$$

$$P = \frac{1}{1+e^{-(m+kx)}}$$

$$P = \frac{1}{1+e^{-(m+kx)}}$$

We can, just as with linear regression, add several dimensions (dependent variables) to the problem:

$$P = \frac{1}{1 + e^{-(m + k_1 x_1 + k_2 x_2 + \cdots + k_{N-1} x_{N-1} k_N x_N)}}$$

To illustrate what this function looks like and the difference from fitting a linear model, we plot both functions:

```
k = 1.
m = -5.
y = lambda x: k*x + m
#p = lambda x: np.exp(k*x+m) / (1+np.exp(k*x+m))
p = lambda x: 1 / (1+np.exp(-1*(k*x+m)))

xx = np.linspace(0,10)
plt.plot(xx,y(xx), label='linear')
plt.plot(xx,p(xx), label='logistic')
plt.plot([0,abs(m)], [0.5,0.5], dashes=(4,4), color='.7')
plt.plot([abs(m),abs(m)], [-.1,.5], dashes=(4,4), color='.7')

# limits, legends and labels
plt.ylim((-.1,1.1))
plt.legend(loc=2)
plt.ylabel('P')
plt.xlabel('xx')
```

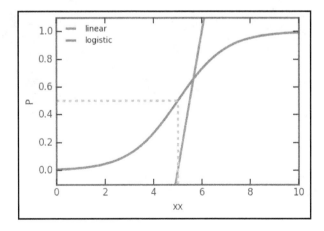

As is clearly seen, the S-shaped curve, our logistic fitting function (more generally called **sigmoid function**), can illustrate binary logistic probabilities much better. Playing around with k and m, we quickly realize that k determines the steepness of the slope and m moves the curve left or right. We also notice that $P(Y|xx=5) = 0.5$, that is, at $xx=5$, the outcome Y (corresponding to P=1) has a 50% probability.

Imagine that we asked students how long they studied for an exam. Can we check how long you need to study to be fairly sure to pass? To investigate this, we need to use logistic regression. It is only possible to pass or fail an exam, that is, it is a binary variable. First, we need to create the data:

```
studytime=[0,0,1.5,2,2.5,3,3.5,4,4,4,5.5,6,6.5,7,7,8.5,9,9,9,10.5,10.5,12,1
2,12,12.5,13,14,15,16,18]
passed=[0,0,0,0,0,0,0,0,0,0,0,1,0,1,1,0,1,1,0,1,1,1,1,1,1,1,1,1,1,1]
data = pd.DataFrame(data=np.array([studytime, passed]).T, columns=['Time',
                    'Pass'])
data.Time.hist(bins=6)
plt.xlabel('Time')
plt.ylabel('No. students');
```

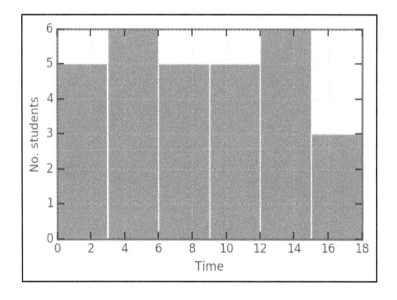

The first thing plotted is the histogram of how much time the students spent studying for the exam. It seems like it is a rather flat distribution. Here, we will check how they did on the exam:

```
plt.plot(data.Time, data.Pass,'o', mew=0, ms=7,)
plt.ylim(-.1,1.1)
```

```
plt.xlim(-0.2,16.2)
plt.xlabel('Time studied')
plt.ylabel('Pass? (0=no, 1=yes)');
```

This plot will now show you how much time someone studied and the outcome of the exam-if they passed given by a value of `1.0` (yes) or if they failed given by a value of `0.0` (no). The *x* axis goes from 0 hours (a student who did not study at all) up to 18 hours (a student who studied more).

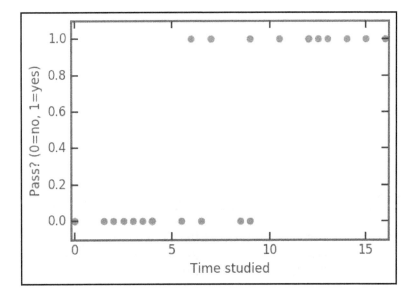

By simply inspecting the figure, it seems like sometime between 5-10 hours is needed to at least pass the exam. Once again, we use statsmodels to fit the data with our model. In statsmodels, there is a `logit` function that performs logistic regression:

```
import statsmodels.api as sm
probfit = sm.Logit(data.Pass, sm.add_constant(data.Time, prepend=True))
```

```
Optimization terminated successfully.
         Current function value: 0.251107
         Iterations 8
```

The optimization worked; if there would have been any problems converging, error messages would have been printed instead. After running the fit, checking the summary is a good idea:

```
fit_results = probfit.fit()
print(fit_results.summary())
```

```
                        Logit Regression Results
==============================================================================
Dep. Variable:                   Pass   No. Observations:                  30
Model:                          Logit   Df Residuals:                      28
Method:                           MLE   Df Model:                           1
Date:                Mon, 21 Dec 2015   Pseudo R-squ.:                 0.6366
Time:                        03:40:43   Log-Likelihood:                -7.5332
converged:                       True   LL-Null:                       -20.728
                                        LLR p-value:                 2.791e-07
==============================================================================
                 coef    std err          z      P>|z|      [95.0% Conf. Int.]
------------------------------------------------------------------------------
const         -5.7980      2.240     -2.588      0.010     -10.188      -1.408
Time           0.8020      0.297      2.703      0.007       0.220       1.384
==============================================================================
```

The const variable is the intercept, that is, k of the fit-function, and Time is the intercept, m. The covariance parameters can be used to estimate the standard deviation by taking the square root of the diagonal of the covariance matrix:

```
logit_pars = fit_results.params
intercept_err, slope_err = np.diag(fit_results.cov_params())**.5
fit_results.cov_params()
```

	const	Time
const	5.017663	-0.635081
Time	-0.635081	0.088035

However, statsmodels also gives the uncertainty in the parameters, as can be seen from the fit summary output:

```
intercept = logit_pars['const']
slope = logit_pars['Time']
print(intercept,slope)
-5.79798670884 0.801979232718
```

```
-5.79798670884 0.801979232718
```

It is also possible to print out the confidence intervals directly:

```
fit_results.conf_int()
```

	0	1
const	-10.188333	-1.407640
Time	0.220444	1.383514

Now it is appropriate to plot the fit on top of the data. We have estimated the parameters of the fit function:

```
plt.plot(data.Time, data.Pass,'o', mew=0, ms=7, label='Data')
p = lambda x,k,m: 1 / (1+np.exp(-1*(k*x+m)))
xx = np.linspace(0,data.Time.max())
l1 = plt.plot(xx, p(xx,slope,intercept), label='Fit')
plt.fill_between(xx, p(xx,slope+slope_err**2, intercept+intercept_err),
p(xx,slope-slope_err**2, intercept-intercept_err), alpha=0.15,
color=l1[0].get_color())
plt.ylim(-.1,1.1)
plt.xlim(-0.2,16.2)
plt.xlabel('Time studied')
plt.ylabel('Pass? (0=no, 1=yes)')
plt.legend(loc=2, numpoints=1);
```

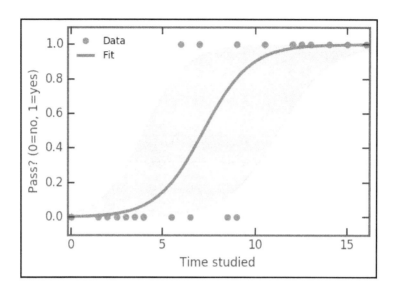

Here, we have not only plotted the best fit curve, but also the curve corresponding to one standard deviation away. The uncertainty encompasses a lot of values. Now, with the estimated parameters, it is possible to calculate how long should we study for a 50% chance of success:

```
target=0.5
x_prob = lambda p,k,m: (np.log(p/(1-p))-m)/k
T_max = x_prob(target, slope-slope_err, intercept-intercept_err)
T_min = x_prob(target, slope+slope_err, intercept+intercept_err)
T_best = x_prob(target, slope, intercept)
print('{0}% sucess rate: {1:.1f} +{2:.1f}/-
{3:.1f}'.format(int(target*100),T_best,T_max-T_best,T_best-T_min))
50% success rate: 7.2 +8.7/-4.0
```

So studying for 7.2 hours for this test, the chance of passing is about 50%. The uncertainty is rather large, and the 50% chance of passing could also be for about 15 hours of studying or as little as three hours. Of course, there is more to studying for an exam than the absolute number of hours put in. However, by not studying at all, the chances of passing are very slim.

Some notes

Logistic regression assumes that the probability at the inflection point, that is, halfway through the S-curve, is 0.5. There is no real reason to assume that this is always true; thus, using a model that allows the inflection point to move could be a more general case. However, this will add another parameter to estimate and, given the quality of the input data, this might not make it easier or increase the reliability.

Summary

In this chapter, we looked at linear, multiple, and logistic regression. We fetched data from online sources, cleaned it up, and mapped it to the data structures that we are interested in. The world of statistics is huge and there are numerous special areas even for these somewhat straightforward concepts and methods. For regression analysis, it is important to note that correlation does not always mean causation, that is, just because there is a correlation between two variables, it does not mean that they depend on one another in nature. There are websites that show these spurious correlations; some of them are quite entertaining (`http://www.tylervigen.com/spurious-correlations`).

In the next chapter, we will look at clustering techniques to find similarities in data. We will start out with an example using the same data that we saved in this chapter when performing multiple regression analysis.

5
Clustering

With data comprising of several separated distributions, how do we find and characterize them? In this chapter, we will look at some ways to identify clusters in data. Groups of points with similar characteristics form clusters. There are many different algorithms and methods to achieve this with good and bad points. We want to detect multiple separate distributions in the data and determine the degree of association (or similarity) with another point or cluster for each point. The degree of association needs to be high if they belong in a cluster together or low if they do not. This can of course, just as previously, be a one-dimensional problem or multi-dimensional problem. One of the inherent difficulties of cluster finding is determining how many clusters there are in the data. Various approaches to define this exist; some where the user needs to input the number of clusters and then the algorithm finds which points belong to which cluster, and some where the starting assumption is that every point is a cluster and then two nearby clusters are combined iteratively on a trial basis to see if they belong together.

In this chapter, we will cover the following topics:

- A short introduction to cluster finding—reminding you of the general problem—and an algorithm to solve it
- Analysis of a dataset in the context of cluster finding-the Cholera outbreak in central London 1854
    - By simple zeroth order analysis, calculating the centroid of the whole dataset
    - By finding the closest water pump for each recorded Cholera-related death
- Using the K-means nearest neighbor algorithm for cluster finding, applying it to data from `Chapter 4`, *Regression*, and identifying two separate distributions
- Using hierarchical clustering by analyzing the distribution of galaxies in a confined slice of the Universe

The algorithms and methods covered here are focused on those available in SciPy.

As before, start a new Notebook and put in the default imports. Perhaps you want to change to interactive Notebook plotting to try it out a bit more. For this chapter, we are adding the following specific imports. The ones related to clustering are from SciPy, while later on, we will need some packages to transform astronomical coordinates. These packages are all preinstalled in the Anaconda Python 3 distribution and have been tested there:

```
import scipy.cluster.hierarchy as hac
import scipy.cluster.vq as vq
```

Introduction to cluster finding

There are many different algorithms for cluster identification. Many of them try to solve a specific problem in the best way. Therefore, the specific algorithm that you want to use might depend on the problem you are trying to solve and also on what algorithms are available in the specific package that you are using.

Some of the first clustering algorithms consisted of simply finding the centroid positions that minimize the distances to all the points in each cluster. The points in each cluster are closer to that centroid than other cluster centroids. As might be obvious at this point, the hardest part with this is figuring out how many clusters there are. If we can determine that, it is fairly straightforward to try various ways of moving the cluster centroid around, calculate the distance to each point, and then figure out where the cluster centroids are. There are also obvious situations where this might not be the best solution, for example, if you have two very elongated clusters next to each other.

Commonly, the distance is the Euclidean distance:

$$\left\| \overline{p} - \mu_i \right\|$$

Here, p is a vector with all the points' positions, that is, $\{p1, p2, \ldots, pN-1, pN\}$ in cluster C_k, and the distances are calculated from the cluster centroid, μ_i. We have to find the cluster centroids that minimize the sum of the absolute distances to the points:

$$min \sum_{i=1}^{K} | \overline{p} - \mu_i |$$

In this first example, we shall first work with fixed cluster centroids.

Starting out simple – John Snow on cholera

In 1854, there was an outbreak of cholera in North-western London, in the neighborhood around Broad Street. The leading theories at the time claimed that cholera spread, just like it was believed the plague spread, through foul, bad air. John Snow, a physician at the time, hypothesized that cholera spread through drinking water. During the outbreak, John tracked the deaths and drew them on a map of the area. Through his analysis, he concluded that most of the cases were centered on the Broad Street water pump. Rumors say that he then removed the handle of the water pump, thus stopping an epidemic. Today, we know that cholera is usually transmitted through contaminated food or water, thus confirming John's hypothesis. We will do a short but instructive reanalysis of John Snow's data.

The data comes from the public data archives of The National Center for Geographic Information and Analysis (http://www.ncgia.ucsb.edu/ and http://www.ncgia.ucsb.edu/pubs/data.php). A cleaned-up map and copy of the data files along with an example of a geospatial information analysis of the data can also be found at https://www.udel.edu/johnmack/frec682/cholera/cholera2.html. A wealth of information about physician and scientist John Snow's life and works can be found at http://johnsnow.matrix.msu.edu.

To start the analysis, we read in the data to a Pandas DataFrame; the data is already formatted into CSV files, readable by Pandas:

```
deaths = pd.read_csv('data/cholera_deaths.txt')
pumps = pd.read_csv('data/cholera_pumps.txt')
```

Each file contains two columns, one for X coordinates and one for Y coordinates. Let's check what it looks like:

```
deaths.head()
```

	X	Y
0	13.588010	11.095600
1	9.878124	12.559180
2	14.653980	10.180440
3	15.220570	9.993003
4	13.162650	12.963190

```
pumps.head()
```

	X	Y
0	8.651201	17.891600
1	10.984780	18.517851
2	13.378190	17.394541
3	14.879830	17.809919
4	8.694768	14.905470

With this information, we can now plot all the pumps and deaths in order to visualize the data:

```
plt.figure(figsize=(4,3.5))
plt.plot(deaths['X'], deaths['Y'],
        marker='o', lw=0, mew=1, mec='0.9', ms=6)
plt.plot(pumps['X'],pumps['Y'],
        marker='s', lw=0, mew=1, mec='0.9', color='k', ms=6)
plt.axis('equal')
plt.xlim((4.0,22.0));
plt.xlabel('X-coordinate')
plt.ylabel('Y-coordinate')
plt.title('John Snow\'s Cholera')
```

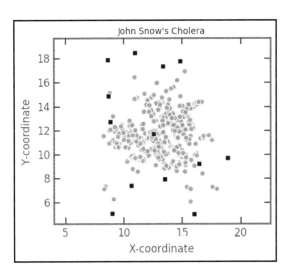

It is fairly easy to see that the pump in the middle is important. As a first data exploration, we will simply calculate the mean centroid of the distribution and plot this in the figure as an ellipse. We calculate the mean and standard deviation along the *x* and *y* axes as the centroid position:

```
fig = plt.figure(figsize=(4,3.5))
ax = fig.add_subplot(111)
plt.plot(deaths['X'], deaths['Y'],
         marker='o', lw=0, mew=1, mec='0.9', ms=6)
plt.plot(pumps['X'],pumps['Y'],
         marker='s', lw=0, mew=1, mec='0.9', color='k', ms=6)

from matplotlib.patches import Ellipse
ellipse = Ellipse(xy=(deaths['X'].mean(), deaths['Y'].mean()),
               width=deaths['X'].std(), height=deaths['Y'].std(),
               zorder=32, fc='None', ec='IndianRed', lw=2)
ax.add_artist(ellipse)
plt.plot(deaths['X'].mean(), deaths['Y'].mean(),
         '.', ms=10, mec='IndianRed', zorder=32)
for i in pumps.index:
    plt.annotate(s='{0}'.format(i), xy=(pumps[['X','Y']].loc[i]),
                 xytext=(-15,6), textcoords='offset points')
plt.axis('equal')
plt.xlim((4.0,22.5))
plt.xlabel('X-coordinate')
plt.ylabel('Y-coordinate')
plt.title('John Snow's Cholera')
```

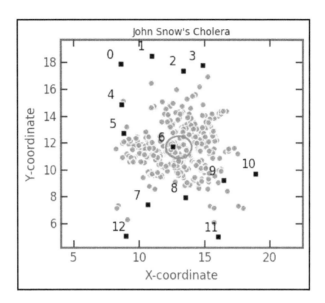

Here, we also plotted the pump index, which we can get from DataFrame with the `pumps.index` method. The next step in the analysis is to see which pump is the closest to each point. We do this by calculating the distance from all pumps to all points. Then, we want to figure out for each point, which pump is the closest.

We save the closest pump to each point in a separate column of the deaths' DataFrame. With this dataset, the for-loop runs fairly quickly. However, the DataFrame subtract method chained with `sum()` and `idxmin()` methods takes a few seconds. I strongly encourage you to play around with various ways to speed this up. We also use the `.apply()` method of DataFrame to square and square root the values. The simple brute force first attempt of this took over a minute to run. The built-in functions and methods helped a lot:

```
deaths_tmp = deaths[['X','Y']].as_matrix()
idx_arr = np.array([], dtype='int')
for i in range(len(deaths)):
    idx_arr = np.append(idx_arr,
                (pumps.subtract(deaths_tmp[i])).apply(lambda
                x:x**2).sum(axis=1).apply(lambda x:x**0.5).idxmin())
deaths['C'] = idx_arr
```

Just quickly check whether everything seems fine by printing out the top rows of the table:

```
deaths.head()
```

	X	Y	C
0	13.588010	11.095600	6
1	9.878124	12.559180	5
2	14.653980	10.180440	9
3	15.220570	9.993003	9
4	13.162650	12.963190	6

Now we want to visualize what we have. With colors, we can show which water pump we associate each death with. To do this, we use a colormap; in this case, the *jet* colormap. By calling the colormap with a value between 0 and 1, it returns a color; thus, we give it the pump indexes and then divide it with the total number of pumps – 12 in our case:

```
fig = plt.figure(figsize=(4,3.5))
ax = fig.add_subplot(111)
np.unique(deaths['C'].values)
plt.scatter(deaths['X'].as_matrix(), deaths['Y'].as_matrix(),
            color=plt.cm.jet(deaths['C']/12.),
            marker='o', lw=0.5, edgecolors='0.5', s=20)
plt.plot(pumps['X'],pumps['Y'],
marker='s', lw=0, mew=1, mec='0.9', color='0.3', ms=6)
for i in pumps.index:
plt.annotate(s='{0}'.format(i), xy=(pumps[['X','Y']].loc[i]),
             xytext=(-15,6), textcoords='offset points',
             ha='right')
ellipse = Ellipse(xy=(deaths['X'].mean(), deaths['Y'].mean()),
                  width=deaths['X'].std(),
                  height=deaths['Y'].std(),
                  zorder=32, fc='None', ec='IndianRed', lw=2)
ax.add_artist(ellipse)
plt.axis('equal')
plt.xlim((4.0,22.5))
plt.xlabel('X-coordinate')
plt.ylabel('Y-coordinate')
plt.title('John Snow's Cholera')
```

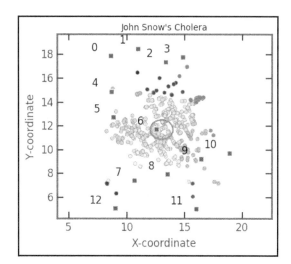

The majority of deaths are dominated by the proximity of the pump in the center. This pump is located on Broad Street.

Now, remember that we have used fixed positions for the cluster centroids. In this case, we are basically working on the assumption that the water pumps are related to the cholera cases. Furthermore, the Euclidean distance is not really the real-life distance. People go along roads to get water and the road there is not necessarily straight. Thus, one would have to map out the streets and calculate the distance to each pump from that. Even so, already at this level, it is clear that there is something with the center pump related to the cholera cases. How would you account for the different distance? To calculate the distance, you would do what is called cost-analysis (c.f. when you hit directions on your sat-nav to go to a place). There are many different ways of doing cost analysis, and it also relates to the problem of finding the correct way through a maze.

In addition to these things, we do not have any data in the time domain, that is, the cholera would possibly spread to other pumps with time and the outbreak might have started at the Broad Street pump and spread to other, nearby pumps. Without time data, it is extra difficult to figure out what happened.

This is the general approach to cluster finding. The coordinates might be attributes instead, length and weight of dogs for example, and the location of the cluster centroid something that we would iteratively move around until we find the best position.

K-means clustering

The K-means algorithm is also referred to as vector quantization. What the algorithm does is finds the cluster (centroid) positions that minimize the distances to all points in the cluster. This is done iteratively; the problem with the algorithm is that it can be a bit greedy, meaning that it will find the nearest minima quickly. This is generally solved with some kind of basin-hopping approach where the nearest minima found is randomly perturbed and the algorithm restarted. Due to this fact, the algorithm is dependent on good initial guesses as input.

Suicide rate versus GDP versus absolute latitude

As mentioned in Chapter 4, *Regression*, we will analyze the data of suicide rates versus GDP versus absolute latitude or **Degrees From Equator** (DFE) for clusters. Our hypothesis from the visual inspection was that there were at least two distinct clusters, one with a higher suicide rate, GDP, and absolute latitude, and one with lower. We saved an HDF file in Chapter 4, *Regression*, that we now read in as a DataFrame. This time, we want to discard all the rows where one or more column entries are NaN or empty. Thus, we use the appropriate DataFrame method for this:

```
TABLE_FILE = 'data/data_ch4.h5'
d2 = pd.read_hdf(TABLE_FILE)
d2 = d2.dropna()
```

Next, while the DataFrame is a very handy format, which we will utilize later on, the input to the cluster algorithms in SciPy does not handle Pandas datatypes natively. Thus, we transfer the data to a NumPy array:

```
rates = d2[['DFE','GDP_CD','Both']].as_matrix().astype('float')
```

Next, to recap, we visualize the data with one histogram of the GDP and one scatterplot for all the data. We do this to aid us in the initial guesses of the cluster centroid positions:

```
plt.subplots(12, figsize=(8,3.5))
plt.subplot(121)
plt.hist(rates.T[1], bins=20,color='SteelBlue')
plt.xticks(rotation=45, ha='right')
plt.yscale('log')
plt.xlabel('GDP')
plt.ylabel('Counts')
plt.subplot(122)
plt.scatter(rates.T[0], rates.T[2],
            s=2e5*rates.T[1]/rates.T[1].max(),
            color='SteelBlue', edgecolors='0.3');
```

```
plt.xlabel('Absolute Latitude (Degrees, 'DFE')')
plt.ylabel('Suicide Rate (per 100')')
plt.subplots_adjust(wspace=0.25);
```

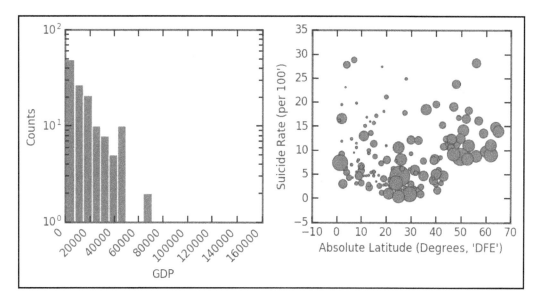

The scatter plot to the right shows the **Suicide Rate** on the y-axis and the **Absolute Latitude** on the x-axis. The size of each point is proportional to the country's GDP. The function to run the clustering k-means takes a special kind of normalized input. The data arrays (columns) have to be normalized by the standard deviation of the array. Although this is straightforward, there is a function included in the module called `whiten`. It will scale the data with the standard deviation:

```
w = vq.whiten(rates)
```

To show what it does to the data, we plot the preceding plots again, but with the output from the `whiten` function:

```
plt.subplots(12, figsize=(8,3.5))
plt.subplot(121)
plt.hist(w[:,1], bins=20, color='SteelBlue')
plt.yscale('log')
plt.subplot(122)
plt.scatter(w.T[0], w.T[2], s=2e5*w.T[1]/w.T[1].max(),
            color='SteelBlue', edgecolors='0.3')
plt.xticks(rotation=45, ha='right');
```

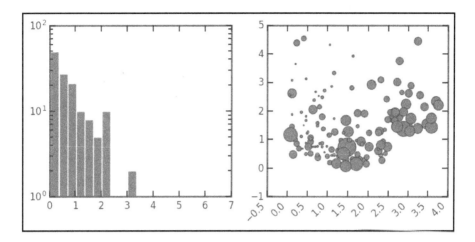

As you can see, all the data is scaled from the previous figure. However, as mentioned, the scaling is just the standard deviation. So let's calculate the scaling and save it to the sc variable:

```
sc = rates.std(axis=0)
```

Now we are ready to estimate the initial guesses for the cluster centroids. Reading off the first plot of the data, we guess the centroids to be at 20 DFE, 200,000 GDP, and 10 suicides, and the second at 45 DFE, 100,000 GDP, and 15 suicides. We put this in an array and scale it with our scale parameter to the same scale as the output from the whiten function. This is then sent to the kmeans2 function of SciPy:

```
init_guess = np.array([[20,20E3,10],[45,100E3,15]])
init_guess /= sc
z2_cb, z2_lbl = vq.kmeans2(w, init_guess, minit='matrix',
                           iter=500)
```

There is another function, kmeans (without the 2), which is a less complex version and does not stop iterating when it reaches a local minima; it stops when the changes between two iterations goes below some level. Thus, the standard k-means algorithm is represented in SciPy by the kmeans2 function. The function outputs the centroids' scaled positions (here, z2_cb) and a lookup table (z2_lbl) telling us which row belongs to which centroid. To get the centroid positions in units we *understand*, we simply multiply with our scaling value:

```
z2_cb_sc = z2_cb * sc
```

At this point, we can plot the results. The following section is rather long and contains many different parts, so we will go through them section by section. However, the code should be run in one cell of the Notebook:

```
# K-means clustering figure START
plt.figure(figsize=(6,4))
plt.scatter(z2_cb_sc[0,0], z2_cb_sc[0,2],
            s=5e2*z2_cb_sc[0,1]/rates.T[1].max(),
            marker='+', color='k',
            edgecolors='k', lw=2, zorder=10, alpha=0.7);
plt.scatter(z2_cb_sc[1,0], z2_cb_sc[1,2],
            s=5e2*z2_cb_sc[1,1]/rates.T[1].max(),
            marker='+', color='k', edgecolors='k', lw=3,
            zorder=10, alpha=0.7);
```

The first steps are quite simple; we set up the figure size and plot the points of the cluster centroids. We hypothesized about two clusters, thus we plot them with two different calls to `plt.scatter`. Here, `z2_cb_sc[1,0]` gets the second cluster x coordinate (DFE) from the array, then switching 0 for 1 gives us the y coordinate (rate). We set the size of the marker to scale with the value of the third data axis, the GDP. We also do this further down for the data, just as in previous plots, so that it is easier to compare and differentiate the clusters. The `zorder` keyword gives the order in-depth of the elements that are plotted; a high `zorder` will put them on top of everything else, and a negative `zorder` will send them to the back.

```
s0 = abs(z2_lbl==0).astype('bool')
s1 = abs(z2_lbl==1).astype('bool')
pattern1 = 5*'x'
pattern2 = 4*'/'
plt.scatter(w.T[0][s0]*sc[0],
            w.T[2][s0]*sc[2],
            s=5e2*rates.T[1][s0]/rates.T[1].max(),
            lw=1,
            hatch=pattern1,
            edgecolors='0.3',
            color=plt.cm.Blues_r(
                rates.T[1][s0]/rates.T[1].max()));
plt.scatter(rates.T[0][s1],
            rates.T[2][s1],
            s=5e2*rates.T[1][s1]/rates.T[1].max(),
            lw=1,
            hatch=pattern2,
            edgecolors='0.4',
            marker='s',
            color=plt.cm.Reds_r(
                rates.T[1][s1]/rates.T[1].max()+0.4))
```

In this section, we plot the points of the clusters. First, we get the selection arrays. They are simply Boolean arrays, which are arrays where the values that correspond to either cluster 0 or 1 are True. Thus s0 is True where cluster id is 0, and s1 is True where cluster id is 1. Next, we define the hatch pattern for the scatterplot markers, which we later give the plotting function as input. The multiplier for the hatch pattern gives the density of the pattern. The scatterplots for the points are created in a similar fashion to the centroids, except the markers are a bit more complex. They are both colorcoded, as in the previous example with cholera deaths, but in a gradient instead of the exact same colors for all points. The gradient is defined by the GDP, which also defines the size of the points. The x and y data sent to the plot is different between the clusters, but they access the same data in the end because we multiply with our scaling factor.

```python
p1 = plt.scatter([],[], hatch='None',
                 s=20E3*5e2/rates.T[1].max(),
                 color='k', edgecolors='None',)
p2 = plt.scatter([],[], hatch='None',
                 s=40E3*5e2/rates.T[1].max(),
                 color='k', edgecolors='None',)
p3 = plt.scatter([],[], hatch='None',
                 s=60E3*5e2/rates.T[1].max(),
                 color='k', edgecolors='None',)
p4 = plt.scatter([],[], hatch='None',
                 s=80E3*5e2/rates.T[1].max(),
                 color='k', edgecolors='None',)
labels = ["20'", "40'", "60'", ">80'"]
plt.legend([p1, p2, p3, p4], labels, ncol=1,
           frameon=True, #fontsize=12,
           handlelength=1, loc=1,
           borderpad=0.75,labelspacing=0.75,
           handletextpad=0.75, title='GDP', scatterpoints=1.5)
plt.ylim((-4,40))
plt.xlim((-4,80))
plt.title('K-means clustering')
plt.xlabel('Absolute Latitude (Degrees, 'DFE')')
plt.ylabel('Suicide Rate (per 100 000)');
```

The last tweak to the plot is made by creating a custom legend. We want to show the different sizes of the points and what GDP they correspond to. As there is a continuous gradient from low to high, we cannot use the plotted points. Thus we create our own, but leave the x and y input coordinates as empty lists. This will not show anything in the plot but we can use them to register in the legend. The various tweaks to the legend function control different aspects of the legend layout. I encourage you to experiment with it to see what happens:

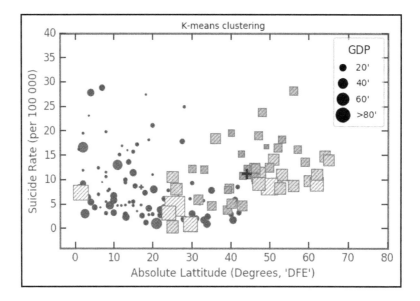

As for the final analysis, two different clusters are identified. Just as our previous hypothesis, there is a cluster with a clear linear trend with relatively higher GDP, which is also located at a higher absolute latitude. Although the identification is rather weak, it is clear that the two groups are separated. Countries with low GDP are clustered closer to the equator. What happens when you add more clusters? Try to add a cluster for the low DFE high-rate countries, visualize it, and think about what this could mean for the conclusion(s).

Hierarchical clustering analysis

Hierarchical clustering is connectivity-based clustering. It assumes that the clusters are connected, or in another word, linked. For example, we can classify animals and plants based on this assumption. We have all developed from something common. This makes it possible for us to assume that every observation is its own cluster on one hand and, on the other, all observations are in one and the same group. This also forms the basis for two approaches to hierarchical clustering algorithms, agglomerative and divisive:

- **Agglomerative clustering** starts out with each point in its own cluster and then merges the two clusters with the lowest dissimilarity, that is, the bottom-up approach

- **Divisive clustering** is, as the name suggests, a top-down approach where we start out with one single cluster that is divided into smaller and smaller clusters

In contrast to k-means, it gives us a way to identify the clusters without initial guesses of the number of clusters or cluster positions. For this example, we will run an agglomerative cluster algorithm in SciPy.

Reading in and reducing the data

Galaxies in the Universe are not randomly distributed, they form clusters and filaments. These structures hint at the complex movement and history of the Universe. There are many different catalogs of galaxy clusters, although the techniques to classify clusters vary and there are several views on this. We will use the Updated Zwicky Catalog, which contains 19,367 galaxies (Falco et al. 1999, PASP 111, 438). The file can be downloaded from `http://tdc-www.harvard.edu/uzc/index.html`. The first Zwicky Catalog of Galaxies and Clusters of Galaxies was released in 1961 (Zwicky et al. 1961-1968. Catalog of Galaxies and Clusters of Galaxies, Vols. 1-6. CalTech).

To start, we import some required packages, read in the file to a DataFrame, and investigate what we have:

```
import astropy.coordinates as coord
import astropy.units as u
import astropy.constants as c
```

Astropy is a community-developed astronomy package to help Astronomers analyze and create powerful software to handle their data (http://www.astropy.org/). We import the coordinates package that can handle astronomical coordinates (**World Coordinate System**–**WCS**) and transforms. The units and constants packages are packages to handle physical units (conversions and so on) and constants (with units); both are extremely handy to do calculations where the units matter:

```
uzcat = pd.read_table('data/uzcJ2000.tab/uzcJ2000.tab',
                sep='\t', header=16, dtype='str',
                names=['ra', 'dec', 'Zmag', 'cz', 'cze', 'T', 'U',
                     'Ne', 'Zname', 'C', 'Ref', 'Oname', 'M', 'N'],
                skiprows=[17])
```

Let's look at the data with the head method:

```
uzcat.head()
```

	ra	dec	Zmag	cz	cze	T	U	Ne	Zname	C	Ref	Oname	M	N
0	000237.9	+163838	14.9	6350	19	A	1	0	000000+16220	F		I5378S		
1	000246.3	+185310	14.8	7864	47	A	0	0	000012+18370	Z	0650	00002+1837		
2	000257.0	+041231	15.5	8695	40	E	0	0	000030+03560	Z	2700	00005+0356		
3	000302.9	+185221	15.5	8007	39	E	0	0	000030+18360	Z	0650	00005+1836		
4	000305.6	-015450	14.3	7298	42	B	0	0	000036-02110	Z	2218	00006-0211		

The first two columns, `ra` and `dec`, are coordinates in the equatorial coordinate system. Basically, if you imagine Earth's latitude and longitude system expanded, we are on the inside. RA, or Right Ascension, is the longitude and Dec, or declination, is the latitude. A consequence of this is that, as we are on the inside of it, East is West and West is East. The third column is the Z magnitude, which is a measure of how bright the galaxy is (in logarithmic units) measured at a certain wavelength of light. The fourth column is the redshift distance in units of km/s (fifth is the uncertainty) with respect to our Sun (that is, Heliocentric distance). This odd unit is the redshift multiplied by the speed of light ($v = cz$, z: `redshift`). Due to the simplicity of this, the v parameter can have speeds that go above the speed of light, that is, non-physical speeds. It assumes that the radial speed of every galaxy in the universe is dominated by the expansion of the universe. Recollecting that in `Chapter 3`, *Learning About Models*, we looked at Hubble's Law, the expansion of the universe increases linearly with distance. While the Hubble constant is constant for short distances, today we know that the expansion speed of the universe (that is, Hubble constant, H) changes at large distances, the change depending on what cosmology is assumed. We will convert this distance to something more graspable later on.

The rest of the columns are described either in the accompanying README file or online at `http://tdc-www.harvard.edu/uzc/uzcjformat.html`.

First, we want to translate the coordinates into something more readable than a string (that is, `ra` and `dec` columns). Equatorial coordinates are given for RA in hours, minutes, and seconds and Dec in degrees, minutes, and seconds. To get degrees from hours, you simply multiply hours by 15 (that is, 360 degrees divided by 24 hours). One of the first reasons to choose this dataset as an example is that because of the coordinate system, the distance is not the Euclidean distance. To be able to use it, we have to translate the coordinates into Cartesian coordinates, which we will do soon. As explained, we now fix the first thing with the coordinates; we convert them into understandable strings:

```
df['ra'] = df['ra'].apply(lambda x: '{0}h{1}m{2}s'.format(
                          x[:2],x[2:4],x[4:]))
df['dec'] = df['dec'].apply(lambda x: '{0}d{1}m{2}s'.format(
                          x[:3],x[3:5],x[5:]))
df.head()
```

	ra	dec	Zmag	cz	cze	T	U	Ne	Zname	C	Ref	Oname	M	N
0	00h02m37.9s	+16d38m38s	14.9	6350	19	A	1	0	000000+16220	F		I5378S		
1	00h02m46.3s	+18d53m10s	14.8	7864	47	A	0	0	000012+18370	Z	0650	00002+1837		
2	00h02m57.0s	+04d12m31s	15.5	8695	40	E	0	0	000030+03560	Z	2700	00005+0356		
3	00h03m02.9s	+18d52m21s	15.5	8007	39	E	0	0	000030+18360	Z	0650	00005+1836		
4	00h03m05.6s	-01d54m50s	14.3	7298	42	B	0	0	000036-02110	Z	2218	00006-0211		

Next, we need to put `np.nan` where the entry is empty (we are checking whether it is an empty string with spaces). With `apply`, you can apply a function to a certain column/row, and `applymap` applies a function to every table entry:

```
uzcat = uzcat.applymap(lambda x: np.nan if
                       isinstance(x, str) and
                       x.isspace() else x)
uzcat['cz'] = uzcat['cz'].astype('float')
```

We also convert the magnitude column to floats by running `mycat.Zmag = mycat.Zmag.astype('float')`. To do an initial visualization of the data, we need to convert the coordinates to radians or degrees, something that matplotlib understands. To do this, we use the convenient Astropy Coordinates package:

```
coords_uzc = coord.SkyCoord(uzcat['ra'], uzcat['dec'], frame='fk5',
                            equinox='J2000')
```

We can now access the coordinates in one object and convert them to various units. For example, `coords_uzc.ra.deg.min()` will return the minimum RA coordinate in units of degrees; replacing `deg` with `rad` will return it in radians. Visualizing it at this level has several reasons; one reason for this is that we want to check what the coordinates cover; what part of the sky we are looking at. To do this, we use a projection method; otherwise, the coordinates do not make sense as they are not common x,y,z coordinates (in this case, the Mollweide projection), so we are looking at the whole sky flattened out:

```
color_czs = (uzcat['cz']+abs(uzcat['cz'].min()))) /
             (uzcat['cz'].max()+abs(uzcat['cz'].min())))
from matplotlib.patheffects import withStroke
whitebg = withStroke(foreground="w", linewidth=2.5)
fig = plt.figure(figsize=(8,3.5))
ax = fig.add_subplot(111, projection="mollweide")
ax.scatter(coords_uzc.ra.radian-np.pi, coords_uzc.dec.radian,
           color=plt.cm.Blues_r(color_czs), alpha=0.6,
           s=4, marker='.', zorder=-1)
plt.grid()
for tick in ax.get_xticklabels():
    tick.set_path_effects([whitebg])
```

As the scatter points are dark, I have also modified the tick labels with path effects, which was introduced in matplotlib 1.4. This makes it much easier to distinguish the coordinate labels:

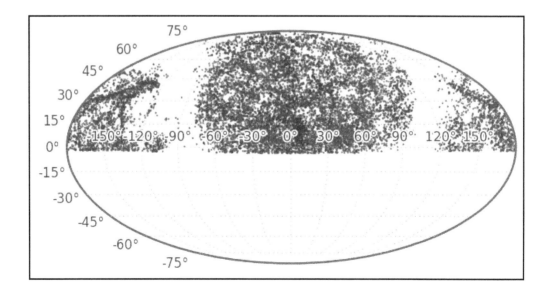

We can see that we have data for the upper part of the sky only. We also see the extent of the Milky Way, its gas and dust is blocking our view beyond it and no galaxies are found there in the dataset. To minimize the data that we look at, we will cut it along the Dec between 15 and 30 degrees. Let's check the distribution of distances that are covered:

```
uzcat['cz'].hist(bins=50)
plt.yscale('log')
plt.xlabel('CZ-distance')
plt.ylabel('Counts')
plt.xticks(rotation=45, ha='right');
```

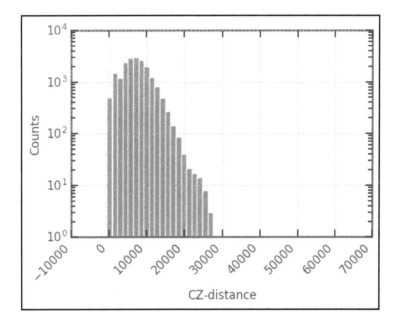

The peak is around 10,000 km/s, and we cut it off at 12,500 km/s. Let's visualize this cut from top-down. Instead of looking at both RA and Dec, we will look at RA and cz. First, we create the selection:

```
uzc_czs = uzcat['cz'].as_matrix()
uzcat['Zmag'] = uzcat['Zmag'].astype('float')
decmin = 15
decmax = 30
ramin = 90
ramax = 295
czmin = 0
czmax = 12500
selection_dec = (coords_uzc.dec.deg>decmin) *
```

```
                        (coords_uzc.dec.deg<decmax)
selection_ra = (coords_uzc.ra.deg>ramin) *
                        (coords_uzc.ra.deg<ramax)
selection_czs = (uzc_czs>czmin) * (uzc_czs<czmax)
selection= selection_dec * selection_ra * selection_czs
```

We export the cz column from the DataFrame just for convenience; we create a separate Boolean array for each selection. This way, we can filter whatever we want. For example, calling coords_uzc.ra.radian[selection_dec*selection_ra] will only filter out the RA and Dec that we are after. Next, we plot it all with only the Dec filter, and then visualize where we are about to cut in cz and RA. I have not explained the cut in RA and cz chosen here, but it was done after looking at the following image:

```
fig = plt.figure( figsize=(6,6))
ax = fig.add_subplot(111, polar=True)
sct = ax.scatter(coords_uzc.ra.radian[selection_dec],
                    uzc_czs[selection_dec],
                    color='SteelBlue',
                    s=uzcat['Zmag'][selection_dec*selection_czs],
                    edgecolors="none",
                    alpha=0.7,
                    zorder=0)
ax.set_rlim(0,20000)
ax.set_theta_offset(np.pi/-2)
ax.set_rlabel_position(65)
ax.set_rticks(range(2500,20001,5000));
ax.plot([(ramin*u.deg).to(u.radian).value,
        (ramin*u.deg).to(u.radian).value], [0,12500],
        color='IndianRed', alpha=0.8, dashes=(10,4))
ax.plot([ramax*np.pi/180., ramax*np.pi/180.], [0,12500],
        color='IndianRed', alpha=0.8, dashes=(10,4))
        theta = np.arange(ramin, ramax, 1)
ax.plot(theta*np.pi/180., np.ones_like(theta)*12500,
        color='IndianRed', alpha=0.8, dashes=(10,4))
```

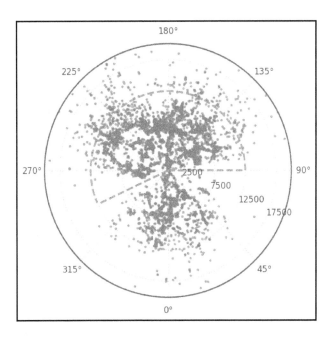

Here, we use a polar plot by passing `polar=True` when we instantiate the subplot and applying the `selection_dec` filters to all `Dec` values above 30 and below 15 degrees. The coordinates need to be given in radians, hence we go over to radians by simply asking for the coordinates in radians as previously described. Next, we customize the plot, rotating the plot 90 degrees clockwise, which is pi/2 in radians. To make it easier to read the radial distance axis labels, we set them to be drawn at 65 degrees and set the distance at which they should be drawn. The last two function calls draw the dashed region, the region which I set as `selection_ra` and `selection_czs`. Next, we plot only the selection points and zoom in a bit:

```
fig = plt.figure( figsize=(6,6))
ax = fig.add_subplot(111, polar=True)
sct = ax.scatter(coords_uzc.ra.radian[selection],
                 uzc_czs[selection],
                 color='SteelBlue',
                 s=uzcat['Zmag'][selection],
                 edgecolors="none",
                 alpha=0.7,
                 zorder=0)
ax.set_rlim(0,12500)
ax.set_theta_offset(np.pi/-2)
ax.set_rlabel_position(65)
ax.set_rticks(range(2500,12501,2500));
```

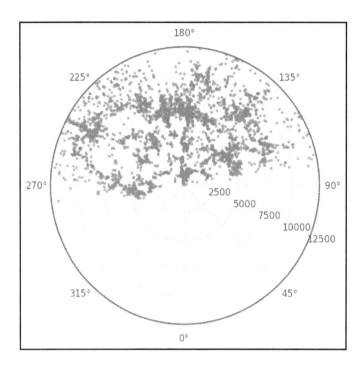

It is important to notice that most coordinates are above the line that 90 to 270 degrees forms. This will later have an effect on the Cartesian coordinates. With a subsection of the total catalog, it is a good idea to create a separate DataFrame to store everything in it, including the coordinates in degrees:

```
mycat = uzcat.copy(deep=True).loc[selection]
mycat['ra_deg'] = coords_uzc.ra.deg[selection]
mycat['dec_deg'] = coords_uzc.dec.deg[selection]
```

Although RA, Dec, and cz is a perfectly understandable coordinate format for astronomers, it is not for most people (it is even hard to digest for astronomers). So we shall now convert these spherical coordinates (Celestial Equatorial Coordinate System) to X, Y, Z. To do this, we use some very convenient functions in the Astropy Coordinates package, which we have already worked with. First, we calculate the actual distance to the galaxies. To do this, we use the Distance function, which can be done with different geometries of the universe/cosmologies, but the default (current) is fine for us:

```
zs = (((mycat['cz'].as_matrix()*u.km/u.s) / c.c).decompose())
dist = coord.Distance(z=zs)
print(dist)
mycat['dist'] = dist
```

We now have everything to calculate the Cartesian coordinates of the galaxies:

```
coords_xyz = coord.SkyCoord(ra=mycat['ra_deg']*u.deg,
                            dec=mycat['dec_deg']*u.deg,
                            distance=dist*u.Mpc,
                            frame='fk5',
                            equinox='J2000')
```

Now is a good time to save these Cartesian coordinates to our catalog:

```
mycat['X'] = coords_xyz.cartesian.x.value
mycat['Y'] = coords_xyz.cartesian.y.value
mycat['Z'] = coords_xyz.cartesian.z.value
```

I suggest running `head()` and `describe()` on the current DataFrame catalog that we have created (that is, `mycat`). Notice then that most X coordinates are negative. Why is this? Remember what RA coordinates most of our selection had? Go back and check the polar plots that we made. The RA is between 90 and 270 degrees; basically the opposite direction of 0 degrees, causing them to have negative X coordinates now. Now I want to plot this; as it is actually three-dimensional data, I will use two plots to visualize the three dimensions:

```
fig, axs = plt.subplots(1,2, figsize=(14,6))
plt.subplot(121)
plt.scatter(mycat['Y'], -1*mycat['X'], s=8,
            color=plt.cm.OrRd_r(10**(mycat.Zmag
                                     -mycat.Zmag.max())),
            edgecolor='None')
plt.xlabel('Y (Mpc)'); plt.ylabel('X (Mpc)')
plt.axis('equal');
plt.subplot(122)
plt.scatter(-1*mycat['X'],mycat['Z'], s=8,
            color=plt.cm.OrRd_r(10**(mycat.Zmag
                                     -mycat.Zmag.max())),
            edgecolor='None')
lstyle = dict(lw=1.5, color='k', dashes=(6,4))
plt.plot([0,150], [0,80], **lstyle)
plt.plot([0,150], [0,45], **lstyle)
plt.plot([0,-25], [0,80], **lstyle)
plt.plot([0,-25], [0,45], **lstyle)
plt.xlabel('X (Mpc)'); plt.ylabel('Z (Mpc)')
plt.axis('equal')
plt.subplots_adjust(wspace=0.25);
```

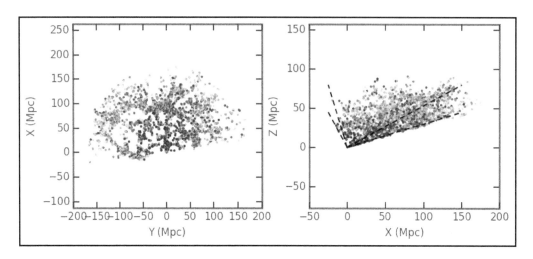

Visualizing it like this gives you a good overview, even if the data is three-dimensional. We could have made the selection after converting to X, Y, and Z coordinates and cut out a cube. Try this out and see how the results of this exercise differ. Furthermore, I recommend that you try to make a three-dimensional plot at this stage; refer to the previous chapter (Chapter 4, *Regression*) for the code. We have now reduced the catalog to cover the region that we are interested in and mapped some of the columns to values easily readable by functions. This is the time to save it in order to make it easier to start where we left off. Just like in the previous chapter, we use the HDF file format:

```
TABLE_FILE = 'data/data_ch5_clustering.h5'
mycat.to_hdf(TABLE_FILE, 'ch5data', mode='w', table=True)
```

As an alternative, if you have problems with the HDF libraries or just want an alternative, you can also save it with the pickle module, which is a standard module in Python:

```
mycat.to_pickle('data/data_ch5_clustering.pick')
```

We will read this data in Chapter 7, *Supervised and Unsupervised Learning*. Now we have reduced the data so that we can run our clusteringanalysis on it.

Hierarchical cluster algorithm

The hierarchical agglomerative clustering algorithm is run in SciPy through the `linkage` function with this array as input. There are two main parameters to set in the linkage function, method and metric:

- **Method** defines the linkage algorithm to use, that is, how we estimate the dissimilarities between two clusters and thus define how clusters are formed
- **Metric** defines the distance metric; in this case, we are working with non-categorical variables, where distance makes sense

In our case, we have converted the data to Cartesian coordinates so that we can use the common Euclidean distance. It is possible to define your own distance function. Possible methods and metrics in the linkage function are listed in the SciPy documentation at `http://docs.scipy.org/`.

The linkage function takes an N by 2 array (N data points), so here we use only the *X* and *Y* coordinates:

```
galpos = np.array([mycat.X,mycat.Y]).T
z_centroid = hac.linkage(galpos, metric = 'euclidean',
                            method = 'centroid')
```

The output here is the linkage matrix. This is the result for the whole run; it contains four columns. To quickly illustrate what it contains, we run a controlled and much smaller example. To visualize the various group levels, we also plot a dendrogram, which is done with the `hac.dendrogram` function that takes the linkage output as input. It visualizes the clustering sequence in a handy way. The root level is the level where the whole dataset is in one cluster. At the other end is a lower level of clustering; however, they are connected to the root level. Each node represents a group of clusters and each node connects to two subnodes. If all levels are plotted, the end node (node at the lowest level) is called a leaf node and contains only one data point (observation). How these are connected is determined by the linkage definition (dissimilarity measuring algorithm):

```
x = np.array([1,2,2,1,6,7,8,5])
y = np.array([8,6,8,7,1,2,2,3])
a = np.array([x,y]).T
z = hac.linkage(a, metric = 'euclidean', method = 'centroid')
fig, axs = plt.subplots(1,2,figsize=(7,3))
axs[0].scatter(x,y, marker='o', s=40, c='IndianRed')
axs[0].set_xlabel('X'); axs[0].set_ylabel('Y');
for i in range(len(x)):
    axs[0].annotate(s=str(i), xy=(x[i]+0.1,y[i]+0.1))
ellipse1 = Ellipse(xy=(1.6,8.2),
```

```
                    width=2., height=1.2,
                    zorder=32, fc='None', ec='k', lw=1.5)
axs[0].add_artist(ellipse1)
d_temp = hac.dendrogram(z, ax=axs[1])
axs[1].annotate(s='8',
                xy=(np.mean(d_temp['icoord'][0][1:-1]),
                d_temp['dcoord'][0][1]),
                xytext=(3,3), textcoords='offset points')
axs[1].annotate(s='9',
                xy=(np.mean(d_temp['icoord'][3][1:-1]),
                d_temp['dcoord'][3][1]),
                xytext=(3,3), textcoords='offset points')
axs[1].annotate(s='10',
                xy=(np.mean(d_temp['icoord'][1][1:-1])-2,
                d_temp['dcoord'][1][1]),
                xytext=(3,3), textcoords='offset points',
                ha='right')
axs[1].annotate(s='Root',
                xy=(np.mean(d_temp['icoord'][-1][1:-1]),
                d_temp['dcoord'][-1][1]-0.3),
                xytext=(5,5), textcoords='offset points',
                va='top', ha='center')
axs[1].set_xlabel('Leafs')
```

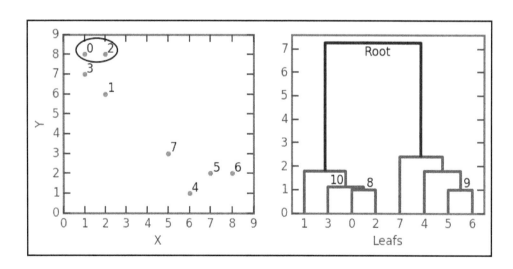

In the linkage output z, the first row is [0., 2., 1., 2.], which says the following: cluster index 0 and 2 form a group, their distance is 1, and the number of leafs (data points) in the group is 2. This group is encircled in the image. The group number is the number of original points plus the iteration number (n+i); in this case, we form cluster 8 (8+0). The third row (NB, not the second!) has the numbers [3., 8., 1.11803399, 3.] in it. It combines cluster index 3, which in this case is just the point because every cluster number less than 8 is a point/leaf with cluster 8, just what we created in the first iteration. The distance between them (with the given metric and method) is 1.111803399 and it contains three leafs. It forms the 10th cluster, that is, 8 + 2 iterations. I have illustrated these nodes in the example dendrogram and also marked cluster group number 10. Think about how it fits into the linkage output described here.

With this knowledge, we can now plot the dendrogram for the main data analysis:

```
fig, ax = plt.subplots(1, figsize=(8,6))
d0 = hac.dendrogram(z_centroid, p=6, truncate_mode='level',
              orientation='right', ax=ax)
```

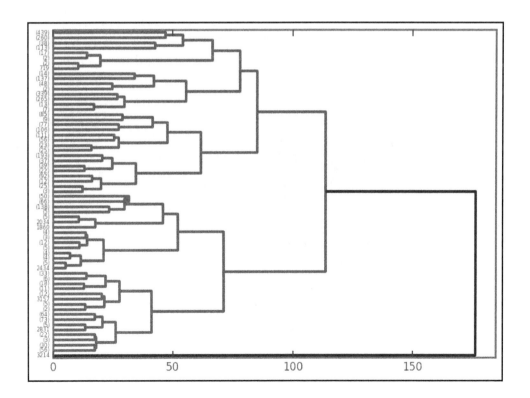

This time, I have added some parameters to the plotting function-we have tipped the whole dendrogram 90 degrees. The height between two nodes is proportional to the dissimilarity between the nodes (the distance method). Cutting this dendrogram across will give a certain amount of clusters. It's interesting to see that the root node divides only once into two clusters, where only one of them continues to divide. To get the clusters at a certain level, we use the `fcluster` function, also part of SciPy's clustering module. I suggest that you try different amount of clusters and plot them. In the following example, I have used 20 clusters:

```
nclust = 20
part_centroid = hac.fcluster(z_centroid, 20, criterion='maxclust')
```

Here, criterion sets the constraints on forming the clusters. Just to check the division of points in each cluster/group, we plot a histogram:

```
plt.figure(figsize=(7,6))
otpt = plt.hist(part_centroid, color='SteelBlue', bins=nclust);
plt.xlabel('Cluster no.'); plt.ylabel('Counts');
```

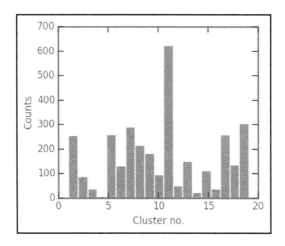

There are a lot of points in the 11th cluster. Of course, this does not tell us much, so now we plot all the clusters. As the position of each cluster, I just calculate the centroid with the mean method of the array object. This is just to mark the location of clusters more clearly:

```
plt.figure(figsize=(6,5))
plt.subplot(111)
part = part_centroid
levels = np.arange(nclust)
colors = plt.cm.rainbow(np.random.rand(len(levels)))
for n, color in zip(levels, colors):
```

```
plt.scatter(mycat['Y'][part==n], -1*mycat['X'][part==n], s=12,
            color=color, edgecolor='None')
plt.plot(mycat['Y'][part==n].mean(),
         -1*mycat['X'][part==n].mean(),
         'o', c='0.7', mec='k', ms=6,
         ls='None', mew=1.5, alpha=0.7)
plt.xlabel('Y (Mpc)'); plt.ylabel('X (Mpc)')
plt.scatter(mycat['Y'], -1*mycat['X'], s=10,
            color='0.7', edgecolor='None',zorder=-1)
plt.title('A slice of the Universe - Clusters identified')
plt.axis('equal');
```

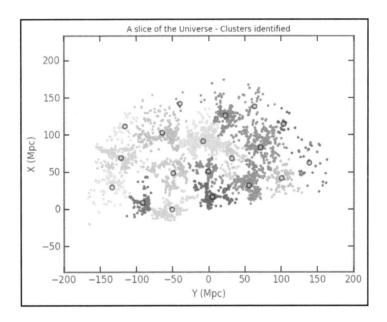

The cluster division looks solid. However, we determined the number of clusters by visually inspecting the effect of changing the number of clusters. This might not be the true or ideal number of clusters. In the previous example, we had a hypothesis of two clusters that we wanted to test, but even in that case the data might be better represented by, for example, three clusters or perhaps none (or one cluster with outliers). We want to have a reproducible way of determining the number of clusters. There are several approaches to this; there is even a dedicated Wikipedia article on how to find the number of clusters (http s://en.wikipedia.org/wiki/Determining_the_number_of_clusters_in_a_data_ set). The main problem with determining the optimum number of clusters is that we have to assume something about the cluster shapes. Hierarchical clustering circumvents this problem slightly by checking all the levels of a cluster with the assumption that each cluster is divided up into smaller clusters.

One approach measures the cluster compactness by calculating the normalized sum of the squared distances (that is, variance) for each cluster and then using this to estimate what percentage of the data that can be described by this variance in cluster size. Incrementally increasing the number of clusters, you get a graph of the increase in the coverage of the cluster by calculating the variance. When the `true` number of clusters has been reached, this variance (or coverage) will stop increasing and flatten out. However, this does not fit all clump shapes; imagine, for example, very elongated ellipses close to each other. In our case, the clusters at medium distances are more filamentary than clumpy (or Gaussian-like).

Summary

We have now identified clusters using a range of methods, from calculating simple centroids manually to advanced hierarchical clustering algorithms in SciPy. There are of course many more packages in Python. We will look at one alternative, the machine learning package, Scikit-learn, in `Chapter 7`, *Supervised and Unsupervised Learning*, to identify clusters. SciPy has these two clustering frameworks, that is, vector quantization and hierarchical clustering, which lay the foundation for cluster analysis and are very useful in many general data analysis problems. In the next chapter, we will look at Bayesian analysis and how to use the PyMC Bayesian inference package in Python to characterize various things in data.

6
Bayesian Methods

Bayesian inference is a different paradigm for statistics; it is not a method or algorithm such as cluster finding or linear regression. It stands next to classical statistical analysis. Everything that we have done so far in this book, and everything that you can do in classical (or frequentist) statistical analysis, you can do in Bayesian statistics. The main difference between frequentist (classical) and Bayesian statistics is that while frequentist assumes that the model parameters are fixed, Bayesian assumes that they have a range, a distribution. Thus, from the frequentist approach, it is easy to create point estimates—mean, variance, or fixed model parameters—directly from the data. The point estimates are unique to the data; each new dataset needs new point estimates.

In this chapter, we will cover the following topics:

- Examples of Bayesian analysis: one where we try to identify a switch point in a time series and another with linear regression, where we compare the methods from `Chapter 4`, *Regression*
- How to assess the MCMC run from Bayesian analysis
- A very short introduction on plotting coordinates on maps, which can be very important when presenting and investigating data

The Bayesian method

From the Bayesian approach, data is seen as fixed. Once we have measured things, the values are fixed. On the other hand, parameters can be described by probability distributions. The probability distribution describes how much is known about a certain parameter. This description might change if we get new data, but the model itself will not change. There is lots of literature on this, and there is no rule of thumb for when to use frequentist or when to use Bayesian analysis.

For simple and fairly well-behaved data, I would say that the frequentist approach is fine when you need a quick estimate. To get more insights and for more constrained problems, that is, when we know more about our parameters and can estimate the prior distributions with more than a simple uniform prior, it is better to use the Bayesian approach. Due to the slightly more intuitive handling of things in Bayesian analysis, it is easier to build more complex models and answer complex questions.

Credible versus confidence intervals

A nice and common way to highlight the differences is to compare the confidence interval of frequentists with the corresponding notion in Bayesian statistics, credible interval. Confidence interval is from the frequentist's approach, where the parameter is fixed. The confidence interval is based on the repetition of the observations. A 98% confidence interval means that repeating the experiment to measure the parameter a large number of times and calculating the interval for each experiment, 98% of the intervals will contain the value of the parameter. This goes back to the fact that the data is random.

Credible (or probability) interval stems from probabilities, that is, the Bayesian approach. This means that the parameter is random and we can say that, given the data, there is a 98% chance that the true value of the parameter is in the interval.

Bayes formula

Bayesian analysis boils down to Bayes formula; thus, a chapter about Bayesian analysis without mentioning Bayes formula would not be worth much. In Bayesian analysis, everything done can be expressed in a probability statement:

$$\boxed{P\left(a \mid b\right)}$$

This is read as probability of a given b, where b is the data and a is the parameter that you are trying to estimate. With Bayesian analysis, we build models that we can test against data. Bayesian analysis (inference) uses probability distribution(s) as input to the model (hypothesis) that we are building (testing).

With some prior knowledge of statistics in our luggage, we write out Bayes formula:

$$P(a \mid b) = \frac{P(b \mid a) P(a)}{P(b)}$$

The Bayes formula follows from conditional probabilities. Describing it in words, the posterior probability is the probability of the observations (given the parameter) times the prior of the parameter divided by an integral over the whole parameter space. It is this denominator that causes trouble with the analysis because, to calculate it, we need to employ some advanced analysis; in these examples, the **Markov Chain Monte Carlo** (**MCMC**) algorithm is used. We assume that you are familiar with the basics of Bayes formula. We will see how to implement the analysis in Python with the help of the PyMC package.

Python packages

One popular Bayesian analysis package in Python is PyMC (`http://pymc-devs.github.io/pymc/`). PyMC is an actively developed package to make Bayesian models and fitting in Python accessible and straightforward. One of the fitting algorithms available is MCMC, which is also one of the most employed. There are other packages such as the feature-rich emcee package (`http://dan.iel.fm/emcee/current/`). We will use PyMC in this book. To install PyMC in Anaconda, open an Anaconda command prompt (or terminal window) and use the conda command to install PyMC:

```
conda install pymc
```

It will check the Anaconda Python package index and download and install/upgrade the necessary dependencies for PyMC. Next, we can start a new Jupyter Notebook and put in the default imports.

U.S. air travel safety record

In this example, we will look at a dataset from the U.S. **National Transportation Safety Board** (**NTSB**). The NTSB has an open database that can be downloaded from their web page, `http://www.ntsb.gov`. One important thing about the data is that it contains *civil aviation accidents and selected incidents within the United States, its territories and possessions, and in international waters*, that is, it is not for the whole world. Basically, it is for U.S.-related accidents only, which makes sense for a U.S. national organization. There are databases that contain the whole world, but with less fields in them. For example, the NTSB dataset contains information about minor injuries for the accident in question. For comparison, and as an opening for exercises, after the Bayesian analysis of the NTSB data, we shall load and have a quick look at a dataset from OpenData by Socrata (`https://opendata.socrata.com`) that covers the whole world. The question that we want to investigate in this section is whether there are any jumps in the statistics for plane accidents with time. An alternative source is the Aviation Safety Network (`https://aviation-safety.net`). One important point before starting the analysis is that we shall once again read in the real raw data and clean it from unwanted parts so that we can focus on the analysis. This takes a few lines of coding, but it is very important to cover this as this shows you what is really happening and you will understand the results and data much better than if I would give you the finished cleaned and reduced data (or even created data with *random* noise).

Getting the NTSB database

To download the data from NTSB, go to their web page (`http://www.ntsb.gov`), click on **Aviation Accident Database**, and select **Download All (Text)**. The data file, `AviationData.txt`, should now be downloaded and saved for you to read in.

The dataset contains date stamps for when a specific accident took place. To be able to read in the dates into a format that Python understands, we need to parse the date strings with the datetime package. The datetime package is a standard package that comes with Python (and the Anaconda distribution):

```
from datetime import datetime
```

Now let's read in the data. To spare you some time, I have redefined the column names so that they are more easily accessible. By now, you should be familiar with the very useful Pandas `read_csv` function:

```
aadata = pd.read_csv('data/AviationData.txt',
                     delimiter='|',
                     skiprows=1,
                     names=['id', 'type', 'number', 'date',
         'location', 'country', 'lat', 'long', 'airport_code',
         'airport_name', 'injury_severity', 'aircraft_damage',
         'aircraft_cat', 'reg_no', 'make', 'model',
         'amateur_built', 'no_engines', 'engine_type', 'FAR_desc',
         'schedule', 'purpose', 'air_carrier', 'fatal',
         'serious', 'minor', 'uninjured',
         'weather', 'broad_phase', 'report_status',
         'pub_date', 'none'])
```

Listing the column names shows that there is a wealth of data here, such as location, latitude, and longitude of the accident, the airport code and name, and so on:

```
aadata.columns
```

```
Index(['id', 'type', 'number', 'date', 'location', 'country', 'lat', 'long',
       'airport_code', 'airport_name', 'injury_severity', 'aircraft_damage',
       'aircraft_cat', 'reg_no', 'make', 'model', 'amateur_built',
       'no_engines', 'engine_type', 'FAR_desc', 'schedule', 'purpose',
       'air_carrier', 'fatal', 'serious', 'minor', 'uninjured', 'weather',
       'broad_phase', 'report_status', 'pub_date', 'none'],
      dtype='object')
```

After looking at the data and trying some of the following things, you will discover that some date entries are empty, that is, just containing whitespace ( ). We could, as before, find the entries with whitespace using the `apply` (-map) function(s) and replace the values. In this case, I will just quickly filter them out with a Boolean array produced by the matching expression, `!=`, that is, not equal to (we only want the rows with dates). This is because, as mentioned in the beginning, we want to see how the accidents vary with time:

```
selection = aadata['date'] != '  '
aadata = aadata[selection]
```

Now the actual date strings are a bit tricky. They have the MONTH/DAY/YEAR format (for me as a European, this is illogical). The standard `datetime` module can do the job as long as we tell it what format the dates are in. In practice, Pandas can parse this when reading the data with the `parse_dates=X` flag, where X is either a column index integer or column name string.

However, sometimes it does not work well without putting in a lot of work, as in our case, so we shall parse it on our own. Here, we parse it into the new column, `datetime`, where each date is converted to a `datetime` object with the `strptime` function. One of the reasons for this is that the date is given with whitespace around it. So it is given as `02/18/2016` instead of `02/18/2016`, which is also why we give the date format specification as `%m/%d/%Y`, that is, with whitespace around it. This way, the `strptime` function knows what it looks like:

```
aadata['datetime'] = [datetime.strptime(x, ' %m/%d/%Y ') for x in
    aadata['date']]
```

Now that we have `datetime` objects, Python knows what the dates mean. Only checking just the year or month could be interesting later on. To have it handy, we save those in separate columns. With a moderate dataset like this, we can create many columns without slowing down things noticeably:

```
aadata['month'] = [int(x.month) for x in aadata['datetime']]
aadata['year'] = [int(x.year) for x in aadata['datetime']]
```

Now we also want the dates as decimal year, so we can bin them year by year and calculate yearly statistics. To do this, we want to see what fraction of a year has passed for a certain date. Here, we write a small function, the solution inspired in part by various answers online. We call the `datetime` function to create objects representing the start and end of the year. We need to put `year+1` here, if we do not do this, `month=12` and `day=31` would yield in nonsensical values around the new year (for example, 2017 when it is still 2016). If you search on Google for this problem, there are a lot of different, good answers and ways of doing this (some requiring additional packages installed):

```
def decyear(date):
    start = datetime(year=date.year, month=1, day=1)
    end = datetime(year=date.year+1, month=1, day=1)
    decimal = (date-start)/(end-start)
    return date.year+decimal
```

With this function, we can apply it to each element in the `datetime` column of our table. As all the column rows contain a `datetime` object already, the function that we just created happily accepts the input:

```
aadata['decyear'] = aadata['datetime'].apply(decyear)
```

Now, the columns `Latitude`, `Longitude`, `uninjured`, `fatalities`, and `serious and minor injuries` should all be floats and not strings for easy calculations and other operations. So we convert them to floats with the `applymap` method. The following code will convert the empty strings to `Nan` values and numbers to floats:

```
cols = ['lat', 'long',
        'fatal',
        'serious',
        'minor',
        'uninjured']
aadata[cols] = aadata[cols].applymap(
        lambda x: np.nan if isinstance(x, str)
                     and x.isspace() else float(x))
```

We are just applying a lambda function, which converts the values to floats and empty strings to NaN, to all the entries in the given columns. Now let's plot the data to see if we need to trim or process it further:

```
plt.figure(figsize=(9,4.5))
plt.step(aadata['decyear'], aadata['fatal'],
        lw=1.75, where='mid', alpha=0.5, label='Fatal')
plt.step(aadata['decyear'], aadata['minor']+200,
        lw=1.75,where='mid', label='Minor')
plt.step(aadata['decyear'], aadata['serious']+200*2,
        lw=1.75, where='mid', label='Serious')
plt.xticks(rotation=45)
plt.legend(loc=(0.01,.4),fontsize=15)
plt.ylim((-10,600))
plt.grid(axis='y')
plt.title('Accident injuries {0}-{1}'.format(
            aadata['year'].min(), aadata['year'].max()))
plt.text(0.15,0.92,'source: NTSB', size=12,
        transform=plt.gca().transAxes, ha='right')
plt.yticks(np.arange(0,600,100), [0,100,0,100,0,100])
plt.xlabel('Year')
plt.ylabel('No injuries recorded')
plt.xlim((aadata['decyear'].min()-0.5,
            aadata['decyear'].max()+0.5));
```

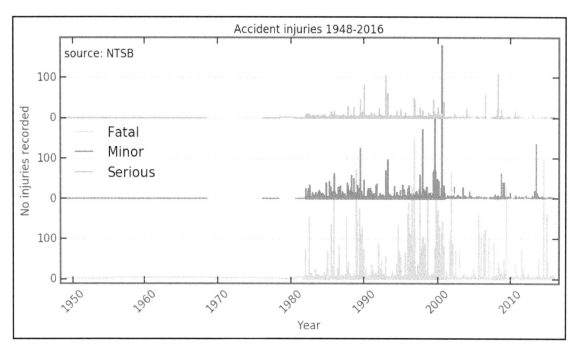

The available data before around 1980 is very sparse and not ideal for statistical interpretation. Before deciding what to do, let's check the data for these entries. To see how many accidents were recorded, we plot the histogram around that time. Here, we employ a filter by combining two Boolean arrays. We also change the `bins` parameter by giving it the years, 1975 to 1990; in this way, we know that the `bins` will be per year:

```
plt.figure(figsize=(9,3))
plt.subplot(121)
year_selection = (aadata['year']>=1975) & (aadata['year']<=2016)
plt.hist(aadata[year_selection]['year'].as_matrix(),
        bins=np.arange(1975,2016+2,1), align='mid')
plt.xlabel('Year'); plt.grid(axis='x')
plt.xticks(rotation=45);
plt.ylabel('Accidents recorded')
plt.subplot(122)
year_selection = (aadata['year']>=1976) & (aadata['year']<=1986)
plt.hist(aadata[year_selection]['year'].as_matrix(),
        bins=np.arange(1976,1986+2,1), align='mid')
plt.xlabel('Year')
plt.xticks(rotation=45);
```

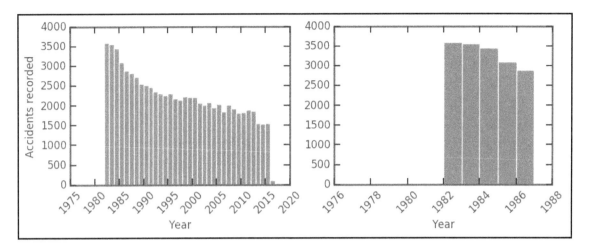

The absolute number of accidents have roughly halved in 35 years; given that the number of passengers has definitely increased, this is very good. The right-hand plot shows that before 1983, there are very few recorded accidents by the NTSB. Listing the table with this criteria shows six recorded accidents:

```
aadata[aadata['year']<=1981]
```

After this thorough inspection, I think it is safe to remove the entries before and including 1981. I do not know the reason for the lack of data; perhaps the NTSB was founded at this point? Their mandate was reformulated to include storing a database of the incidents? In any case, let's exclude these entries:

```
aadata = aadata[ aadata['year']>1981 ]
```

Creating the same figure as before, this is what we can see:

```
plt.figure(figsize=(10,5))
plt.step(aadata['decyear'], aadata['fatal'],
        lw=1.75, where='mid', alpha=0.5, label='Fatal')
plt.step(aadata['decyear'], aadata['minor']+200,
        lw=1.75,where='mid', label='Minor')
plt.step(aadata['decyear'], aadata['serious']+200*2,
        lw=1.75, where='mid', label='Serious')
plt.xticks(rotation=45)
plt.legend(loc=(0.8,0.74),fontsize=15)
plt.ylim((-10,600))
plt.grid(axis='x')
plt.title('Accidents {0}-{1}'.format(
        aadata['year'].min(), aadata['year'].max()))
```

```
plt.text(0.135,0.95,'source: NTSB', size=12,
         transform=plt.gca().transAxes, ha='right')
plt.yticks(np.arange(0,600,100), [0,100,0,100,0,100])
plt.xlabel('Year')
plt.ylabel('No injuries recorded')
plt.xlim((aadata['decyear'].min()-0.5,
          aadata['decyear'].max()+0.5));
```

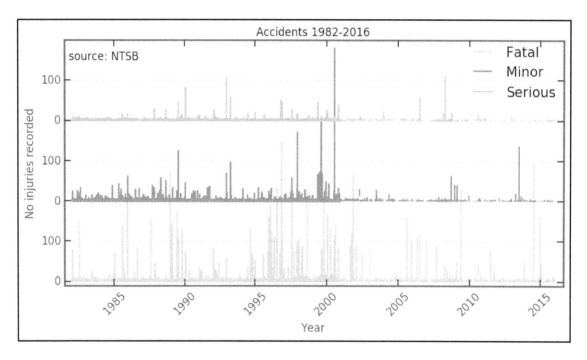

We now have a cleaned dataset that we can work with. It is still hard to distinguish any trends, but around the millennium shift, there is a change in the trend. However, to further see what might be happening, we want to bin the data and look at various key numbers.

Binning the data

In this section, we will bin the data by year. This is so that we can get a better overview of overall trends in the data, which takes us to the next step in the characterization and analysis.

As mentioned before, we want to bin the data per year to look at the trends per year. We did binning before in `Chapter 4`, *Regression*; we use the `groupby` method of our Pandas `DataFrame`. There are two ways to define the bins here, we can use NumPy's `digitize` function or we can use Pandas cut function. I have used the digitize function here as it is more generally useful; you might not always use Pandas for your data (for some reason):

```
bins = np.arange(aadata.year.min(), aadata.year.max()+1, 1 )
yearly_dig = aadata.groupby(np.digitize(aadata.year, bins))
```

We can now calculate statistics for each bin. We can get the sum, maximum, mean, and so on:

```
yearly_dig.mean().head()
```

	lat	long	fatal	serious	minor	uninjured	month	year	decyear
1	30.757778	-88.355555	0.443978	0.203699	0.279474	2.317168	6.488450	1982	1982.495213
2	47.080556	-117.368611	0.358996	0.190059	0.296213	4.258810	6.652137	1983	1983.508864
3	NaN	NaN	0.356749	0.202322	0.303919	3.621739	6.553659	1984	1984.502076
4	NaN	NaN	0.534198	0.198379	0.359507	3.663855	6.477390	1985	1985.494267
5	NaN	NaN	0.410435	0.215454	0.338097	4.138531	6.480556	1986	1986.495181

Additionally, ensure that you get the years out:

```
np.floor(yearly_dig['year'].mean()).as_matrix()
```

```
array([ 1982., 1983., 1984., 1985., 1986., 1987., 1988., 1989.,
        1990., 1991., 1992., 1993., 1994., 1995., 1996., 1997.,
        1998., 1999., 2000., 2001., 2002., 2003., 2004., 2005.,
        2006., 2007., 2008., 2009., 2010., 2011., 2012., 2013.,
        2014., 2015., 2016.])
```

More importantly, we can visualize it. The following function will plot a bar plot and stack the various fields on top of each other. As input, it takes the Pandas `groups` object, a list of field names (< 3), and which field name to use as x axis. Then, there are some customizations and tweaks to make it look better. Noteworthy among them is the `fig.autofmt_xdate(rotation=90, ha='center')` function, which will format the dates for you automatically. You can send it various parameters; in this case, we use it to rotate and horizontally align the x tick labels (as dates):

```
def plot_trend(groups, fields=['Fatal'], which='year', what='max'):
    fig, ax = plt.subplots(1,1,figsize=(9,3.5))
    x = np.floor(groups.mean()[which.lower()]).as_matrix()
    width = 0.9
    colors = ['LightSalmon', 'SteelBlue', 'Green']
    bottom = np.zeros( len(groups.max()[fields[0].lower()]) )
    for i in range(len(fields)):
        if what=='max':
            ax.bar(x, groups.max()[fields[int(i)].lower()],
                    width, color=colors[int(i)],
                    label=fields[int(i)], align='center',
                    bottom=bottom, zorder=4)
    bottom += groups.max()[
    fields[int(i)].lower()
    ].as_matrix()
        elif what=='mean':
            ax.bar(x, groups.mean()[fields[int(i)].lower()],
                    width, color=colors[int(i)],
                    label=fields[int(i)],
                    align='center', bottom=bottom, zorder=4)
            bottom += groups.mean()[
                                fields[int(i)].lower()
                                ].as_matrix()
    ax.legend(loc=2, ncol=2, frameon=False)
    ax.grid(b=True, which='major',
            axis='y', color='0.65',linestyle='-', zorder=-1)
    ax.yaxis.set_ticks_position('left')
    ax.xaxis.set_ticks_position('bottom')
    for tic1, tic2 in zip(
                            ax.xaxis.get_major_ticks(),
                            ax.yaxis.get_major_ticks()
                            ):
        tic1.tick1On = tic1.tick2On = False
        tic2.tick1On = tic2.tick2On = False
    for spine in ['left','right','top','bottom']:
        ax.spines[spine].set_color('w')
    xticks = np.arange(x.min(), x.max()+1, 1)
    ax.set_xticks(xticks)
    ax.set_xticklabels([str(int(x)) for x in xticks])
```

```
fig.autofmt_xdate(rotation=90, ha='center')
ax.set_xlim((xticks.min()-1.5, xticks.max()+0.5))
ax.set_ylim((0,bottom.max()*1.15))
if what=='max':
    ax.set_title('Plane accidents maximum injuries')
    ax.set_ylabel('Max value')
elif what=='mean':
    ax.set_title('Plane accidents mean injuries')
    ax.set_ylabel('Mean value')
ax.set_xlabel(str(which))
return ax
```

Now, let's use it to plot the maximum fatal, serious, and minor injuries for each year in the timespan, 1982 to 2016:

```
ax = plot_trend(yearly_dig, fields=['Fatal','Serious','Minor'],
    which='Year')
```

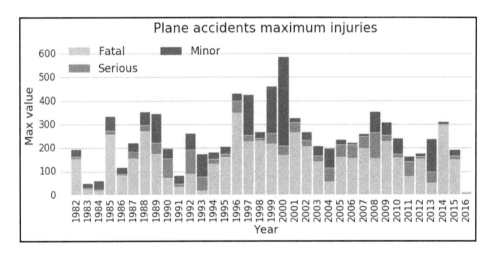

The dominant bars are the ones for fatal—at least from this visual inspection—so when things go really bad in an airplane accident, most people contract fatal injuries. What is curious here is that there seems to be a change in the maximum value, a jump somewhere between 1991 and 1996. After that, it looks like the mean of the maximum number of fatalities is higher. This is what we will try to model with Bayesian inference in the next section.

Bayesian analysis of the data

Now we can dive into the Bayesian part of this analysis. You should always inspect the data in the manner that we have done in the previous exercises. These steps are commonly skipped in text and even fabricated data is used; this paints a simplified picture of data analysis. We have to work with the data to get somewhere and understand what analysis is feasible. First, we need to import the PyMC package and plot function from the Matplot submodule. This function plots a summary of the parameters' posterior distribution, trace (that is, each iteration), and autocorrelation:

```
import pymc
from pymc import Matplot as mcplt
```

To start the analysis, we store the x and y values, year, and maximum fatalities in arrays:

```
x = np.floor(yearly_dig.mean()['year']).as_matrix()
y = yearly_dig.max()['fatal'].as_matrix()
```

Now we develop our model by defining a function with all the parameters and data. It is a discrete process, so we use a Poisson distribution. Furthermore, we use the exponential distribution for the early and late mean rate; this is appropriate for this stochastic process. Try plotting a histogram of the fatalities to see what distribution it has. For the year where the jump/switch takes place, we use a discrete uniform distribution, that is, it is flat for all the values between the lower and upper bounds and zero elsewhere. The variable that is determined by the various stochastic variables, late, early mean, and the switch point is the mean value before and after the jump. As it depends on (stochastic) variables, it is called a deterministic variable. In the code, this is marked by the `@pymc.deterministic()` decorator. This is the process that we are trying to model. There are several distributions built into PyMC, but you can also define your own. However, for most problems, the built-in ones should do the trick. The various available distributions are in the `pymc.distributions` submodule:

```
def model_fatalities(y=y):
    s = pymc.DiscreteUniform('s', lower=5, upper=18, value=14)
    e = pymc.Exponential('e', beta=1.)
    l = pymc.Exponential('l', beta=1.)
    @pymc.deterministic(plot=False)
    def m(s=s, e=e, l=l):
        meanval = np.empty(len(y))
        meanval[:s] = e
        meanval[s:] = l
        return meanval
    D = pymc.Poisson('D', mu=m, value=y, observed=True)
    return locals()
```

The `return locals()` is a somewhat simply way to send all the local variables back. As we have a good overview of what those are, this is not a problem to use. We have now defined the model; to use it in the MCMC sampler, we give the mode as input to the MCMC class:

```
np.random.seed(1234)
MDL = pymc.MCMC(model_fatalities(y=y))
```

To use the standard sampler, we can simply call the `MDL.sample(N)` method, where `N` is the number of iterations to run. There are additional parameters as well; you can give it a burn-in period, a period where no results are considered. This is part of the MCMC algorithm, where it can sometimes be good to let it run for a few iterations that are discarded so that it can start converging. Second, we can give a thin argument; this is how often it should save the outcome of the iteration. In our case, I run it 50,000 times, with 5,000 iterations as burn-in and thin by two. Try running with various numbers to see if the outcome changes, how it changes, and how well the parameters are estimated:

```
MDL.sample(5e4, 5e3, 2)
```

```
[-----------------100%-----------------] 50000 of 50000 complete in 8.6 sec
```

The step method, that is, how to move around in the parameter space, can also be changed. To check what step method we have, we run the following command:

```
MDL.step_method_dict
```

```
{<pymc.distributions.new_dist_class.<locals>.new_class 'l' at 0x7f841e56b470>: [<pymc.StepMethods.Metropolis at 0x7f841e56b390>],
 <pymc.distributions.new_dist_class.<locals>.new_class 'e' at 0x7f841e56b358>: [<pymc.StepMethods.Metropolis at 0x7f841e56b208>],
 <pymc.distributions.new_dist_class.<locals>.new_class 's' at 0x7f841e56b3c8>: [<pymc.StepMethods.DiscreteMetropolis at 0x7f841e56b2e8>]}
```

To change the step method, perhaps to the Adaptive Metropolis algorithm, which uses an adaptive step size (length), we would import it and run the following:

```
from pymc import AdaptiveMetropolis
MDL = pymc.MCMC(model_fatalities(y=y))
MDL.use_step_method(AdaptiveMetropolis, MDL.e)
MDL.use_step_method(AdaptiveMetropolis, MDL.l)
MDL.sample(5e4, 5e3, 2)
```

We are not going to do this here though; this is for problems where the variables are highly correlated. I leave this as an exercise for you to test, together with different prior parameter distributions.

Now we have the whole run in the MDL object. From this object, we can estimate the parameters and plot their posterior distribution. There are convenient functions to do all of this. The following code shows you how to pull out the mean of the posterior distribution and standard deviation. This is where credible interval comes in; we have credible intervals for the parameters, not confidence intervals:

```
early = MDL.stats()['e']['mean']
earlyerr = MDL.stats()['e']['standard deviation']
late = MDL.stats()['l']['mean']
lateerr = MDL.stats()['l']['standard deviation']
spt = MDL.stats()['s']['mean']
spterr = MDL.stats()['s']['standard deviation']
```

Before plotting the results and all the numbers, we must check the results of the MCMC run, to do this we plot the trace, posterior distribution, and autocorrelation for all the stochastic parameters. We do this with the `plot` function from the `pymc.Matplot` module that we imported in the beginning:

```
mcplt.plot(MDL)
```

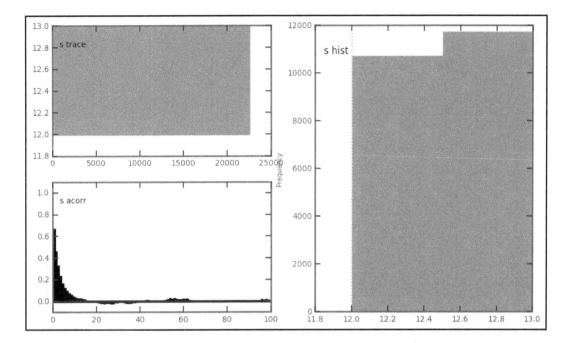

The function plots all three things in one figure. This is very convenient for a quick assessment of the results. It is important to look at all the plots; they give clues to how well the run went:

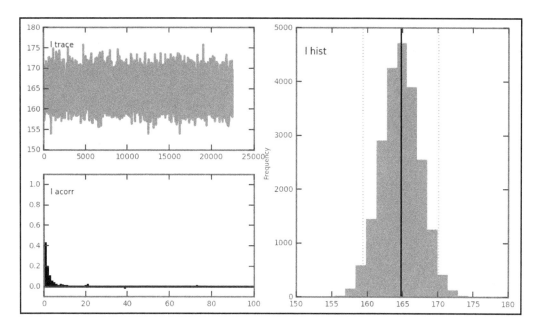

For each stochastic variable, the trace, autocorrelation, and posterior distribution is plotted:

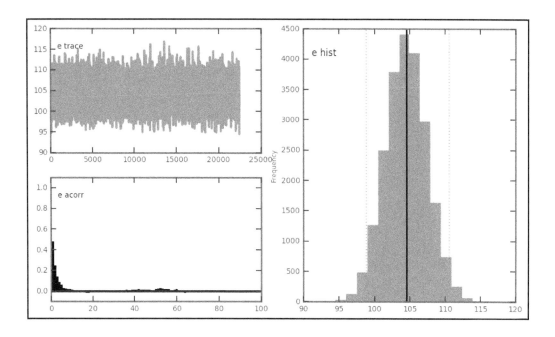

In our case, this gives one figure each for e, l, and s. In each figure, the top left-hand plot shows the trace or time series. The trace is the value for each iteration. It can be accessed with MDL.trace('l')[:] for the late parameter. Try getting the trace and plotting the trace versus iteration and histogram for it; they should look the same as these. For a good model setup, the trace should fluctuate randomly around the best estimate, just like the trace for the early and later parameter. The autocorrelation plot should have a peak at 0; if the plot shows a significant amount of values at higher x values, it is a sign that you need to increase the thin variable. The trace and posterior distribution for the jump/switch point looks different. However, because it is a discrete variable and is constrained within one year, it just shows one peak and the trace follows this. Thus, the switch point is well-constrained with a very small credible interval. Each of the plots in the figures can be drawn individually with related functions in the pymc.Matplot module (mcplt here). The autocorrelation plot for the l variable can be produced with the following command:

```
mcplt.autocorrelation(MDL.l)
```

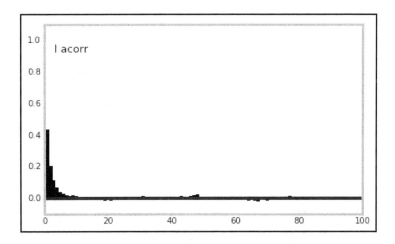

Now that we have constructed a model, run the sampler, and extracted the best estimate parameters, we can plot the results. The jump/switch point identified by the model is simply an index in the array of years, so we need to find which year the index/position corresponds to. To do this, we use NumPy's floor function to round down, and then we can convert it to an integer and slice the x array, which is our year array created in the beginning:

```
s = int(np.floor(spt))
print(spt, spterr, x[s])
```

The preceding code gives `12.524`, `0.499423667841`, and `1994.0` as an output.

To construct the plot with the results, we can once again use the function defined previously, but this time we are only looking at the fatal injuries, so we give a different field parameter. To plot the credible intervals, I use the `fill_between` function here; it is a very handy function and does exactly what it says. Furthermore, instead of the `text` function, which just places `text` in the figure, I use the more powerful annotate function, where we can customize it with a nice box around it:

```
ax = plot_trend(yearly_dig, fields=['Fatal'], which='Year')
ax.plot([x[0]-1.5,x[s]],[early,early], 'k', lw=2)
ax.fill_between([x[0]-1.5,x[s]],
                [early-3*earlyerr,early-3*earlyerr],
                [early+3*earlyerr,early+3*earlyerr],
              color='0.3', alpha=0.5, zorder=2)
ax.plot([x[s],x[-1]+0.5],[late,late], 'k', lw=2)
ax.fill_between([x[s],x[-1]+0.5],
                [late-3*lateerr,late-3*lateerr],
                [late+3*lateerr,late+3*lateerr],
              color='0.3', alpha=0.5, zorder=2)
ax.axvline(int(x[s]), color='0.4', dashes=(3,3), lw=2)
bbox_args = dict(boxstyle="round", fc="w", alpha=0.85)
ax.annotate('{0:.1f}$\pm${1:.1f}'.format(early, earlyerr),
            xy=(x[s]-1,early),
            bbox=bbox_args, ha='right', va='center')
ax.annotate('{0:.1f}$\pm${1:.1f}'.format(late, lateerr),
            xy=(x[s]+1,late),
            bbox=bbox_args, ha='left',va='center')
ax.annotate('{0}'.format(int(x[s])),xy=(int(x[s]),300),
            bbox=bbox_args, ha='center',va='center');
```

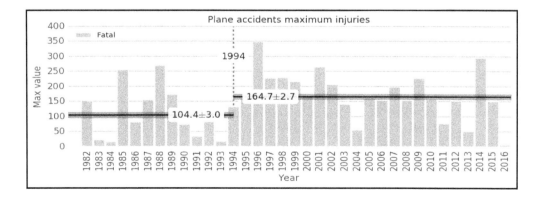

Given the data, the parameters are in the ranges, `104.5+/-3.0` and `164.7+/- 2.7`, with a 95% credibility (that is, `+/-1` sigma). The mean maximum number of fatalities in a year have increased and made a jump around 1994 from `104.5` to `164.7` people. Although from the plot it looks around the year 2004 and 2012-2013, the maximum values do not follow the same trend. Even if this is a simple model, it is hard to argue for a more complex model and the results are significant. The goal should, of course, be to have zero fatalities for every year.

We analyzed what the statistics look like on a per year basis; what if we look at the statistics over the year? To do this, we need to bin per month. So in the next section, this is what we will do.

Binning by month

Repeat the binning procedure that we have, but by month:

```
bins = np.arange(1, 12+1, 1 )
monthly_dig = aadata.groupby(np.digitize(aadata.month, bins))
monthly_dig.mean().head()
```

	lat	long	fatal	serious	minor	uninjured	month	year	decyear
1	35.355070	-91.799283	1.024984	0.351452	0.482369	7.505215	1	1996.595841	1996.637186
2	35.211711	-92.921433	0.890277	0.295262	0.486586	6.861646	2	1996.190641	1996.313377
3	36.439443	-93.719725	0.673851	0.281289	0.428362	6.491056	3	1996.299847	1996.503531
4	37.187038	-93.330245	0.651183	0.304870	0.489868	5.455664	4	1996.292600	1996.579883
5	37.816921	-94.954229	0.671199	0.272957	0.445699	5.194848	5	1996.382683	1996.754983

Now we can do the same but per month; just send the right parameters to the `plot_trend` function that we have created:

```
ax = plot_trend(monthly_dig, fields=['Fatal', 'Serious', 'Minor'],
    which='Month')
ax.set_xlim(0.5,12.5);
```

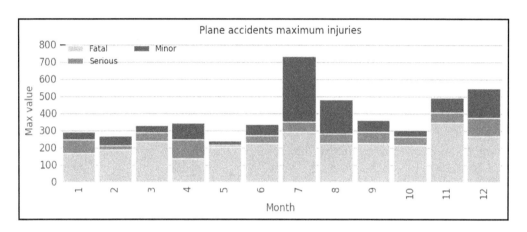

While there is no strong trend, we can note that months 7 and 8, July and August, together with months 11 and 12, November and December, have higher values. Summer and Christmas are popular times of the year to travel, so it is probably a reflection of the yearly variation in the amount of travelers. More travelers means an increase in the number of accidents (with constant risk), thus a greater chance for high fatality accidents. Another question is what the mean variation looks like; what we have worked with so far is the maximum. I have added a parameter in the plotting function, `what`, and set it to `mean`, which will cause the mean to be plotted. I leave this as an exercise; you will see something peculiar with the mean. Try to create different plots to investigate! Also, do not forget to check the mean per month and year.

This last plot highlights something else as well—the total number of passengers might affect the outcome. To get the total number of passengers in the U.S., you can run the following:

```
from pandas.io import wb
airpasstot = wb.download(indicator='IS.AIR.PSGR',
        country=['USA'], start=1982, end=2014)
```

However, looking at this data and comparing it with the data that we have worked with here is left as an exercise for you.

To give you a taste of some of the powerful visualizations that are possible with Python, I want to quickly plot the coordinates of each accident on a map. This is of course not necessary in this case, but it is good to visualize results sometimes, and in Python, it is not obvious how to do it. So this part is not necessary for this chapter, but it is good to know the basics of how to plot things on a map in Python, as many things that we study depend on location on the Earth.

Plotting coordinates

To plot the coordinates, we (unfortunately) have to install packages. Even more unfortunate is that it depends on what operating system and Python distribution you are running. The two packages that we will quickly cover here are the basemap module of the mpl_toolkits package and the cartopy package.

The first one, mpl_toolkits, does not work on Windows (as of April 2016). To install basemap from mpl_toolkits in Anaconda on Mac and Linux, run `conda install -c https://conda.anaconda.org/anaconda basemap`. This should install basemap and all its dependencies.

The second package, cartopy, depends on the GEOS and proj.4 libraries, so they need to be installed first. This can be a bit tedious, but once the GEOS (version greater than 3.3.3) and proj.4 libraries (version greater than 4.8.0) are installed, cartopy can be installed with the `pip` command-line tool, `pip install cartopy`. Once again, in Windows, the prebuilt binaries of proj.4 is version 4.4.6, making it very difficult to install cartopy as well.

For this quick exercise, we grab the latitudes and longitudes of each accident in separate arrays as the plotting commands might be sensitive with the input format and might not support the Pandas Series:

```
lats, lons = aadata['lat'].as_matrix(), aadata['long'].as_matrix()
```

Cartopy

First out is cartopy, where we first create a figure, then add axes to it, where we have to specify the lower left and top right edges of the axes inside the figure and additionally, give it a projection, which is taken from the CRS module of cartopy. When importing the CRS module, we also import the formatters for longitude and latitude, which will just add N, S, E, and W to the x and y tick labels. Importing the matplotlib ticker module, we can specify the exact locations of the tick labels. We could probably do this in the same manner with the ticks function.

As we are plotting the coordinates of the accidents, it is nice to have a background showing the Earth. Therefore, we load an image of the Earth with the `ax.stock_img()` command. It is possible to load coastlines, countries, and other things. To view examples and other possibilities including different projections, see the cartopy website (`http://scitools.org.uk/cartopy`). We then create a scatter plot with latitude and longitude as coordinates and scale the size of the markers proportional to the total fatalities. Then, we plot the gridlines, meridians, and latitude great circles. After this, we just customize the tick locations and labels with the imported formatters and tick location setters:

```
import cartopy.crs as ccrs
from cartopy.mpl.gridliner import LONGITUDE_FORMATTER, LATITUDE_FORMATTER
import matplotlib.ticker as mticker
fig = plt.figure(figsize=(12,10))
ax = fig.add_axes([0,0,1,1], projection=ccrs.PlateCarree())
ax.stock_img()
ax.scatter(aadata['long'],aadata['lat'] ,
           color='IndianRed', s=aadata['fatal']*2,
           transform=ccrs.Geodetic())
gl = ax.gridlines(crs=ccrs.PlateCarree(), draw_labels=True,
                  linewidth=2, color='gray',
                  alpha=0.5, linestyle='--')
gl.xlabels_top = False
gl.ylabels_right = False
gl.xlocator = mticker.FixedLocator(np.arange(-180,180+1,60))
gl.xformatter = LONGITUDE_FORMATTER
gl.yformatter = LATITUDE_FORMATTER
```

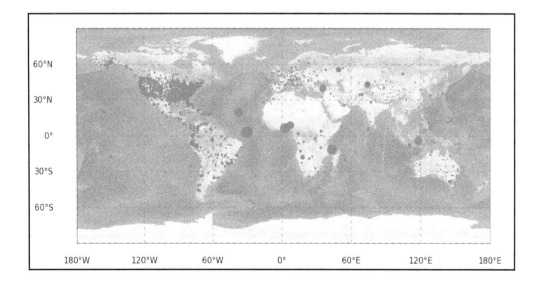

It seems that most of the registered accidents occurred over land. I leave the further tinkering of the figure to you. Looking at statistics over the world, it is useful to be able to plot the spatial distribution of the parameters.

Mpl toolkits – basemap

As promised, we now produce the exact same plot in the basemap module of mpl_toolkits. Here, we only need to import the basemap module and no other tick-modifying functions. The projection is not set in creating the axes, instead it is created by calling the basemap function with the wanted projection. Previously, we called the Carree projection; this is simply the Equidistant Cylindrical projection, and in basemap, this is obtained by giving it the projection string, `cyl`, for cylindrical. The resolution parameter is given as `c`, for coarse. To get the same background image, call the `shadedrelief` command. There are other backgrounds, such as Earth by night, for example. It is possible to draw only coastlines or country borders. In basemap, there are built-in functions for a lot of things; thus, instead of calling matplotlib functions, we now call methods of the `map` object to create meridians and latitudes. I have also included the functions to draw coastlines and country borders, but commented them out. Try uncommenting them and perhaps comment out the drawing of the background image:

```
from mpl_toolkits.basemap import Basemap
fig = plt.figure(figsize=(11,10))
ax = fig.add_axes([0,0,1,1])
map = Basemap(projection='cyl', resolution='c')
map.shadedrelief()
#map.drawcoastlines()
#map.drawcountries()
map.drawparallels(np.arange(-90,90,30),labels=[1,0,0,0],
                color='grey')
map.drawmeridians(np.arange(map.lonmin,map.lonmax+30,60),
                labels=[0,0,0,1], color='grey')
x, y = map(lons, lats)
map.scatter(x, y, color='IndianRed', s=aadata['fatal']*2);
```

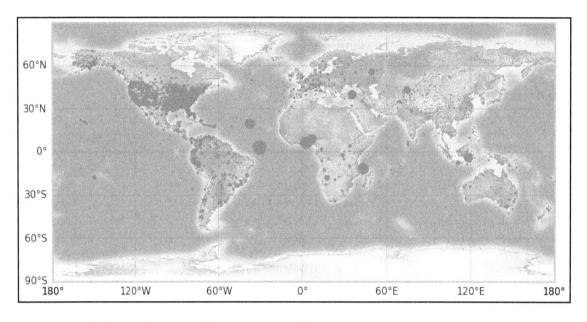

I leave any further tinkering of the coordinate plotting to you. However, you have the first steps here. As the main goal of this chapter is Bayesian analysis, we shall now continue with the data analysis examples.

Climate change – CO_2 in the atmosphere

With Bayesian analysis, we can fit any model; anything that we can do with frequentist or classical statistics, we can do with Bayesian statistics. In this next example, we will perform linear regression with both Bayesian inference and frequentist approaches. As we have covered the model creation and date parsing, we will go through things a little bit more quickly in this example. The data that we are going to use is the atmospheric CO_2 over a span of about 1,000 years and the growth rate over the past 40 years, and then fit a linear function to the growth rate over the past 50-60 years.

Getting the data

The data for the last 50-60 years is from **National Oceanic and Atmospheric Administration** (**NOAA**) marine stations, **surface sites**. It can be found at `http://www.es rl.noaa.gov/gmd/ccgg/trends/global.html`, where you can download two datasets, growth rates, and annual means. The direct links to the data tables are `ftp://aftp.cmdl. noaa.gov/products/trends/co2/co2_gr_gl.txt` for the growth rates (that is, gr) and `ftp://aftp.cmdl.noaa.gov/products/trends/co2/co2_annmean_gl.txt` for the global means (annual in this case). The data reference is Ed Dlugokencky and Pieter Tans, NOAA/ESRL (`hhtp://www.esrl.noaa.gov/gmd/ccgg/trends/`).

To go further back, we need ice core samples from the South Pole, the SIPLE station ice core that goes about 200 years into the past. At `http://cdiac.ornl.gov/trends/co2/siple .html`, there is more information and a direct link to the data, `http://cdiac.ornl.gov/f tp/trends/co2/siple2.013`. The data reference is *Neftel,A., H. Friedli, E. Moor, H. Lötscher, H. Oeschger, U. Siegenthaler, and B. Stauffer, 1994. Historical CO$_2$ record from the Siple Station ice core. In Trends: A Compendium of Data on Global Change. Carbon Dioxide Information Analysis Center, Oak Ridge National Laboratory, U.S. Department of Energy, Oak Ridge, Tenn., U.S.A.* For data even further back, a 1,000 years, we use ice cores from the Law Dome; more information can be found at `http://cdiac.ornl.gov/trends/co2/lawdome.html` with a direct link to the data, `http://cdiac.ornl.gov/ftp/trends/co2/lawdome.smoothe d.yr75`, and the reference is *D.M. Etheridge, L.P. Steele, R.L. Langenfelds, R.J. Francey, J.-M. Barnola, and V.I. Morgan, 1998. Historical CO$_2$ records from the Law Dome DE08, DE08-2, and DSS ice cores. In Trends: A Compendium of Data on Global Change. Carbon Dioxide Information Analysis Center, Oak Ridge National Laboratory, U.S. Department of Energy, Oak Ridge, Tenn., U.S.A.*

As we have done a few times now, we read in the data with the Pandas csv reader:

```
co2_gr = pd.read_csv('data/co2_gr_gl.txt',
                delim_whitespace=True,
                skiprows=62,
                names=['year', 'rate', 'err'])
co2_now = pd.read_csv('data/co2_annmean_gl.txt',
                delim_whitespace=True,
                skiprows=57,
                names=['year', 'co2', 'err'])
co2_200 = pd.read_csv('data/siple2.013.dat',
                delim_whitespace=True,
                skiprows=36,
                names=['depth', 'year', 'co2'])
co2_1000 = pd.read_csv('data/lawdome.smoothed.yr75.dat',
                delim_whitespace=True,
```

```
skiprows=22,
names=['year', 'co2'])
```

There are some additional comments in the last rows of the SIPLE ice core file:

```
co2_200.tail()
```

	depth	year	co2
20	86.80	1943	307.9
21	81.22	1953	312.7
22	Data	in	the
23	table	were	published
24	CO2	concentrations	are

We remove them by slicing the data frame excluding the last three rows:

```
co2_200 = co2_200[:-3]
```

As the Pandas csv reader could not parse the last three rows into floats/integers, the dtype is not right; as it also reads in text, it will use the most generic and accepting data type. First, check the data type of all the datasets to see that we do not have to fix any of the others:

```
print( co2_200['year'].dtype, co2_1000['co2'].dtype,
    co2_now['co2'].dtype, co2_gr['rate'].dtype)
```

```
object float64 float64 float64
```

The co2_200 DataFrame has the wrong dtype, as expected. We change it with Pandas' to_numeric function and check whether it works:

```
co2_200['year'] = pd.to_numeric(co2_200['year'])
co2_200['co2'] = pd.to_numeric(co2_200['co2'])
co2_200['co2'].dtype,co2_200['year'].dtype
```

```
(dtype('float64'), dtype('int64'))
```

64-bit integer and float is now the new data type of the year and co2 columns respectively, which is exactly what we need.

Creating and sampling the model

Now let's visualize all of this. The dataset can be separated in two, as explained previously—one for the absolute CO_2 concentration and one for the growth rate. The unit of the CO_2 concentration is expressed as a mole fraction in dry air (the South Pole is one of the driest places on Earth); in this case, the fraction is expressed in parts per million:

```
fig, axs = plt.subplots(1,2,figsize=(10,4))

ax2 = axs[0]
ax2.errorbar(co2_now['year'], co2_now['co2'],
            #yerr=co2_now['err'],
            color='SteelBlue',
            ls='None',
            elinewidth=1.5,
            capthick=1.5,
            marker='.',
            ms=6)
ax2.plot(co2_1000['year'], co2_1000['co2'],
            color='Green',
            ls='None',
            marker='.',
            ms=6)
ax2.plot(co2_200['year'], co2_200['co2'],
            color='IndianRed',
            ls='None',
            marker='.',
            ms=6)
ax2.axvline(1800, lw=2, color='Gray', dashes=(6,5))
ax2.axvline(co2_gr['year'][0], lw=2,
color='SteelBlue', dashes=(6,5))
print(co2_gr['year'][0])
ax2.legend(['Recent',
            'LAW ice core',
            'SIPLE ice core'],fontsize=15, loc=2)
labels = ax2.get_xticklabels()
plt.setp(labels, rotation=33, ha='right')
ax2.set_ylabel('CO$_2$ (ppm)')
ax2.set_xlabel('Year')
ax2.set_title('Past CO$_2$')

ax1 = axs[1]
ax1.errorbar(co2_gr['year'], co2_gr['rate'],
            yerr=co2_gr['err'],
            color='SteelBlue',
            ls='None',
            elinewidth=1.5,
```

```
                capthick=1.5,
                marker='.',
                ms=8)
labels = ax1.get_xticklabels()
plt.setp(labels, rotation=33, ha='right')
ax1.set_ylabel('CO$_2$ growth (ppm/yr)')
ax1.set_xlabel('Year')
ax1.set_xlim((1957,2016))
ax1.set_title('Growth rate since 1960');
```

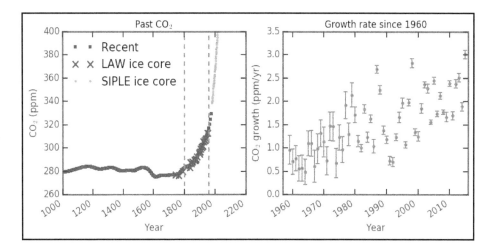

The left-hand plot showing the absolute CO_2 level shows that the ice cores connect to the present day measurements very well. The first vertical dashed line marks the rough start of the industrial revolution (the year 1800). Even though it took some 50 years to really get the steam going (pun intended), this shows where the curve starts an exponential increase that has continued to this day. This correlation between the sharp changes from rather stable measurements to an exponential increase precisely after introducing coal burning steam engines is a strong evidence for manmade climate change. The second vertical line shows where the modern, direct measurements start, that is, 1959. They fit very well with the historical record extracted from ice cores. In the right-hand plot, we basically have a zoom in of that modern time period, from 1959 until today; however, it shows the growth of CO_2 in the atmosphere in ppm (as covered earlier). The data seems to have some distribution in the uncertainties (signifying an upgrade in the measuring technique/instrument). Out of curiosity, let's check this first:

```
_ = plt.hist(co2_gr['err'], bins=20)
plt.xlabel('Uncertainty')
plt.ylabel('Count');
```

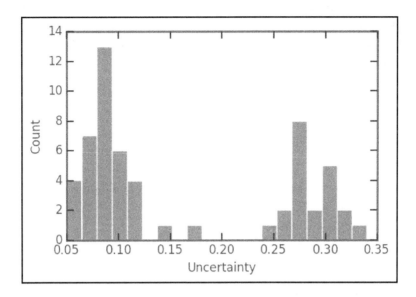

Indeed, it has two peaks where the oldest values are the most uncertain. Just like our previous example, let's first convert the values that we want to NumPy arrays:

```
x = co2_gr['year'].as_matrix()
y = co2_gr['rate'].as_matrix()
y_error = co2_gr['err'].as_matrix()
```

Now that we have done this, we define our model of a linear slope with the same method as for the airplane accidents. It is simply a function that returns the stochastic and deterministic variables. In our case, it is a linear function, taking slope and intercept; this time, we assume that they are normally distributed, which is not an unreasonable assumption. The normal distribution takes a minimum of two parameters, `mu` and `tau` (from PyMC documentation), which is just the position and width of the Gaussian normal distribution:

```
def model(x, y):
    slope = pymc.Normal('slope', 0.1, 1.)
    intercept = pymc.Normal('intercept', -50., 10.)
    @pymc.deterministic(plot=False)
    def linear(x=x, slope=slope, intercept=intercept):
        return x * slope + intercept
    f = pymc.Normal('f', mu=linear,
        tau=1.0/y_error, value=y, observed=True)
    return locals()
```

As before, we initiate the model with a call to MCMC and then sample from it half a million times, a burn-in of 50,000 and thin by 100 this time. I encourage you to first run with something low, such as four, or even omit it (that is, `MDL.sample(5e5, 5e4)`), plot the diagnostics (as follows), and compare the results:

```
MDL = pymc.MCMC(model(x,y))
MDL.sample(5e5, 5e4, 100)
```

```
[------------------100%------------------] 500000 of 500000 complete in 41.5 sec
```

You just ran half a million iterations in less than a minute! Due to the thinning, the post-sampling analysis is a bit quicker:

```
y_min = MDL.stats()['linear']['quantiles'][2.5]
y_max = MDL.stats()['linear']['quantiles'][97.5]
y_fit = MDL.stats()['linear']['mean']

slope = MDL.stats()['slope']['mean']
slope_err = MDL.stats()['slope']['standard deviation']
intercept = MDL.stats()['intercept']['mean']
intercept_err = MDL.stats()['intercept']['standard deviation']
```

We should also create the plots for the time series, posterior distribution, and autocorrelation:

```
mcplt.plot(MDL)
```

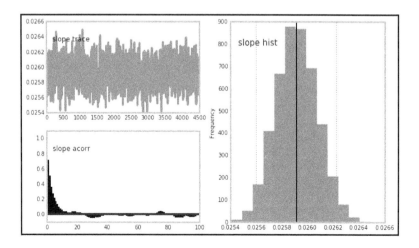

The trace, posterior distribution, and autocorrelation plots all look very good—sharp, well-defined peaks and stable time series. This is also true for the intercept variable:

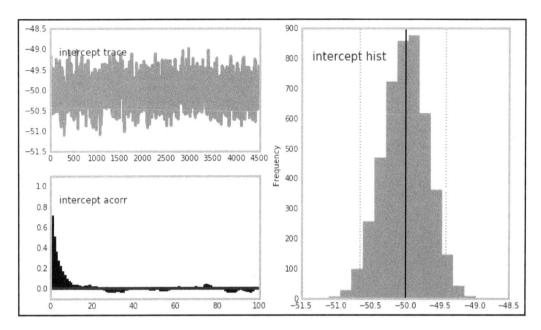

Before we plot the results, I also want us to use one of the other packages, the statsmodels ordinary least square fitting. Just as before, we import the formula package so that we can simply give Pandas the column names that we want to find the relationship between:

```
import statsmodels.formula.api as smf
from statsmodels.sandbox.regression.predstd import wls_prediction_std
ols_results = smf.ols("rate ~ year", co2_gr).fit()
```

We then grab the best fitting parameters and their uncertainty. Here, I flip the parameter tuples for convenience:

```
prstd, iv_l, iv_u = wls_prediction_std(ols_results)
ols_params = np.flipud(ols_results.params)
ols_err = np.flipud(np.diag(ols_results.cov_params())**.5)
```

We can now compare the two methods, least square (frequentist) and Bayesian model fitting:

```
print('OLS: slope:{0:.3f}, intercept:{1:.2f}'.format(*ols_params))
print('Bay: slope:{0:.3f}, intercept:{1:.2f}'.format(slope, intercept))
```

```
OLS: slope:0.027, intercept:-51.81
Bay: slope:0.026, intercept:-50.01
```

The Bayesian method seems to find the best estimates of the parameters just below the ordinary least square method. The parameters are close enough for us to call it even, but consistently closer to zero—an interesting observation. We will get back to this same dataset when we look at machine learning algorithms in the next chapter. I also want to look at the confidence versus credible intervals. We do this for the OLS and Bayesian model fit with the following method:

```
ols_results.conf_int(alpha=0.05)
```

	0	1
Intercept	-66.531103	-37.092365
year	0.019425	0.034240

The `alpha=0.05` gives the confidence interval level, where it means the 95% confidence interval (that is, `1-0.05=0.95`):

```
MDL.stats(['intercept','slope'])
```

```
{'intercept': {'95% HPD interval': array([-50.64990877, -49.42168758]),
  'mc error': 0.011931753405578262,
  'mean': -50.008066085637815,
  'n': 4500,
  'quantiles': {2.5: -50.646760270081515,
   25: -50.228993605017173,
   50: -50.004119841092979,
   75: -49.789140434449351,
   97.5: -49.412790669964195},
  'standard deviation': 0.31970980437231761},
 'slope': {'95% HPD interval': array([ 0.02560229,  0.02622579]),
  'mc error': 6.0141748688389682e-06,
  'mean': 0.0259157602742307,
  'n': 4500,
  'quantiles': {2.5: 0.025609913276748567,
   25: 0.0258033738263553462,
   50: 0.02591258446734945,
   75: 0.026027359901668552,
   97.5: 0.026237852465415799},
  'standard deviation': 0.00016186303140381465}}
```

So the confidence level for the intercept is `[-66.5, -37.1]` for the OLS fit, and the credible interval from the Bayesian fit is `[-50.6,-49.4]`. This highlights the difference between the two methods. Let's now finally plot the results, and I want to draw both the fits in the same plot:

```
plt.figure(figsize=(10,6))
plt.title('Growth rate since 1960');
plt.errorbar(x,y,yerr=y_error,
        color='SteelBlue', ls='None',
        elinewidth=1.5, capthick=1.5,
        marker='.', ms=8,
        label='Observed')
plt.xlabel('Year')
plt.ylabel('CO$_2$ growth rate (ppm/yr)')
plt.plot(x, y_fit,
        'k', lw=2, label='pymc')
plt.fill_between(x, y_min, y_max,
        color='0.5', alpha=0.5,
        label='Uncertainty')
plt.plot([x.min(), x.max()],
        [ols_results.fittedvalues.min(), ols_results.fittedvalues.max()],
        'r', dashes=(13,2), lw=1.5, label='OLS', zorder=32)
plt.legend(loc=2, numpoints=1);
```

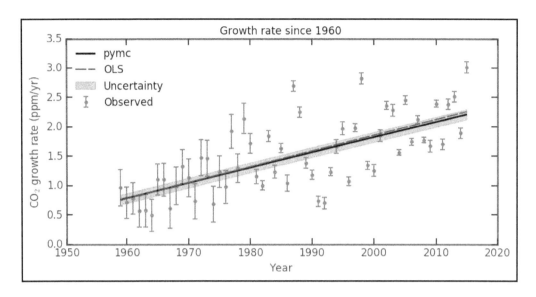

Here, I use the matplotlib function, `fill_between`, to show the credible interval of the function. The fit of the data looks good, and after looking at it a few times, you might realize that it looks as if it is divided into two—two linear segments with some offset divided around 1985. One exercise for you is to test this hypothesis: create a function with two linear segments with a break in a certain year, and then try to constrain the model and compare the results. Why could this be? Perhaps they changed the instrument; if you remember, the two parts of the data also have different uncertainties, so a difference in systematic error is not completely unlikely.

Summary

We have discussed how to test models and hypotheses with Bayesian analysis using the Python package, PyMC. It is a powerful package that gives out more intuitive results, where you see how the parameters are characterized. Not all posterior distributions are shaped like Gaussian, but the trace and autocorrelation should look similar for well-constrained parameters.

In the next chapter, we will dive into some of the machine learning algorithms available in Python and look at how they can identify clusters, classify data, and do linear regression. As in this chapter, we will compare the linear fit with that of Bayesian analysis and OLS. We will compare the cluster findings with the analysis that we did of galaxies in the universe in Chapter 5, *Clustering*.

7
Supervised and Unsupervised Learning

The amount of data collected for various purposes in society has increased enormously in the last few decades. Machine learning is a way of making sense of all this data by leveraging what we know about the data. In the generalized picture of machine learning, the computer first learns from a given dataset (training) and creates a generalized model to represent it. With this model, it is possible to predict various outcomes, results, and groupings (classes). In this chapter, we will cover the following topics:

- Linear regression with machine learning algorithms
- Clustering with machine learning algorithms
- Feature selection—a preprocessing method to select what is most important
- Classification with different machine learning algorithms and kernels

Before getting started, I will give you a brief introduction to machine learning and the package that we will use: Scikit-learn.

Introduction to machine learning

There are three main categories of machine learning: supervised, unsupervised, and reinforced. Given a simple dataset with input x and output y, supervised learning is when both x and y have known labels. The algorithm maps x to y and after training, it can predict y values with x as input. Contrary to this, unsupervised learning is when only x is labeled and the algorithm finds a label for y itself. Reinforced learning is when the computer learns without the need to map the input to an outcome and instead responds to the input. This is how algorithms that play chess or other games work.

They try to predict how to react to input without a clearly quantifiable outcome, instead seeking reinforcement; one example being to play the game continuously until it ends without making a mistake (that is, win). One feature-rich and popular package for machine learning in Python is Scikit-learn.

Scikit-learn

Scikit-learn is part of the SciPy Toolkits, which are packages that are affiliated with SciPy. More information on SciPy toolkits and a list of available ones can be found at `https://www.scipy.org/scikits.html`. The first release of Scikit-learn came in 2007, but the first publication presenting the package in 2011 was Machine Learning in Python, Pedregosa et al., JMLR 12, pp. 2825-2830, 2011. For a wealth of examples, documentation, and reading, see the Scikit-learn web page (`http://scikit-learn.org`). The package is well-maintained and the documentation is excellent and very extensive in coverage.

After this brief introduction, we do as we did in the previous chapters—we start a Jupyter Notebook and run the standard imports.

Now we also, of course, want to import Scikit-learn. The following code imports it and also prints out the version number of the installed Scikit-learn:

```
import sklearn
sklearn.__version__
```

Next, I have created a function that removes the right and top axis in a plot or a grid of plots. It comes in handy when producing figures; it is important to be able to present the data and results from the analysis in a clear and focused way. Removing unnecessary lines in a plot is part of this and also saves text space. The name of the `despine` function is inspired by the equivalent function in the excellent package, Seaborn, which can help you make nice figures as well (`https://stanford.edu/~mwaskom/software/seaborn/`):

```
def despine(axs):
    # to be able to handle subplot grids
    # it assumes the input is a list of
    # axes instances, if it is not a list,
    # it puts it in one
    if type(axs) != type([]):
        axs = [axs]
    for ax in axs:
        ax.yaxis.set_ticks_position('left')
        ax.xaxis.set_ticks_position('bottom')
        ax.spines['bottom'].set_position(('outward', 10))
        ax.spines['left'].set_position(('outward', 10))
```

Linear regression

There are many different linear regression models built-in in Scikit-learn, **Ordinary Least Squares (OLS)** and **Least Absolute Shrinkage and Selection Operator (LASSO)** to name two. The difference between these two can be approximated by different loss functions, which is the function that is worked on by the machine learning algorithm. In LASSO, there is an added penalty going away from the fitted function, whereas OLS is simply the least square equation. However, the routine is still different from the OLS that we covered earlier; the underlying algorithm to reach the answer is a machine learning algorithm. One such common algorithm is gradient decent. Here, we shall take the climate data from the previous chapter and fit a linear function to it with two methods, then we will compare the results from the OLS model with that of PyMC's Bayesian inference (Chapter 6, *Bayesian Methods*) and statsmodels' OLS (Chapter 4, *Regression*).

Climate data

We begin by reading in the data on the CO_2 growth rate for the past 60 years:

```
co2_gr = pd.read_csv('data/co2_gr_gl.txt',
                delim_whitespace=True,
                skiprows=62,
                names=['year', 'rate', 'err'])
```

To refresh your memory, we plot the data again. We now use our despine function to remove two of the axes:

```
fig, ax = plt.subplots(1,1)
ax.errorbar(co2_gr['year'], co2_gr['rate'],
            yerr=co2_gr['err'],
            ls='None',
            elinewidth=1.5,
            capthick=1.5,
            marker='.',
            ms=8)
despine(ax)
plt.minorticks_on()
labels = ax.get_xticklabels()
plt.setp(labels, rotation=33, ha='right')
ax.set_ylabel('CO$_2$ growth')
ax.set_xlabel('Year')
ax.set_xlim((1957,2016))
ax.set_title('CO$_2$ growth rate');
```

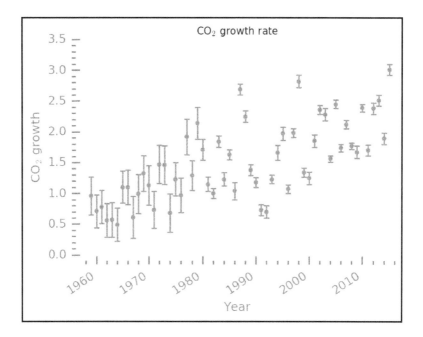

The data has a lot of spread in the middle of the range, roughly between 1980 and 2000. In one way, it looks like two lines with a jump at 1985 could be fitted. However, it is not clear why this would be the case; perhaps the two distributions of uncertainties have something to do with it?

In Scikit-learn, the learning is done by first initiating the estimator, an object where we call the fit method to train the dataset. This means that we first have to import the estimator. In this example, I will show you two different estimators and the resulting fits that they produce. The first is the simple linear model and the second is the LASSO estimator. There are many different linear models in Scikit-learn: RANSAC, Theil-Sen, and linear models based on **stochastic gradient descent** (**SGD**) learning, to name a few. After going through this example, you should look at another estimator and try it out. We first import the ones that we will work with, and also the `cross_validation` function, which we will use to separate the dataset into two parts—training and testing:

```
from sklearn.linear_model import LinearRegression, Lasso
from sklearn import cross_validation
```

As we want to be able to validate our fit and see how good it is, we do not use all of the data. We use the `train_test_split` function in `cross_validation` to put 25% of the data in a testing set and 75% in the training set. Play around with different values and see how the fit results change in the end. Then, we store the x and y values in appropriate structures. The x values have to have one extra axis. This could also be done with the `x_train.reshape(-1,1)` code; the way we do it here gives the same effect. We also create an array to later plot the fit with x values that we know span the whole range and a bit more:

```
x_test, x_train, y_test, y_train = cross_validation.train_test_split(
    co2_gr['year'], co2_gr['rate'],
    test_size=0.75,
    random_state=0)
X train = x_train[:, np.newaxis]
X_test = x_test[:, np.newaxis]
line_x = np.array([1955, 2025])
```

In the training and test data split, we also make use of the `random_state` parameter so that the random seed is the same and we get the same division of the training and testing set by running it multiple times (for exact reproducibility). We are now ready to train the data, the first is the simple linear regression model. To run the machine learning algorithms on the training set, we first create an estimator object/class and then we simply train the model by calling the `fit` method with the training x and y values as input:

```
est_lin = LinearRegression()
est_lin.fit(X_train, y_train)
lin_pred = est_lin.predict(line_x.reshape(-1, 1))
```

Here, I also added a calculation of the predicted y values from the array that we created earlier, and to show an alternative way of restructuring the input array, I used the reshape method. Next is the LASSO model, and we do exactly the same, except that in creating the model object we now have the option of giving it extra parameters. The `alpha` parameter is basically what separates this model from the preceding simple linear regression model. If it is set to zero, the model becomes the same as the linear model. The LASSO model alpha input modifies the loss function and the default value is 1. Try different values, although 0 is not good to choose as the model is not made to operate without the added penalty to the loss function:

```
est_lasso = Lasso(alpha=0.7)
est_lasso.fit(X_train, y_train)
lasso_pred = est_lasso.predict(line_x.reshape(2, 1))
```

To see the results, we first print out the estimates of the coefficients, mean square discrepancy or error (mean squared residuals), and variance score. The variance score is a method in the Scikit-learn model (estimator) that we create. While a variance score of 1 means that it is able to predict the values perfectly, a score of 0 means that no values were predicted and there is no (linear) relationship between the variables. The coefficients are accessed with `estimator.coeff_` and `estimator.intercept_`. To get the mean square error, we simply take the difference between the predicted and observed values, which are calculated with `estimator.predict(x)`, where x is x values where you want to predict y values. This should be calculated on the test data and not the training set. We first create a function to calculate this and print the relevant diagnostics:

```
def printstuff(estimator, A, b):
    name = estimator.__str__().split('(')[0]
    print('+'*6, name, '+'*6)
    print('Slope: {0:.3f} Intercept:{1:.2f} '.format(
            estimator.coef_[0], estimator.intercept_))
    print("Mean squared residuals: {0:.2f}".format(
            np.mean((estimator.predict(A) - b)**2)) )
    print('Variance score: {0:.2f}'.format(
            estimator.score(A, b)) )
```

With this function, we can now print the results of the fitting in a way that gives us the estimated slope and intercept, mean squared residuals, and variance score:

```
printstuff(est_lin, X_test, y_test)
printstuff(est_lasso, X_test, y_test)
```

```
++++++ LinearRegression ++++++
Slope: 0.027 Intercept:-51.60
Mean squared residuals: 0.17
Variance score: 0.56
++++++ Lasso ++++++
Slope: 0.024 Intercept:-46.16
Mean squared residuals: 0.17
Variance score: 0.56
```

The LASSO model estimates lower values to the slope and intercept, but gives a similar mean squared residuals and variance score to the linear regression model. The spread in the data is too much to conclude whether any of them produce more reliable estimates. We can, of course, plot all of these results in a figure together with the data:

```
fig = plt.figure()
ax = fig.add_subplot(111)
ax.scatter(X_train, y_train, marker='s',
        label='Train', color='IndianRed')
```

```
ax.scatter(X_test, y_test, label='Test',
        color='SteelBlue')
ax.plot(line_x, lin_pred, color='Green',
        label='Linreg', lw=2)
ax.plot(line_x, lasso_pred, color='Coral',
        dashes=(5,4), label='LASSO', lw=2)
ax.set_xlabel('Year')
ax.set_ylabel('CO$_2$ growth rate')
ax.legend(loc=2, fontsize=10, numpoints=1)
despine(ax)
plt.minorticks_on()
ax.locator_params(axis='x', nbins=5)
ax.locator_params(axis='y', nbins=7)
ax.set_xlim(1950,2030)
ax.set_title('CO$_2$ growth rate');
```

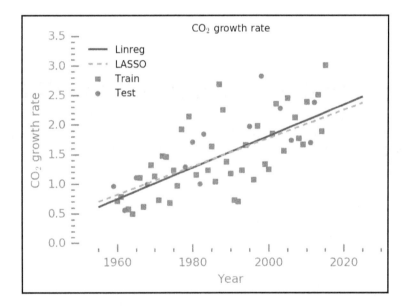

The fits differ slightly, but are definitely within each other's uncertainty. The spread in the data points is relatively large. The squares show the training set and the circles show the testing (validation) set. Extrapolating outside this range would, however, predict significantly different values.

We can calculate the R^2 score, just as before with classical OLS regression:

```
from sklearn.metrics import r2_score
r2_lin = r2_score(co2_gr['rate'],
                  est_lin.predict(
                    co2_gr['year'].reshape(-1,1)))
r2_lasso = r2_score(co2_gr['rate'],
                    est_lasso.predict(
                      co2_gr['year'].reshape(-1,1)))
print('LinearSVC: {0:.2f}\nLASSO:\
\t   {1:.2f}'.format(r2_lin, r2_lasso))
```

```
LinearSVC: 0.49
LASSO:     0.48
```

The R^2 values are relatively high, despite the significant spread in the data points and limited size of the data.

Checking with Bayesian analysis and OLS

We will quickly make a comparison with both the statsmodels' OLS regression and Bayesian inference with a linear model. The Bayesian inference and OLS fits are the same as in Chapter 6, *Bayesian Methods*, and a small version is repeated here:

```
import pymc
x = co2_gr['year'].as_matrix()
y = co2_gr['rate'].as_matrix()
y_error = co2_gr['err'].as_matrix()
def model(x, y):
    slope = pymc.Normal('slope', 0.1, 1.)
    intercept = pymc.Normal('intercept', -50., 10.)
    @pymc.deterministic(plot=False)
    def linear(x=x, slope=slope, intercept=intercept):
        return x * slope + intercept
    f = pymc.Normal('f', mu=linear, tau=1.0/y_error,
value=y, observed=True)
    return locals()
MDL = pymc.MCMC(model(x,y))
MDL.sample(5e5, 5e4, 100)
y_fit = MDL.stats()['linear']['mean']
slope = MDL.stats()['slope']['mean']
intercept = MDL.stats()['intercept']['mean']
```

For the OLS model, we again use the formula framework to express the relationship between our variables:

```
import statsmodels.formula.api as smf
from statsmodels.sandbox.regression.predstd import wls_prediction_std
ols_results = smf.ols("rate ~ year", co2_gr).fit()
ols_params = np.flipud(ols_results.params)
```

Now that we have the results from all three methods, let's print out the slope and intercept for them:

```
print('    Slope  Intercept \nML : \
{0:.3f} {1:.3f} \nOLS: {2:.3f} \
{3:.3f} \nBay: {4:.3f} \
{5:.3f}'.format(est_lin.coef_[0], est_lin.intercept_,
            ols_params[0],ols_params[1],
            slope, intercept) )
```

```
        Slope  Intercept
ML : 0.027 -51.597
OLS: 0.027 -51.812
Bay: 0.026 -49.998
```

While the overall results are similar, Bayesian inference seems to estimate absolute values that are lower than the other methods. We can now visualize these different estimates together with the data:

```
fig = plt.figure()
ax = fig.add_subplot(111)
ax.errorbar(x, y, yerr=y_error, ls='None',
        elinewidth=1.5, capthick=1.5,
        marker='.', ms=8, label='Observed')
ax.set_xlabel('Year')
ax.set_ylabel('CO$_2$ growth rate')
ax.plot([x.min(), x.max()],
        [ols_results.fittedvalues.min(),
         ols_results.fittedvalues.max()],
        lw=1.5, label='OLS',
        dashes=(13,5))
ax.plot(x, y_fit, lw=1.5,
        label='pymc')
ax.plot([x.min(), x.max()],
        est_lin.predict([[x.min(), ], [x.max(), ]]),
        label='Scikit-learn', lw=1.5)
despine(ax)
ax.locator_params(axis='x', nbins=7)
```

```
ax.locator_params(axis='y', nbins=4)
ax.set_xlim((1955,2018))
ax.legend(loc=2, numpoints=1)
ax.set_title('CO$_2$ growth rate');
```

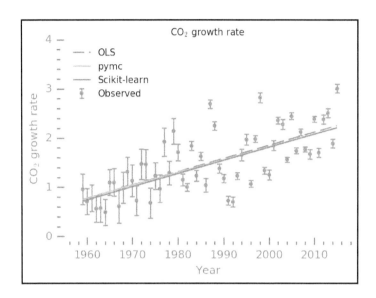

This might look like a very small difference; however, if we use these different results to extrapolate 30, 50, or even 100 years into the future, these will yield significantly different results. This example shows you how simple it is to try out different methods and models in Scikit-learn. It is also possible to create your own. Next up, we will look at one cluster identification model in Scikit-learn, DBSCAN.

Clustering

In this example, we will look at a cluster finding algorithm in Scikit-learn called **DBSCAN**. DBSCAN stands for Density-Based Spatial Clustering of Applications with Noise, and is a clustering algorithm that favors groups of points and can identify points outside any of these groups (clusters) as noise (outliers). As with the linear machine learning methods, Scikit-learn makes it very easy to work with it. We first read in the data from Chapter 5, *Clustering*, with Pandas' read_pickle function:

```
TABLE_FILE = 'data/test.pick'
mycat = pd.read_pickle(TABLE_FILE)
```

As with the previous dataset, to refresh your memory, we plot the data. It contains a slice of the mapped nearby Universe, that is, galaxies with determined positions (direction and distance from us). As before, we scale the color with the Z-magnitude, as found in the data table:

```
fig,ax = plt.subplots(1,2, figsize=(10,2.5))
plt.subplot(121)
plt.scatter(mycat['Y'], -1*mycat['X'],
            s=8,
            color=plt.cm.viridis_r(
                    10**(mycat.Zmag-mycat.Zmag.max()) ),
            edgecolor='None')
plt.xlabel('Y (Mpc)'); plt.ylabel('X (Mpc)')
ax = plt.gca()
despine(ax)
ax.locator_params(axis='x', nbins=5)
ax.locator_params(axis='y', nbins=5)
plt.axis('equal')
plt.subplot(122)
c_arr = 10**(mycat.Zmag-mycat.Zmag.max())
plt.scatter(-1*mycat['X'],mycat['Z'],
            s=8,
            color=plt.cm.viridis_r(c_arr),
            edgecolor='None')
lstyle = dict(lw=1.5, color='k', dashes=(6,4))
ax = plt.gca()
despine(ax)
ax.locator_params(axis='x', nbins=5)
ax.locator_params(axis='y', nbins=5)
plt.plot([0,150], [0,80], **lstyle)
plt.plot([0,150], [0,45], **lstyle)
plt.plot([0,-25], [0,80], **lstyle)
plt.plot([0,-25], [0,45], **lstyle)
plt.xlabel('X (Mpc)'); plt.ylabel('Z (Mpc)')
plt.subplots_adjust(wspace=0.3)
plt.axis('equal');
plt.ylim((-10,110));
```

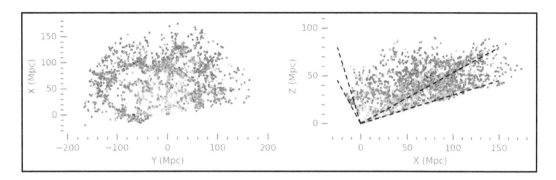

The data spans extremely large scales and many galaxies in the given directions. To start using machine learning for cluster finding, we import the relevant objects from Scikit-learn:

```
from sklearn.cluster import DBSCAN
from sklearn import metrics
from sklearn.preprocessing import StandardScaler
```

The first import is simply the DBSCAN method, and the second import is the metrics module with which we can calculate various statistics on the clustering algorithm. The StandardScaler class is simply to scale the data, as in Chapter 5, *Clustering*. Next, we set up the input data; every row should contain the coordinates of a feature/point scaled. This scaled coordinate list is then input into the DBSCAN method:

```
A = np.array([mycat['Y'], -1*mycat['X'], mycat['Z']]).T
A_scaled = StandardScaler().fit_transform(A)
dbout = DBSCAN(eps=0.15, min_samples=5).fit(A_scaled)
```

The DBSCAN object is instantiated with several parameters. The eps parameter limits the size of the cluster in terms of the distance within which at least min_samples have to lie for it to be a cluster (remember, in scaled units). The dbout object now stores all the results of the fit. The dbout.labels_ array contains all the labels for each point; points not in any cluster are given a -1 label. Let's check whether we have any:

```
(dbout.labels_==-1).any()
```

It prints out True, so we have noise. Another important method that the output object has is core_sample_indices_. It contains the core samples from which each cluster is expanded and formed. It is almost like the centroid positions in k-means clustering. We now create a Boolean array for the core sample indices and also a list of the unique labels in the results. This is the recommended way according to the Scikit-learn documentation.

```
csmask = np.zeros_like(dbout.labels_, dtype=bool)
csmask[dbout.core_sample_indices_] = True
unique_labels = set(dbout.labels_)
```

Without the true labels of the clusters, it is tricky to measure the success of the cluster finding. Normally, you would calculate the silhouette score, which is a score that scales with the distance between the centroid and samples in the same cluster and nearby clusters. The higher the silhouette score, the better the cluster finding was at defining the cluster. However, this assumes clusters that are centered around one point, not a filamentary structure. To show you how to calculate and interpret the silhouette score, we go through it for this example, but keep in mind that it might not be a representative method in this case. We will calculate the silhouette score and also print out the number of clusters found. Remember that the labels array also contains the noise labels (that is, −1):

```
n_clusters = len(set(labels)) - [0,1][-1 in labels]
print('Estimated number of clusters: %d' % n_clusters)
print("Silhouette Coefficient: %0.3f"
        % metrics.silhouette_score(A_scaled, dbout.labels_))
```

```
Estimated number of clusters: 8
Silhouette Coefficient: -0.143
```

Silhouette score values close to zero indicate that the clusters overlap. Now we will plot all the results and check what it looks like. I have tried to plot the core samples differently by increasing their marker size and decreasing the size of non-core samples. I also shuffled the colors in an attempt at making different clusters stand out against their neighbors:

```
colors = plt.cm.viridis(np.linspace(0.3, 1, len(unique_labels)))
np.random.seed(0)
np.random.shuffle(colors)
for lbl, col in zip(unique_labels, colors):
    if lbl == -1:
        # Black used for noise.
        col = 'DarkRed'; m1=m2= '+'; s = 10; a = 0.5
    else:
        m1='.';m2='.'; s=5; a=1
    cmmask = (dbout.labels_ == lbl)
    xy = A[cmmask & csmask]
    plt.scatter(xy[:, 0], xy[:, 1], color=col,
                marker=m1,
                s=s+1,
                alpha=a)
    xy = A[cmmask & ~csmask]
    plt.scatter(xy[:, 0], xy[:, 1], color=col,
```

```
            marker=m2,
            s=s-2,
            alpha=a)
despine(plt.gca())
noiseArtist = plt.Line2D((0,1),(0,0),
                    color='DarkRed',
                    marker='+',
                    linestyle='',
                    ms=4, mew=1,
                    alpha=0.7)
clusterArtist = plt.Line2D((0,1),(0,0),
                    color='k',
                    marker='.',
                    linestyle='',
                    ms=4, mew=1)
plt.legend([noiseArtist, clusterArtist],
            ['Outliers','Clusters'],
            numpoints=1)
plt.title('A slice of the Universe')
plt.xlabel('X [Mpc]')
plt.ylabel('Y [Mpc]');
```

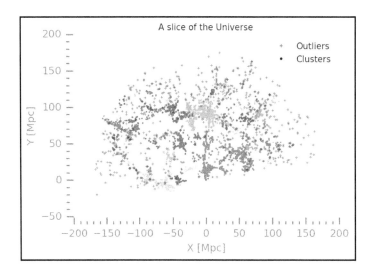

The algorithm also finds noise (outliers), which are plotted in red crosses here. Try to tweak the displaying of the core and non-core samples so that they stand out more. Furthermore, you should try different parameters for the DBSCAN method and see how the outcome is affected. Another thing would be to go back to Chapter 5, *Clustering*, and put 66 clusters in the hierarchical cluster algorithm that we tried there with the same dataset and compare.

Seeds classification

We will now look at three main groups of classification (learning) models: **Support Vector Machine** (**SVM**), Nearest Neighbor, and Random Forest. SVM simply divides the space in *N* regions, separated by a boundary. The boundary can be allowed to have different shapes, for example, there is a linear boundary or quadratic boundary. The Nearest Neighbor classification identifies the k-nearest neighbors and classifies the current data point depending on what class the k-nearest neighbors belong to. The Random Forest classifier is a decision tree learning method, which, in simple terms, creates rules from the given training data to be able to classify new data. A set of if-statements in a row is what gives it the name decision tree.

The data that we are going to use comes from the the UCI Machine Learning repository (Lichman, M. (2013)-http://archive.ics.uci.edu/ml. (Irvine, CA: University of California, School of Information and Computer Science). The dataset contains several measured attributes of three different types of wheat grains (M. Charytanowicz, J. Niewczas, P. Kulczycki, P.A. Kowalski, S. Lukasik, S. Zak,*A Complete Gradient Clustering Algorithm for Features Analysis of X-ray Images*, in: Information Technologies in Biomedicine, Ewa Pietka, Jacek Kawa (eds.), Springer-Verlag, Berlin-Heidelberg, 2010, pp. 15-24.).

We want to create a classifier, something that, if we measure specific parameters of a seed, can tell what type of seed it is. With the dataset, a description of the columns are supplied, which can also be found on the UCI web page for the dataset. There are eight columns, seven for the parameters and one for the known type of the seed (that is, the label). I have created a text file for this; in case you are running a Linux-based system, you can list the contents with Jupyter magic:

```
%%bash
less data/seeds.desc
```

```
1. area A,
2. perimeter P,
3. compactness C = 4*pi*A/P^2,
4. length of kernel,
5. width of kernel,
6. asymmetry coefficient
7. length of kernel groove.
8. group
```

If you are running Microsoft Windows, you can use the `more` command, that is, `more data/seeds.desc`, which gives you the same output but in a pop-up window, not as convenient but still useful.

Now that we know what columns are there, we can read it into a Pandas DataFrame:

```
seeds = pd.read_csv('data/seeds_dataset.txt',
    delim_whitespace=True,
    names=['A', 'P', 'C', 'lkern', 'wkern',
    'asym', 'lgro', 'gr'])
```

As always, list the contents of what was read:

```
seeds.head()
```

	A	P	C	lkern	wkern	asym	lgro	gr
0	15.26	14.84	0.8710	5.763	3.312	2.221	5.220	1
1	14.88	14.57	0.8811	5.554	3.333	1.018	4.956	1
2	14.29	14.09	0.9050	5.291	3.337	2.699	4.825	1
3	13.84	13.94	0.8955	5.324	3.379	2.259	4.805	1
4	16.14	14.99	0.9034	5.658	3.562	1.355	5.175	1

Visualizing the data

We could just run the whole classification process on all seven parameters in the dataset. This is computationally expensive, and the costs increase very quickly when increasing the amount of data. To make a first attempt at selecting only the attributes that matter for classification, I want to visually inspect the distribution of the values for the attributes for the different types of grains. To do this, we first create a selection filter for the different groups:

```
gr1 = seeds.gr == 1
gr2 = seeds.gr == 2
gr3 = seeds.gr == 3
```

To only plot the relevant parameters, we also create a list of the ones that we want to see (that is, not the type of grain):

```
pars = ['A','C','P','asym','lgro','lkern','wkern']
```

With Pandas' built-in `histogram` function, we can plot the attributes for each group. I have added some extra commands to make the figures look a bit better and more clutter-free:

```
axes = seeds[pars][gr1].hist(figsize=(8,6))
despine(list(axes.flatten()))
_ = [ax.grid() for ax in list(axes.flatten())]
_ = [ax.locator_params(axis='x', nbins=4) for ax in
    list(axes.flatten())]
_ = [ax.locator_params(axis='y', nbins=2) for ax in
    list(axes.flatten())]
plt.subplots_adjust(wspace=0.5, hspace=0.7)
```

Once again, we use the `despine` function to make the plots clearer. The preceding code will plot all of the attributes for the first group, `gr1`. The histogram will show you how the values are distributed:

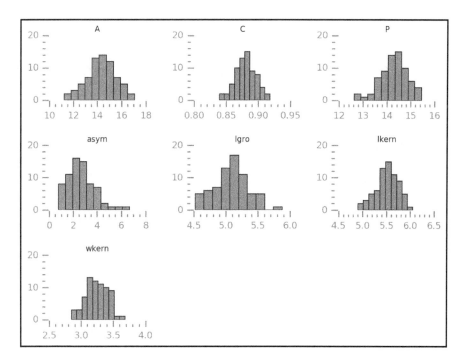

With the selection filters, it is easy to plot the other groups:

```
axes = seeds[pars][gr2].hist(figsize=(8,6))
despine(list(axes.flatten()))
_ = [ax.grid() for ax in list(axes.flatten())]
_ = [ax.locator_params(axis='x', nbins=4) for ax in
```

```
        list(axes.flatten())]
_ = [ax.locator_params(axis='y', nbins=2) for ax in
        list(axes.flatten())]
plt.subplots_adjust(wspace=0.5, hspace=0.7)
```

By plotting all the groups, we can look at how the distribution of values for the attributes differ. We are trying to identify the ones that differ the most between groups:

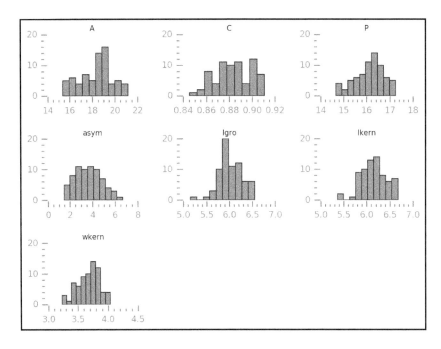

```
axes = seeds[pars][gr3].hist(figsize=(8,6))
despine(list(axes.flatten()))
_ = [ax.grid() for ax in list(axes.flatten())]
_ = [ax.locator_params(axis='x', nbins=5) for ax in
        list(axes.flatten())]
_ = [ax.locator_params(axis='y', nbins=2) for ax in
        list(axes.flatten())]
plt.subplots_adjust(wspace=0.5, hspace=0.7)
```

After plotting this last group, we can look at each attribute and find the attribute where the distribution is separate for each group. This way, we can use it to distinguish the various groups (types of seeds), that is, classify them:

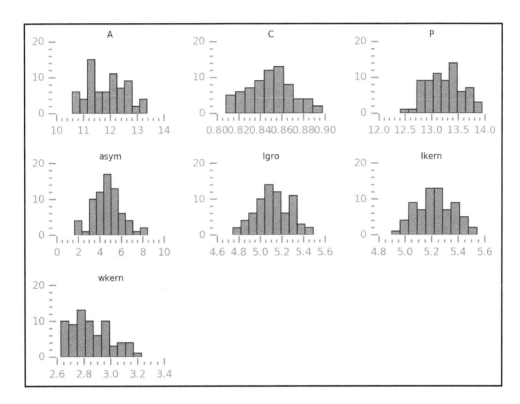

From this, I would argue that porosity and groove length are good parameters due to their fairly well-defined and, for the three groups, separated peaks. To check this, we plot them against each other. We also want to mark the various groups of grains:

```
fig = plt.figure()
ax = fig.add_subplot(111)
ax.scatter(seeds.P[gr1], seeds.lgro[gr1],
        color='LightCoral')
ax.scatter(seeds.P[gr2], seeds.lgro[gr2],
        color='SteelBlue', marker='s')
ax.scatter(seeds.P[gr3], seeds.lgro[gr3],
        color='Green', marker='<');
ax.text(seeds.P[gr1].mean(), seeds.lgro[gr1].mean(),
        '1', bbox=dict(color='w', alpha=0.7,
                boxstyle="Round"))
ax.text(seeds.P[gr2].mean(), seeds.lgro[gr2].mean(),
```

```
            '2', bbox=dict(color='w', alpha=0.7,
                   boxstyle="Round"))
ax.text(seeds.P[gr3].mean(), seeds.lgro[gr3].mean(),
            '3', bbox=dict(color='w', alpha=0.7,
                   boxstyle="Round"))
ax.set_xlabel('Porosity')
ax.set_ylabel('Groove length')
ax.set_title('Seed parameters')
despine(ax)
plt.minorticks_on()
ax.locator_params(axis='x', nbins=5)
ax.locator_params(axis='y', nbins=4)
ax.set_xlim(11.8,18)
ax.set_ylim(3.8,7.1);
```

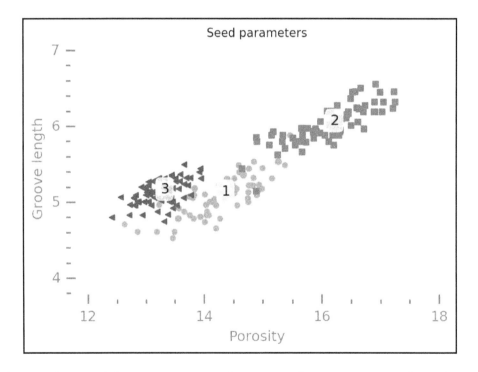

Now, this is only two of the parameters; we have several more. However, from this, it seems that it is the hardest to separate groups 1 and 3, that is, the circles and triangles.

Feature selection

Built-in into Scikit-learn are several ways of determining the best parameters to look at. This is sometimes called feature selection, which is trying to determine which parameters have the biggest differences between each other and are best suited to describe the various groups as exactly that-distinct groups. Here, we use one where we can give a number, K (not to be confused with K in K-means), which determines up to what number of features it should select the best ones.

First, we store the seeds table as a matrix, a NumPy array, and then we separate the data and labels:

```
X_raw = seeds.as_matrix()
X_pre, labels = X_raw[:,:-1], X_raw[:,-1]
```

Now we can import the selection algorithm and run it on the data. Note that we also import the chi2 estimator and supply it to the selection object. This means that chi-squared minimization will be used to determine the best parameters:

```
from sklearn.feature_selection import SelectKBest
from sklearn.feature_selection import chi2
X_best = SelectKBest(chi2, k=2).fit_transform(X_pre, labels)
```

It has now selected two columns; to check which columns, we print out the first few rows of the selection and the raw data:

```
X_best[:5]
```

```
array([[ 15.26 ,    2.221],
       [ 14.88 ,    1.018],
       [ 14.29 ,    2.699],
       [ 13.84 ,    2.259],
       [ 16.14 ,    1.355]])
```

```
seeds.head()
```

	A	P	C	lkern	wkern	asym	lgro	gr
0	15.26	14.84	0.8710	5.763	3.312	2.221	5.220	1
1	14.88	14.57	0.8811	5.554	3.333	1.018	4.956	1
2	14.29	14.09	0.9050	5.291	3.337	2.699	4.825	1
3	13.84	13.94	0.8955	5.324	3.379	2.259	4.805	1
4	16.14	14.99	0.9034	5.658	3.562	1.355	5.175	1

The area (A) and asymmetry (asym) coefficients are the two best parameters to work with according to this selection algorithm. Before we run it through one of the machine learning algorithms for classification, we plot all of the data again, but this time the features are selected by the algorithm:

```
fig = plt.figure()
ax = fig.add_subplot(111)
ax.scatter(seeds.A[gr1], seeds.asym[gr1],
        color='LightCoral')
ax.text(seeds.A[gr1].mean(), seeds.asym[gr1].mean(),
        '1', bbox=dict(color='w', alpha=0.7,
        boxstyle="Round"))
ax.scatter(seeds.A[gr2], seeds.asym[gr2],
        color='SteelBlue',
        marker='s')
ax.text(seeds.A[gr2].mean(), seeds.asym[gr2].mean(),
        '2', bbox=dict(color='w', alpha=0.7,
        boxstyle="Round"))
ax.scatter(seeds.A[gr3], seeds.asym[gr3],
        color='Green',
        marker='<')
ax.text(seeds.A[gr3].mean(), seeds.asym[gr3].mean(),
        '3', bbox=dict(color='w', alpha=0.7,
        boxstyle="Round"))
ax.set_xlabel('Area')
ax.set_ylabel('Asymmetry')
ax.set_title('Seed parameters')
despine(ax)
plt.minorticks_on()
ax.locator_params(axis='x', nbins=5)
ax.locator_params(axis='y', nbins=3)
ax.set_xlim(9.6,22)
ax.set_ylim(-0.6,10);
```

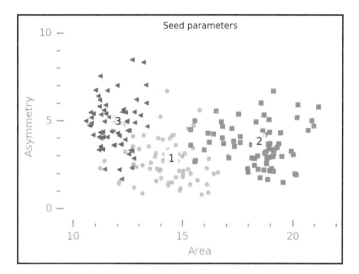

Compared with the previous similar plot, the points are more spread out, and perhaps the circles and triangles are more separated with less overlap—it is hard to assess.

Classifying the data

To start classifying the data, we prepare a few things first. We import the SVM module and K-nearest neighbor along with the random forest estimators. Within the SVM module is the **Support Vector Classification** (**SVC**) estimator, the main estimator for SVM. SVC can be run with different kernels; we will cover the linear, radial basis function, and polynomial kernels. I will give a short explanation of them before we run them.

To visualize the classification, I want to plot the boundaries, and we will use contour lines to do this. For this, we need to create a grid of points and evaluate them with our trained classifier:

```
from sklearn import svm
from sklearn.neighbors import KNeighborsClassifier

res = 0.01
#X, y  = X_best[::2], labels[::2]
X, y  = X_best, labels
x_min, x_max = X[:, 0].min() - 1, X[:, 0].max() + 1
y_min, y_max = X[:, 1].min() - 1, X[:, 1].max() + 1
xx, yy = np.meshgrid(np.arange(x_min, x_max, res),
                     np.arange(y_min, y_max, res))
```

Here, we write a function to draw the results. To draw the boundaries, the x and y grid that we created previously is used. It is passed to the estimator's predict(xxyy) method. Here, input is the estimator, output from the machine learning classification model (that is, different SVMs, K-Nearest Neighbor, and Random Forest), and title of the plot. The contour plot draws the boundaries, and you can change ax.contour to ax.contourf to get filled contours. Now that we have a function to take care of the visualization, we can focus on testing the different models (called kernels):

```
def plot_results(clf, title):
    fig = plt.figure()
    ax = fig.add_subplot(111)
    plt.subplots_adjust(wspace=0.2, hspace=0.4)
    xxyy = np.vstack((xx.flatten(), yy.flatten())).T
    Z = clf.predict(xxyy)
    Z = Z.reshape(xx.shape)
    ax.contour(xx, yy, Z,
               colors=['Green','LightCoral', 'SteelBlue'],
               alpha=0.7, zorder=-1)
    ax.scatter(seeds.A[gr1], seeds.asym[gr1],
               color='LightCoral')
    ax.scatter(seeds.A[gr2], seeds.asym[gr2],
               color='SteelBlue', marker='s')
    ax.scatter(seeds.A[gr3], seeds.asym[gr3],
               color='Green', marker='<')
    ax.text(seeds.A[gr1].mean(), seeds.asym[gr1].mean(),
            '1', bbox=dict(color='w', alpha=0.7,
            boxstyle="Round"))
    ax.text(seeds.A[gr2].mean(), seeds.asym[gr2].mean(),
            '2', bbox=dict(color='w', alpha=0.7,
            boxstyle="Round"))
    ax.text(seeds.A[gr3].mean(), seeds.asym[gr3].mean(),
            '3', bbox=dict(color='w', alpha=0.7,
            boxstyle="Round"))
    despine(ax)
    plt.minorticks_on()
    ax.locator_params(axis='x', nbins=5)
    ax.locator_params(axis='y', nbins=3)
    ax.set_xlabel('Area')
    ax.set_ylabel('Asymmetry')
    ax.set_title(title, size=10)
    ax.set_xlim(9.6,22)
    ax.set_ylim(-0.6,10);
```

The SVC linear kernel

One simple kernel in SVC is the linear kernel, which assumes linear boundaries. As input, it takes C, the parameter determining the sensitivity to noisy data; with very noisy data, you can decrease this parameter. To get the linear kernel, run the classification on our data, and plot the results with our function, we run the following:

```
svc = svm.SVC(kernel='linear', C=1.).fit(X, y)
plot_results(svc, 'SVC-Linear')
```

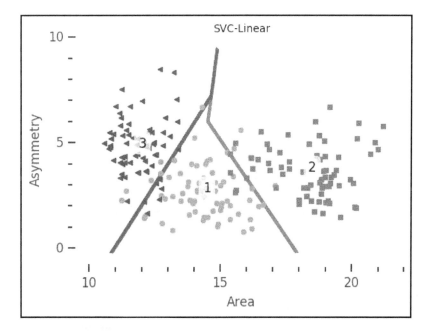

As you can see, the boundaries are linear, and it does a reasonable job in dividing the various points into groups that correspond to the ones created by the researchers.

The SVC Radial Basis Function

The next kernel, the **Radial Basis Function** (RBF), is the kernel used if no input kernel is given to the SVC call; it is basically a Gaussian kernel. The result is a kernel (region) that is built up by a linear combination of Gaussians. In addition to the C parameter, the gamma parameter can be given here; it is the inverse width of the Gaussian(s), so it gives the steepness of the boundary:

```
rbf_svc = svm.SVC(kernel='rbf', gamma=0.4, C=1.).fit(X, y)
plot_results(rbf_svc, 'SVC-Radial Basis Function')
```

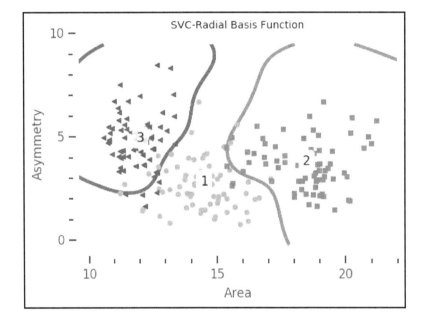

Here, the boundaries are smoother. The borders in the center are roughly the same as with the linear kernel, but they differ going away from the dense regions.

The SVC polynomial

The last SVC kernel that we will cover is the polynomial, and it is exactly what it sounds like, a polynomial. As input, it takes the degree:

```
poly_svc = svm.SVC(kernel='poly', degree=3, C=1.).fit(X, y)
plot_results(poly_svc, 'SVC-Polynomial')
```

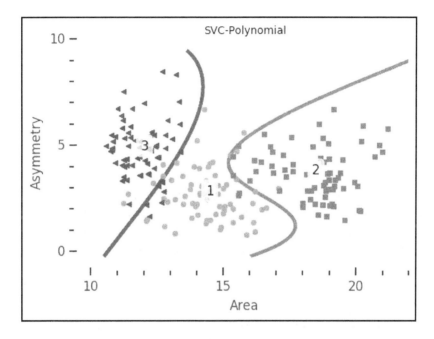

The borders are thus represented by polynomials. I suggest that you try to change the degree to something else and see what happens with the borders.

K-Nearest Neighbour

Now we use the K-Nearest Neighbor. As input, this takes the weight and number of neighbors to compare with. The default weight is one that assumes uniform weights of all n_neighbors nearby points; changing the weights keyword to distance assumes that weights decrease with distance:

```
knn = KNeighborsClassifier(weights = 'uniform', n_neighbors=5).fit(X, y)
plot_results(knn, 'k-Nearest Neighbours')
```

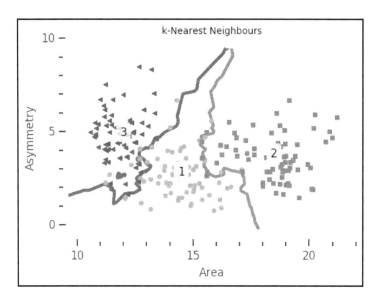

This resembles some of the SVC kernels, but adapted to even smaller changes. Try changing weights to 'distance' and also changing the `n_neighbors` parameter and see how the results change. What happens when you change `n_neighbors` to something larger than 30; which of the other classifiers does it almost exactly replicate?

Random Forest

As a last example classifier, we use the Random Forest method. You can think of it as the dendrogram for hierarchical clustering in `Chapter 5`, *Clustering*; however, each branch is a rule to classify the data here. We give the object three inputs: `max_depth`, `n_estimators`, and `max_features`. The first, `max_depth`, determines how far each decision tree should go, and `n_estimators` gives *how many decision trees there are in the forest*. This is not really intuitive, so to show you what it is, first put `n_estimators=1`, run the code, and look at the output. Then, change to another, higher number and look at the new output:

```
rfc = RandomForestClassifier(
                            max_depth=3,
                            n_estimators=10,
                            max_features='auto').fit(X, y)
plot_results(rfc, 'Random Forest Classifier')
```

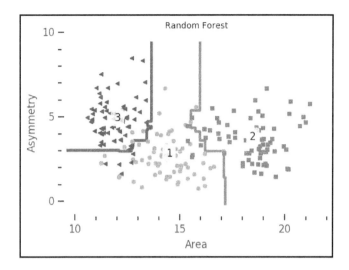

The number of trees in the forest is how many decision trees to build up the classifier with. The resulting plot shows that the random forest classifier is simple yet able to classify fairly complex problems. SVC together with the linear kernel is also simple, but you could imagine how the random forest classifier would be able to classify a more complex problem with fairly low depth and few estimators. I suggest that you take some time and play around with the input parameters for all the classifiers and see how the results change.

Choosing your classifier

The preceding examples show you different results for the SVC (with various kernels), kNN, and Random Forest classifiers. However, when should you use one over the other? In general, try all of the methods on the given problem. The main advantages of SVC are highlighted in these examples—it is very versatile with many different kernels. Decision trees, like the random forest, run the risk of becoming too complex and thus overfitting the data. Also highlighted in the preceding examples, kNN is very good for classifications where the boundary is clearly not linear, as you can see in the results of the preceding image for kNN. There are also other kernels and classifiers. For example, a comparison of 179 classifiers was done for the article, *Do we Need Hundreds of Classifiers to Solve Real World Classification Problems?* (M. Fernandez-Delgado, 2014, JMLR, 15, 3133-3181). All of the common classifiers are covered in the study. However, as stated before, the important thing is to try various classifiers on your data to see what works.

Summary

In this chapter, we looked at various machine learning methods to do regression, clustering, and classification. We compared linear regression using machine learning tools with the same problem in Bayesian inference and standard OLS. Furthermore, we compared the results from the clustering machine learning algorithm, DBSCAN, with what we obtained for hierarchical clustering in Chapter 5, *Clustering*. We concluded by looking at several classification algorithms available in Scikit-learn and how they performed on the same dataset.

With the UCI machine learning repository, finding practice data is not hard. I suggest you visit http://archive.ics.uci.edu/ml and look for a dataset to try any of the new things that we have gone through here.

8
Time Series Analysis

Sometimes the data that we will analyze is a variable measured at fixed time intervals; when we have such data, we are talking about a time series. More specifically, at each step of the time series, there is more than one possible outcome and part of the outcome for each step is randomized and might only depend on a few steps back in time. For these reasons, simple linear regression does not work. In time series analysis, we build models to explain the variations in time, which is sometimes referred to as *longitudinal analysis*.

This chapter covers the following topics in time series analysis:

- Time series modeling, its usefulness, and how Pandas handles data
- Various common patterns in time series
- The concept of stationarity and how to test and make your data stationary
- Resampling, smoothing, and calculating rolling statistics
- How to model the known variations and make short forecasts

We start off with some more information about time series and what insights analyzing it can give.

Introduction

Time series analysis is important in several types of situations; it can be used, for example, to describe changes of a variable in time, predict or forecast through modeling the known variations, and then extrapolate these forward in time or assess how certain external stimuli affects a certain time series variable.

There are three main types of modeling and forecasting methods:

- *Extrapolation*, which is the time series analysis we are focusing on in this chapter. This method simply uses historical data from which a model is built and then used to forecast/predict (that is, extrapolate) into the future.
- *Judgemental*, which is used in, for example, decision making and is common where judgment or beliefs (that is, probabilities) need to be incorporated. This can be the case when no historical time series data exists.
- *Econometric*, which is a regression-based method and usually tries to quantify how and to what extent certain variables/events affect the outcome of the time series. As the name suggests, this is sometimes used in economy studies.

There are other methods such as the *Naïve approach* (using the last historical value or values as the forecast); however, we are going to focus on the method most useful for time series analysis in general—the extrapolation method. Most industries use time series analysis at some point in their workflow. Two obvious examples are as follows:

- **Retail**: How much of a certain product should be kept in stock and how much will be sold?
- **Finance**: Managing assets, given the stock data of the previous months, will the stock go up or down tomorrow?

> The important thing here is that we are trying to model variations that in part are random, thus some things are impossible to model. Where the time series is fully randomized, the best forecast and model is just a mean and spread.

A time series dataset can be seen as a series of y values at a fixed interval in time, thus no x axis values are part of the data. This can be expressed as follows:

$$y_i = \{y_{i-1}, y_{i-2}, \dots, y_{N-1}, y_N\}$$

Here, each y in the set is just each value at a certain point in time. With these things covered, you are ready to learn about time series analysis in Python with Pandas and statsmodels.

As usual, open Jupyter, start a new notebook, and type in the default imports. I added a few imports as we will use them throughout the chapter. The extra imports, except the default ones (described in Chapter 1, *Tools of the Trade*) are as follows:

```
from pandas.io import data, wb
import scipy.stats as st
```

```
from statsmodels.tsa import stattools as stt
from statsmodels import tsa
import statsmodels.api as smapi
```

Here, just as mentioned before, you have to replace `pandas.io` with `pandas_datareader` if you have the Pandas version where it is split into a separate package. Furthermore, I will make use of the `despine()` function that we defined earlier, so make sure that you have it in a cell. As you can see, the main package that I will use is statsmodels; it has some nice functions to make time series analysis a bit easier. The statsmodels developers are working on upgrading the time series analysis to include more advanced functions, so keep an eye out for updates. To start off the analysis, I will read in the first data and go through some unique methods and characteristics that a Pandas time series object has.

Pandas and time series data

In Pandas, there is a certain data type for time series data. This is a normal Pandas DataFrame or Series where the index is a column of the `datetime` objects. It has to be this kind of object for Pandas to recognize it as dates and for it to understand what to do with the dates. To show you how it works, let us read in a time series dataset.

The first data that we are reading in is the mean measured daily temperature at Fisher River near Dallas, USA from 1st January, 1988 to 31st December, 1991. The data can be downloaded from DataMarket in several formats (`https://datamarket.com/data/set/235d/`), and it can also be acquired from `http://ftp.uni-bayreuth.de/math/statlib/datasets/hipel-mcleod`. Here, I have the data in CSV format. The data comes from the Time Series Data Library (`https://datamarket.com/data/list/?q=provider:tsdl`) and originated in Hipel and McLeod (1994).

The data has two columns: the first with the date and the second with the mean measured temperature on that day. To read in the dates, we need to give a date parsing function to the Pandas CSV data reader, which takes a date in string format and converts it to a `datetime` object, just as we discussed in previous chapters (for example, *Chapter 6, Bayesian Methods*). Opening the data file, you can see that the dates are formatted as year-month-day. Thus, we create a date parsing function for this:

```
dateparse = lambda d: pd.datetime.strptime(d, '%Y-%m-%d')
```

With this date parsing function, we can now read in the data as before:

```
temp = pd.read_csv('data/mean-daily-temperature-fisher-river.csv',
                   parse_dates=['Date'],
                   index_col='Date',
                   date_parser=dateparse)
```

As the columns in the file are named, that is, the first row of the data shows **Date** and **Temp**, we let the reader know that the index column-the column to take as the index-is the column with the **Date** name. We also tell it to parse this column with the date parsing function, which is also given by us. Looking at the first few entries, we can see that it is a full DataFrame object:

```
temp.head()
```

Date	Temp
1988-01-01	-23.0
1988-01-02	-20.5
1988-01-03	-22.0
1988-01-04	-30.5
1988-01-05	-31.0

To make our analysis easier and as we are working with a univariate dataset, we can extract only the Pandas series out of it. This is just the column in the DataFrame. With the following, we end up with a Series object:

```
temp = temp.iloc[:,0]
```

The Series object still has the dates as index; in fact, printing out the index attribute shows that we have indeed parsed the date as index:

```
temp.index
```

```
DatetimeIndex(['1988-01-01', '1988-01-02', '1988-01-03', '1988-01-04',
               '1988-01-05', '1988-01-06', '1988-01-07', '1988-01-08',
               '1988-01-09', '1988-01-10',
               ...
               '1991-12-22', '1991-12-23', '1991-12-24', '1991-12-25',
               '1991-12-26', '1991-12-27', '1991-12-28', '1991-12-29',
               '1991-12-30', '1991-12-31'],
              dtype='datetime64[ns]', name='Date', length=1461, freq=None)
```

The `dtype='datetime64[ns]'` value shows that we are storing the index as the date with a very high precision. As always, we first visualize the data to see what we are dealing with:

```
temp.plot(lw=1.5)
despine(plt.gca())
plt.gcf().autofmt_xdate()
plt.ylabel('Temperature');
```

As always, these lines simply call the Pandas Series method plot, change the line width (`lw`), then get the current axis (`plt.gca()`), which is sent to the `despine()` function, and then set the *y* label:

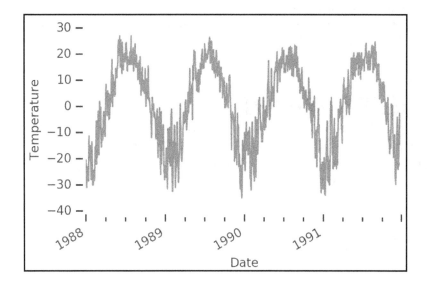

As you can see, there is a strong pattern in the data. As it is repeated in each year, it is a special type of cyclical pattern, a seasonal pattern. To check some of the statistics, we call the `describe()` method of the Series object that we have:

```
temp.describe()
```

```
count      1461.000000
mean          0.803320
std          15.154634
min         -35.000000
25%         -11.250000
50%           2.000000
75%          14.500000
max          27.000000
Name: Temp, dtype: float64
```

In the printed statistics, we can see that the minimum temperature is **-35**, pretty cold. We also see that there are a lot of measurements, enough for us to work with, and in time series analysis it is very important to have enough data. When we do not have enough data, we have to employ more sophisticated models such as the judgmental models described in the introduction. We now have time series data to work with, and we will start off with looking at how to slice these objects in Pandas.

Indexing and slicing

Time series in Pandas can be indexed and sliced in many different ways, but it cannot be with integer indexes. Our index is dates, remember? Thus, to get all the data within the year 1988, we simply index with that year as a string. In the following code, we index it with the year 1988 and then plot the values:

```
temp['1988'].plot(lw=1.5)
despine(plt.gca())
plt.gcf().autofmt_xdate()
plt.minorticks_off()
plt.ylabel('Temperature');
```

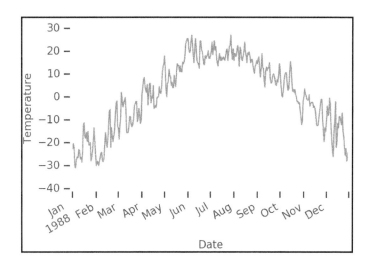

The plot shows how the temperature varied over the year 1988, going from almost -30 to roughly +25 and then back to below zero around late October. As you probably suspected, you can also index to a whole month, by just giving the year and month:

```
temp['1988-01'].plot(ls='dotted', marker='.')
despine(plt.gca())
plt.gcf().autofmt_xdate()
plt.ylabel('Temperature');
```

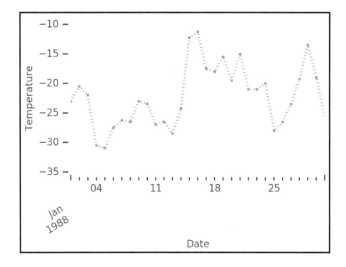

The variation within one month, here January, is quite large, around 20 degrees from minimum to maximum. You can also slice with two indexes, just like a normal array. Try making a plot for a few months by slicing, for example, `temp['1988-06': '1989-06']`.

Just as you can filter out certain values with a normal array, you can filter out certain values in a time series. To only get the values when the temperature was strictly below -25, you do like you always would—do a comparison that returns a Boolean array:

```
temp[temp < -25].head()
```

```
Date
1988-01-04     -30.50
1988-01-05     -31.00
1988-01-06     -27.50
1988-01-07     -26.25
1988-01-08     -26.50
Name: Temp, dtype: float64
```

To finish off this section, make a plot with each year plotted in the same figure as follows:

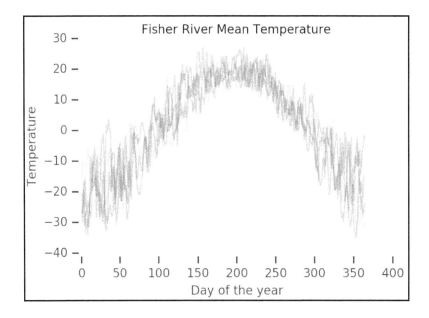

As could be strongly hinted at from the first plot of this data, it has a seasonal component, which is not at all surprising for such a dataset (outdoor temperature). However, try to make this plot yourself by slicing. Can you also add the months on the x axis? Perhaps try to make one for only one month but all years, say April or May. The next step that we will cover is how to manipulate and calculate various estimates on the time series.

Resampling, smoothing, and other estimates

Another useful method to visualize and make some of the initial analysis of the data is resampling, smoothing, and other rolling estimates. When resampling, a frequency keyword needs to be passed to the function. This is a combination of integers and letters, where the letters signify the type of the integer. To give you an idea, some of the frequency specifiers are as follows:

B, business, or D, calendar day

W, weekly

M, calendar month end or MS for start

Q, calendar quarter end or QS for start

A, calendar year end, or AS for start

H, hourly, T, minutely

Most of these can be modified by adding a `B` at the start of the specifier to change it to Business (month, quarter, year, and so on), and there are a few other keywords/descriptors that can be found in the Pandas documentation. Now let's try some of these out in the following examples. As this chapter contains several real-world data examples, which we use to highlight different things, feel free to play around with the data analysis. To resample the data by year, we simply pass an `A` to the `resample()` method:

```
temp.resample('A').head()
```

```
Date
1988-12-31    1.138661
1989-12-31   -0.006164
1990-12-31    0.815753
1991-12-31    1.264110
Freq: A-DEC, Name: Temp, dtype: float64
```

Here, the values are basically the mean of the year, with the label at the end of the year. Now let's make a plot with some of the resampling options to clearly show the variations that happen over these years.

 How the `resample()` method works might change a bit in upcoming releases of Pandas. If you are running a version higher than 0.17.1, you should consult the Pandas documentation for more information.

First off, we plot the raw data, then we plot the data resampled to weekly basis, and lastly to yearly basis. However, if we give the frequency descriptor `A` on a yearly basis, it will simply be at the end of the year. It would be nice to show the year-to-year variation where the point is centered not in the beginning of the year but in the middle of the year. To accomplish this, we use the `AS` descriptor, giving us the data resampled over a year with the labels at the start, and then add an offset of roughly half a year with the `loffset='178 D'` keyword:

```
temp.plot(lw=1.5, color='SkyBlue')
temp.resample('W').plot(lw=1, color='Green')
temp.resample('AS', loffset='178 D').plot(color='k')
plt.ylim(-50,30)
plt.ylabel('Temperature')
plt.title('Fisher River Mean Temperature')
plt.legend(['Raw', 'Binned Weekly', 'Binned Yearly'], loc=3)
despine(plt.gca());
```

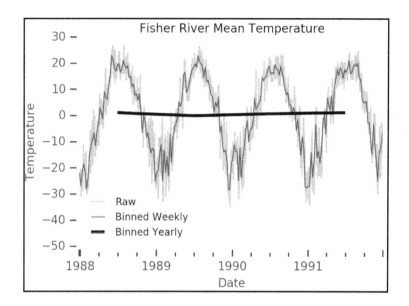

To make the legend more visible, I simply added some space with the `plt.ylim()` function. Now try to make a plot that looks like the following figure, with one month and six months resampling, plotted over the raw data:

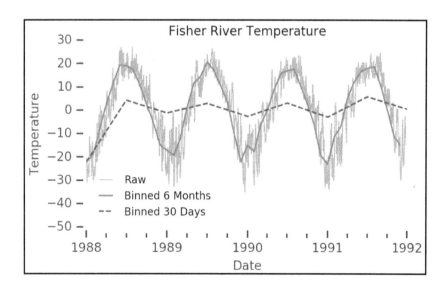

Sometimes we want to calculate a rolling value of something. While the resampling might look like a rolling mean, there is a specific function for it in Pandas. One of the things that we can do with this is combine the rolling mean over the time series and the minimum and maximum values in a region around it to highlight the variation to a nice figure. In the following figure, we plot the rolling mean in a window of 60, meaning that if the data is sampled in days, it will be 60 days. Furthermore, we have told the rolling mean to be centered in the window. To get the minimum and maximum from the raw data, we resample to months, take the minimum and maximum values, and fill the plot between them:

```
temp.plot(lw=1, alpha=0.5)
pd.rolling_mean(temp, center=True, window=60).plot(color='Green')
plt.fill_between(temp.resample('M', label='left',
                              loffset='15 D').index,
                 y1=temp.resample('M', how='max').values,
                 y2=temp.resample('M', how='min').values,
                 color='0.85')
plt.gcf().autofmt_xdate()
plt.ylabel('Temperature')
despine(plt.gca())
plt.title('Fisher River Temperature');
```

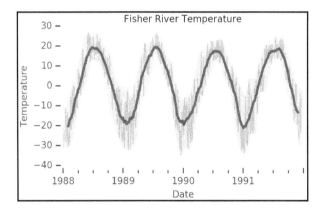

This already looks very good; the rolling mean reproduces the large-scale year-to-year variations of the temperature. While this is a kind of time series analysis and might be enough for first-order analysis and to get a handle of the data, we will look at some more complex methods to model variations. You can calculate other rolling values, such as the covariance:

```
pd.rolling_cov(temp, center=True, window=10).plot(color='Green')
despine(plt.gca());
```

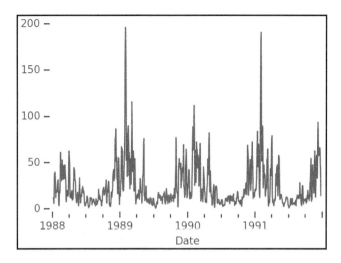

In this case, the covariance is in a window of 10 days and seems very high around the shift of the year. Another rolling value to calculate is the variance:

```
pd.rolling_var(temp, center=True, window=14).plot(color='Green')
despine(plt.gca());
```

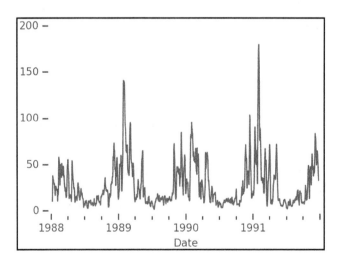

As we shall cover later on, analyzing the variance over time is very important for time series analysis. Try changing the window for both covariance and variance and see how they differ.

We calculated the rolling mean before and saw that it seems to follow the large-scale year-to-year variations of the data. Let's calculate the residuals to subtract this rolling mean from the raw data:

```
temp_residual = temp-pd.rolling_mean(temp, center=True, window=60)
```

Visualizing the residuals, we can see that there is still some periodicity in it. To analyze a time series, we need the data to contain as few of these large-scale patterns as possible:

```
temp_residual.plot(lw=1.5, color='Coral')
despine(plt.gca())
plt.gcf().autofmt_xdate()
plt.title('Residuals')
plt.ylabel('Temperature');
```

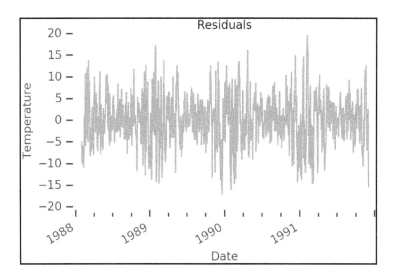

Time series analysis is mostly based on the fact that the current value might depend on only a few of the previous values and to a varying extent. So to analyze the data, we need to get rid of these. This naturally leads us to the next topic—stationarity. In the next section, we will discuss this, show you how to test if your data is stationary, and a couple of ways to make it stationary if it is not.

Stationarity

Most time series modeling depends on the data being stationary. The easiest definition of a stationary time series is that most of its statistical characteristics are all roughly constant over time. For statistical characteristics, the mean, variance, and autocorrelation are most commonly mentioned. For this to be true, we cannot have any trends, that is, data cannot increase monotonically over time. There cannot be long cycles of ups and downs either. If any of these things are true, the mean will change over time and the variance too. There are other more complex mathematical tests, such as the following (Augmented) Dickey-Fuller test. We focus on this test here as it is conveniently available in statsmodels.

The fact is that when doing time series analysis, we first need to make sure that the data is stationary. The easiest way to check whether your data is stationary in Python is to do an Augmented Dickey-Fuller test. This is a statistical test that estimates if your dataset is stationary. The statsmodels package has a function that tests this and sends back the diagnostics. The value of the test (we will call it the *ADF* value) needs to be compared to the critical values at 1, 5, and 10%. If the ADF value is below the critical value at 5% and the p-value (yes, the statistical p-value) is small, around less than 0.05, we can reject the null hypothesis that the data is not stationary at a 95% confidence level.

To make it easier to figure out if the results show whether the time series is stationary or not, let's write a small function that runs the function and summarizes the output:

```
def is_stationary(df, maxlag=15, autolag=None, regression='ct'):
    """Run the Augmented Dickey-Fuller test from Statsmodels
    and print output.
    """
    outpt = stt.adfuller(df,maxlag=maxlag, autolag=autolag,
                         regression=regression)
    print('adf\t\t {0:.3f}'.format(outpt[0]))
    print('p\t\t {0:.3g}'.format(outpt[1]))
    print('crit. val.\t 1%: {0:.3f}, \
        5%: {1:.3f}, 10%: {2:.3f}'.format(outpt[4]["1%"],
        outpt[4]["5%"], outpt[4]["10%"]))
    print('stationary?\t {0}'.format(['true', 'false']\
        [outpt[0]>outpt[4]['5%']]))
    return outpt
```

We are now ready to test the stationarity of a dataset, so let's read one in.

This dataset can be downloaded from DataMarket (https://datamarket.com/data/set /22n4/). The data comes from the Time Series Data Library (https://datamarket.com/d ata/list/?q=provider:tsdl) and originated in Abraham and Ledolter (1983). It shows the monthly car sales in Quebec from 1960 to 1968. As before, we use a date parser to get a Pandas time series DataFrame directly:

```
carsales = pd.read_csv('data/monthly-car-sales\
                       -in-quebec-1960.csv',
                       parse_dates=['Month'],
                       index_col='Month',
                       date_parser=lambda d: \
                       pd.datetime.strptime(d, '%Y-%m'))
```

To go over to a Pandas Series object instead of DataFrame, we do the same thing as before:

```
carsales = carsales.iloc[:,0]
```

Plotting the dataset shows some interesting things. The data has some strong seasonal trends, that is, cyclical patterns within each year. It also has a slow upward trend but more on that later:

```
plt.plot(carsales)
despine(plt.gca())
plt.gcf().autofmt_xdate()
plt.xlim('1960','1969')
plt.xlabel('Year')
plt.ylabel('Sales')
plt.title('Monthly Car Sales');
```

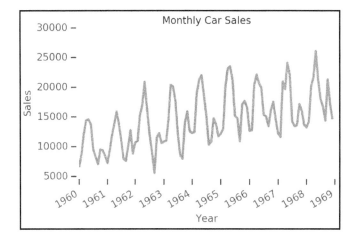

We can now run our small wrapper to test if it is stationary:

```
is_stationary(carsales);
```

```
adf            -1.673
p              0.763
crit. val.     1%: -4.060, 5%: -3.459, 10%: -3.155
stationary?    false
```

It is not! Well, this is not a huge surprise as it had all those patterns. This takes us to the next section, where we will look at various patterns and components that time series is made up of.

Patterns and components

In time series, there are mainly four different patterns or components:

- **Trend**: A slow but significant change of the values over time
- **Season**: A change that is cyclical and has a period of less than one year
- **Cycle**: A change that is cyclical and has a period of longer than one year
- **Random**: A component that is random; the best model for purely random data is the mean, given that it has a distribution corresponding to the normal distribution

Thus, before we can analyze our data, it needs to be stationary, and for it to be stationary, we need to take care of the patterns: trend, season, and cycle. The analysis that you will perform will be on part of the time series that does not fit into any of these patterns, with the random component being part of the uncertainty of the model.

Decomposing components

One method of taking care of the various components and making the time series stationary is decomposing. There are different ways of identifying the components; in statsmodels, there is a function to decompose all of them in one go. So let's import it and run our time series through it:

```
from statsmodels.tsa.seasonal import seasonal_decompose
carsales_decomp = seasonal_decompose(carsales, freq=12)
```

The function takes a frequency as input; this relates to the season so input the seasonal period that you think your data has. In this case, I took 12 as, by looking at the data, it seems like a yearly period. The returned object contains several attributes that are Pandas Series, so let's extract them from the returned object:

```
carsales_trend = carsales_decomp.trend
carsales_seasonal = carsales_decomp.seasonal
carsales_residual = carsales_decomp.resid
```

To visualize what these different components are now, we plot them in a figure:

```
def change_plot(ax):
    despine(ax)
    ax.locator_params(axis='y', nbins=5)
    plt.setp(ax.get_xticklabels(), rotation=90, ha='center')

plt.figure(figsize=(9,4.5))

plt.subplot(221)
plt.plot(carsales, color='Green')
change_plot(plt.gca())
plt.title('Sales', color='Green')
xl = plt.xlim()
yl = plt.ylim()

plt.subplot(222)
plt.plot(carsales.index,carsales_trend,
        color='Coral')
change_plot(plt.gca())
plt.title('Trend', color='Coral')
plt.gca().yaxis.tick_right()
plt.gca().yaxis.set_label_position("right")
plt.xlim(xl)
plt.ylim(yl)

plt.subplot(223)
plt.plot(carsales.index,carsales_seasonal,
```

```
            color='SteelBlue')
change_plot(plt.gca())
plt.gca().xaxis.tick_top()
plt.gca().xaxis.set_major_formatter(plt.NullFormatter())
plt.xlabel('Seasonality', color='SteelBlue', labelpad=-20)
plt.xlim(xl)
plt.ylim((-8000,8000))

plt.subplot(224)
plt.plot(carsales.index,carsales_residual,
            color='IndianRed')
change_plot(plt.gca())
plt.xlim(xl)
plt.gca().yaxis.tick_right()
plt.gca().yaxis.set_label_position("right")
plt.gca().xaxis.tick_top()
plt.gca().xaxis.set_major_formatter(plt.NullFormatter())
plt.ylim((-8000,8000))
plt.xlabel('Residuals', color='IndianRed', labelpad=-20)

plt.tight_layout()
plt.subplots_adjust(hspace=0.55)
```

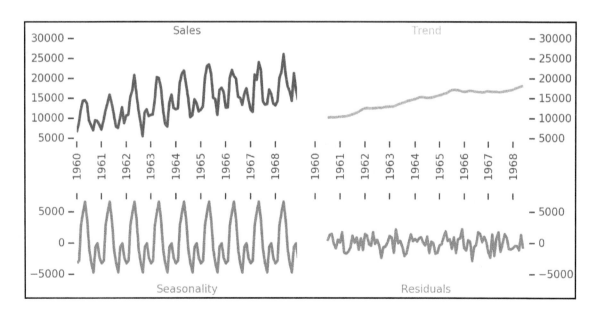

Here, we can see all the different components—the raw sales are shown on the upper left, while the general trend of the data is shown on the upper right. The identified seasonality is on the lower left and the residuals after breaking these two out is on the lower right. The seasonal component has multiple periodic peaks. This seasonal component is really interesting as it accounts for a majority of the annual variation in sales. Let's take a closer look at it by plotting the detrended data (that is, the trend subtracted off the raw sales figures) and seasonality changes (during one year):

```
fig = plt.figure(figsize=(7,1.5) )

ax1 = fig.add_axes([0.1,0.1,0.6,0.9])
ax1.plot(carsales-carsales_trend,
         color='Green', label='Detrended data')
ax1.plot(carsales_seasonal,
         color='Coral', label='Seasonal component')
kwrds=dict(lw=1.5, color='0.6', alpha=0.8)
d1 = pd.datetime(1960,9,1)
dd = pd.Timedelta('365 Days')
[ax1.axvline(d1+dd*i, dashes=(3,5),**kwrds) for i in range(9)]
d2 = pd.datetime(1960,5,1)
[ax1.axvline(d2+dd*i, dashes=(2,2),**kwrds) for i in range(9)]
ax1.set_ylim((-12000,10000))

ax1.locator_params(axis='y', nbins=4)
ax1.set_xlabel('Year')
ax1.set_title('Sales Seasonality')
ax1.set_ylabel('Sales')
ax1.legend(loc=0, ncol=2, frameon=True);

ax2 = fig.add_axes([0.8,0.1,0.4,0.9])
ax2.plot(carsales_seasonal['1960':'1960'],
         color='Coral', label='Seasonal component')
ax2.set_ylim((-12000,10000))
[ax2.axvline(d1+dd*i, dashes=(3,5),**kwrds) for i in range(1)]
d2 = pd.datetime(1960,5,1)
[ax2.axvline(d2+dd*i, dashes=(2,2),**kwrds) for i in range(1)]
despine([ax1, ax2])

import matplotlib.dates as mpldates
yrsfmt = mpldates.DateFormatter('%b')
ax2.xaxis.set_major_formatter(yrsfmt)
labels = ax2.get_xticklabels()
plt.setp(labels, rotation=90);
```

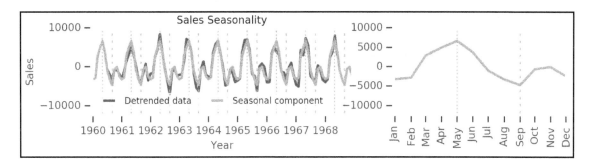

As you can see here, the seasonal component is really significant. While this is rather obvious for this dataset, it is a good start in time series analysis when you can break the data up into pieces like this, and it gives a wealth of insight into what is happening. Let's save this seasonal component for one year:

```
carsales_seasonal_component = carsales_seasonal['1960'].values
```

The residuals, which are left after subtracting the trend and seasonality, should now be stationary, right? They look like they are stationary. Let's check with our wrapper function. To do this, we first need to get rid of NaN values:

```
carsales_residual.dropna(inplace=True)
is_stationary(carsales_residual.dropna());
```

adf	-4.501
p	0.0015
crit. val.	1%: -4.072, 5%: -3.465, 10%: -3.159
stationary?	true

It is now stationary; this would mean that we can continue to analyze the time series and start modeling it. There are some possible bugs in the current version of statsmodels when trying to re-include the seasonal and trend components in the models of the residuals. Due to this, we have tried to do it in a different way.

Before we start making the time series models, I want to look a bit more at the residuals. We can use what we have learned in the first few chapters and check whether the residuals are normally distributed. First, we plot the histogram for the values and overplot a fitted Gaussian probability density distribution:

```
loc, shape = st.norm.fit(carsales_residual)
x=range(-3000,3000)
y = st.norm.pdf(x, loc, shape)
n, bins, patches = plt.hist(carsales_residual, bins=20, normed=True)
plt.plot(x,y, color='Coral')
despine(plt.gca())
plt.title('Residuals')
plt.xlabel('Value'); plt.ylabel('Counts');
```

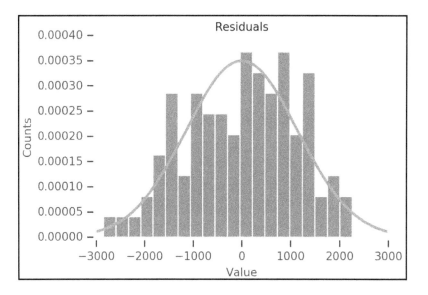

Another check that we used was the probability plot, so let's run it on this as well. However, instead of letting it plot the figure, as we did previously, we will do it ourselves. To do this, we catch the output of `probplot()` and do not give it any axes or plotting functions as input. After we get the variables, we just plot them and a line with the given coefficients:

```
(osm,osr), (slope, intercept, r) = st.probplot(carsales_residual,
                                        dist='norm', fit=True)
line_func = lambda x: slope*x + intercept
plt.plot(osm,osr,
         '.', label='Data', color='Coral')
plt.plot(osm, line_func(osm),
         color='SteelBlue',
```

```
        dashes=(20,5), label='Fit')
plt.xlabel('Quantiles'); plt.ylabel('Ordered Values')
despine(plt.gca())
plt.text(1, -14, 'R$^2$={0:.3f}'.format(r))
plt.title('Probability Plot')
plt.legend(loc='best', numpoints=4, handlelength=4);
```

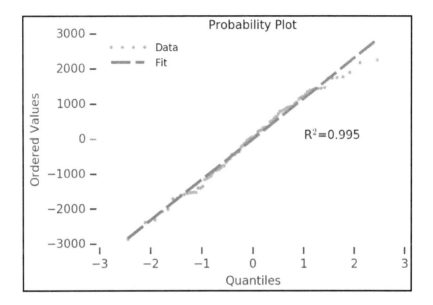

The residuals look like they are normally distributed—the high R^2 value also shows that it is statistically significant. Now that we have checked the residuals of the automatic decomposition, we can go over to the next method of making the data stationary.

Differencing

With differencing, we simply take the difference between two adjacent values. To do this, there is a convenient `diff()` method in Pandas. The following plot shows you the difference with the data shifted by one period:

```
carsales.diff(1).plot(label='1 period', title='Carsales')
plt.legend(loc='best')
despine(plt.gca())
```

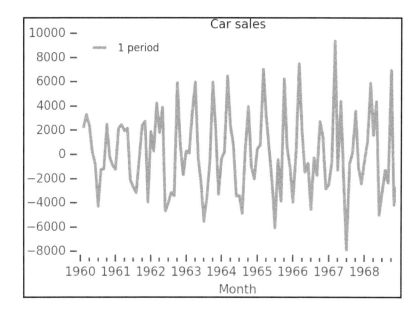

Remember that this is on the raw data—the data with the strong trend and seasonality. While the trend has disappeared, it seems that some of the seasonality is still there; however, let's check whether this is a stationary time series:

```
is_stationary(carsales.diff(1).dropna())
```

adf	-3.124
p	0.101
crit. val.	1%: -4.061, 5%: -3.459, 10%: -3.156
stationary?	false

No, the p-value is higher than 0.05 and the ADF value is higher than at least 5%, so we cannot reject the null hypothesis. Let's run `diff()` again, but with both `1` and `12` periods (that is, 12 months, one year):

```
carsales.diff(1).plot(label='1 period', title='Carsales',
                      dashes=(15,5))
carsales.diff(1).diff(12).plot(label='1 and 12 period(s)',
                               color='Coral')
plt.legend(loc='best')
despine(plt.gca())
plt.xlabel('Date')
```

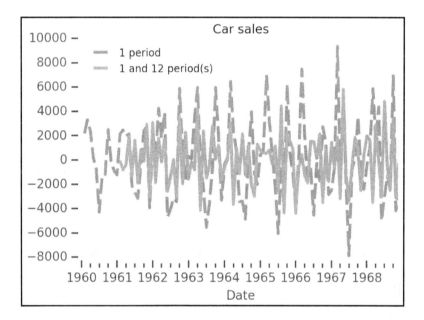

It is very hard to judge from this whether it is more or less stationary. We have to run the wrapper on the output to check:

```
is_stationary(carsales.diff(1).diff(12).dropna());
```

adf	-3.875
p	0.0131
crit. val.	1%: -4.077, 5%: -3.467, 10%: -3.160
stationary?	true

This is much better; we seem to have gotten rid of the seasonal and trend components.

I encourage you to use the first example dataset and check some of the things that we covered in this section. How do the various cyclic/seasonal components decompose? What values do you have to use for it to work? In the next section, we will go through some of the general models for time series and how they are used in statsmodels.

Time series models

Modeling time series can become very complex; here, we will go through some of the most employed models one by one and explain some of the ideas behind them. We will start with the autoregressive model, continue with the moving average model, and finish off with the combined autoregressive integrated moving average model. To start off this section, import the statsmodel time series model framework:

```
from statsmodels.tsa.arima_model import ARIMA
```

The `ARIMA` function takes a Pandas time series and model parameters as input and sends back a model object. To use a combination of the decomposition and differencing method in order to make the time series stationary, I first removed the seasonal component broken out by the statsmodels function and then took the first difference and checked whether it was stationary:

```
is_stationary((carsales-carsales_seasonal).diff(1).dropna());
```

```
adf              -3.611
p                0.0289
crit. val.       1%: -4.061, 5%: -3.459, 10%: -3.156
stationary?      true
```

It is stationary—the ADF value is lower than the 5% critical value and p-value is smaller than 0.05. I will save these steps in separate data structures to be used in the modeling:

```
ts = carsales-carsales_seasonal
tsdiff = ts.diff(1)
```

We are now ready to go through the various models.

Autoregressive – AR

For an autoregressive model, we use the values of a number of previous steps to model a value. The important parameter is how many previous steps to use for the model; here, this is parameter p. There are ways to estimate the p parameter beforehand, but sometimes a normal fitting routine of running models with different values and checking against available data is a good way to choose between parameters. The $AR(p)$ (AR of p) model can be expressed in a simple way as follows:

$$y_i = a_0 + \sum_{j=1}^{p} a_j y_{i-j} + \epsilon$$

Here, j runs from 1 to p. Note that it shows that the current value y_i is a function of p previous values and a random/uncertainty contribution, ϵ. That is, each value has a part that we can model and a random contribution that we want to minimize. Furthermore, it is important to notice the a parameter-these parameters/coefficients (sometimes also called weights) can be tweaked through fitting to make the model better at reproducing values. They basically control how much each of the previous values matter for the model. While the p parameter is important, it is also important to fit the model to the available historical data to tweak the parameters.

To run this model, we simply give the `order` variable as input to the ARIMA function. It should be a tuple with three values-the first value gives the p value, the second gives the middle value d for how many times to difference the data, and the third and last input is the q for the moving of the average model. To run an AR model with $p=1$ and $d=1$ and then fit it to the data, we simply run the following in a cell:

```
model = ARIMA(ts, order=(1, 1, 0))
arres = model.fit()
```

Now we have fitted the parameters that we showed in the preceding equation. To visualize the fit, there is a convenient function in the fit result object, `arres` in this case:

```
arres.plot_predict(start='1961-12-01', end='1970-01-01', alpha=0.10)
plt.legend(loc='upper left')
despine(plt.gca())
plt.xlabel('Year')
print(arres.aic, arres.bic)
```

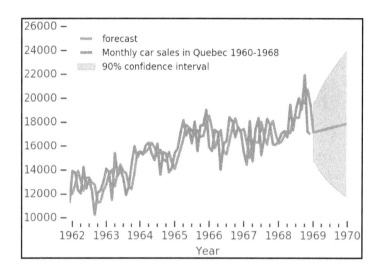

You can clearly see how the AR model kind of shifts the existing historical data when it forecasts them; the important thing is the prediction that goes beyond the sample. The 90% confidence interval is also plotted in the grey area; the prediction is mainly the first few values. After this, it converges to a constant trend. In the last line of the preceding code, I also print the **AIC** and **BIC** (`print(arres.aic, arres.bic)`), which is the **Akaike Information Criterion** and **Bayesian Information Criterion**. They are both used as an estimate of how good one model is with respect to another. The lower these values are in comparison to what another model has, the better the model (relatively). In this case, the printout is `1870.3331809826666` and `1878.35166749`.

While this model is not perfect, it gives you some estimate of the *future* sales. In the next section, we will create a moving average model.

Moving average – MA

In the moving average model, an average of the previous q values is calculated (called μ) and the random contribution is modeled in the same way as the autoregressive model, assuming that the current value is a function of the mean of q previous values and a small random variation modified with parameters/coefficients, here b. This can be expressed as follows:

$$y_i = \mu + \epsilon_i + \sum_{j=1}^{q} b_j \epsilon_{i-j}$$

Here, j runs from 1 to q and the average of the previous values can be expressed as follows:

$$\mu = \sum_{j=1}^{q} y_{i-j}$$

This model assumes in essence that the current value is modeled well by an average of the q previous values, thus it is called the moving average model.

Just like before, we initiate the model with the ARIMA function, but this time with different input so that we can use the MA model:

```
model = ARIMA(ts, order=(0, 1, 1))
mares = model.fit()
```

Plotting this and printing the AIC and BIC shows that it is actually a better model to predict future values:

```
mares.plot_predict(start='1961-12-01', end='1970-01-01', alpha=0.10)
plt.legend(loc='upper left')
despine(plt.gca())
plt.xlabel('Year')
print(mares.aic, mares.bic)
```

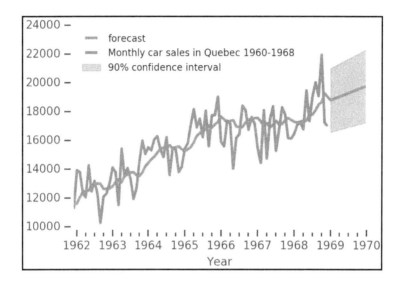

The AIC and BIC are `1853.0753124033156` and `1861.09379891`, which is slightly lower than the AR model. Judging by the look of it, this model is better at extrapolating the rough trend of the historical data into the future. In the next section, we will make a compound model of both AR and MA models. Before we do this, I will show you two ways of selecting the p and q parameters.

Selecting p and q

The p and q parameters of the AR and MA models should be selected based on how well the resulting model fits the historical data. The AIC or BIC should be compared between the results and the one with the lowest value should be chosen.

Automatic function

The statsmodels package of course has a convenience function for this. We will see how to run this on the data:

```
tsa.stattools.arma_order_select_ic(tsdiff.dropna(), max_ar=2, max_ma=2,
                                   ic='aic')
```

```
{'aic':                 0            1            2
   0   1893.258581   1853.075312   1853.070371
   1   1870.333181   1852.567740   1853.880900
   2   1866.617420   1853.644132                NaN, 'aic_min_order': (1, 1)}
```

The output that it prints shows that we should use AR(1) and MA(1) models, and as the input to this is `tsdiff`, *d* should be 1 as well.

The (Partial) AutoCorrelation Function

While the convenient automatic function does a good job, it runs the whole modeling for various parameter inputs. Another way of estimating *p* and *q* is plotting the **autocorrelation function** (**ACF**) and **partial autocorrelation function** (**PACF**). To do this, we first compute them:

```
acf = stt.acf(tsdiff.dropna(), nlags=10)
pacf = stt.pacf(tsdiff.dropna(), nlags=10)
```

After this, we can plot both and also the critical limits. The limits for the values should be 5% of the (partial) autocorrelation for a stationary time series, which is *1.96/(N-d)*, where *N* is the number of data points and *d* is the number of times you have differenced the data. Let's plot the ACF and PACF. In this figure, I also plotted the values suggested by the automatic routine, 1 and 1:

```
fig, (ax1, ax2) = plt.subplots(1,2, figsize=(8,2))
ax1.axhline(y=0,color='gray')
ax1.axhline(y=-1.96/ (len(ts)-1)**.5,
            linestyle='--',color='gray')
ax1.axhline(y=1.96/ (len(ts)-1) **.5,
            linestyle='--',color='gray')
ax1.axvline(x=1,ls=':',color='gray')
ax1.plot(acf)
ax1.set_title('ACF')

ax2.axhline(y=0,color='gray')
```

```
ax2.axhline(y=-1.96/ (len(ts)-1) **.5,
            linestyle='--',color='gray')
ax2.axhline(y=1.96/ (len(ts)-1) **.5,
            linestyle='--',color='gray')
ax2.axvline(x=1,ls=':',color='gray')
ax2.plot(pacf)
ax2.set_title('PACF')

despine([ax1,ax2])
```

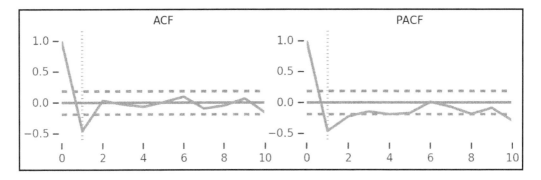

As you can see, both the curves cross the critical limit at p=1 and q=1. This is how you can also estimate the *p* and *q* parameters, by checking where they cross the critical value and stabilize within the limits. Now we are ready to run the compound model.

Autoregressive Integrated Moving Average – ARIMA

The last model that we will look at is the **autoregressive integrated moving average** (**ARIMA**) model. Just as the name suggests, it is a combination of both the previous models. It is run with the same function as before, but for the input tuple, we use all of them. To illustrate some of the functionality, I will run it with a different value of *d* than the preceding models:

```
model = ARIMA(ts, order=(1, 0, 1))
arimares = model.fit()
```

The following figure shows you the prediction and estimate for the historical values:

```
arimares.plot_predict(start='1961-12-01', end='1970-01-01', alpha=0.10)
plt.legend(loc='upper left')
despine(plt.gca())
plt.xlabel('Year')
print(arimares.aic, arimares.bic)
```

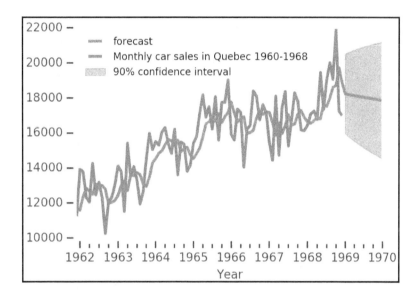

The AIC and BIC are `1880.0061559512924` and `1890.73468086`, which is slightly worse than the previous MA model. I suggest that you try to change the input *p*, *d*, and *q* parameters, perhaps to *(1,1,1)*. Play around with different values and difference the data one extra time to see what happens.

Summary

In this chapter, we looked at the many and interesting aspects of time series analysis in Python with Pandas and statsmodels, how they handle the data, and some of the basic manipulation functions that are available. We also looked at the concept of stationarity, how to test your time series for it, and how to transform a non-stationary series into a stationary one. You also found out the various patterns and components that time series can be built up by, and finally, we went through how to create ARIMA models and predict future values based on previous historical data.

This chapter concludes the book. We have covered many different analysis techniques and general statistical knowledge and how to use them in Python to your benefit. With the knowledge in this book, you can start exploring data, any kind of data. In addition to these chapters, there is an appendix. In `Appendix`, *More on Jupyter Notebook and matplotlib Styles*, I will look at Jupyter Notebook tips and extensions (plugins). I will also provide some links to further resources, including various data repositories for you to find data to download and create your own hypothesis to test.

As mentioned before, it is important to take the time to play around with data and try different algorithms and compare the results. I hope that you have also realized that much of the work in data analysis happens before actually applying the analysis method/algorithm to the data and making a figure with the results, and that making good figures that show all the results without getting bloated is very difficult. In general, with the analysis of real-world data, the process is difficult, and when done, you have to present it all in an easy way for everyone else to understand. With the content taught in this book, you should be able to produce a solid analysis of almost any data and appealing figures in your report that clearly highlight your results.

More on Jupyter Notebook and matplotlib Styles

In this appendix, we will cover several things that will help you when doing data analysis in Jupyter Notebook and compiling reports. This appendix covers the following topics:

- General Jupyter Notebook tips and tricks:

    - Useful keyboard shortcuts to speed up your workflow
    - A short introduction to the Markdown syntax to edit text cells
    - A few other useful tips

- Jupyter Notebook extensions
- **Matplotlib** styles for pretty plotting from the start
- Useful resources such as data repositories, Python packages, and similar

The various tips and tricks are not crucial for data analysis in Python, but it is very useful to make the workflow better and easier to pick up right where you left off in a project. Let's jump right in and start off by looking closer at some good things about Jupyter Notebook.

Jupyter Notebook

Jupyter Notebook is an interactive web application that sends/receives data from a programming language kernel. In this book, we have worked in Python; it is also possible to work in several other programming languages in Jupyter Notebook. The notebook format has support for what it calls checkpoints—when you save, it will create a checkpoint and you can always roll back to that previous checkpoint from **File** | **Revert to Checkpoint** in the menu.

One of the most important problems that Jupyter Notebook solves is that it provides a full record of your data analysis session; this record along with the data files is all that anyone needs to reproduce your analysis. The record may contain, except the code, (structured) text, images, videos, equations, and even interactive widgets. The notebook can be compiled into other formats that are easier to share, such as PDF and HTML. In addition to these things, it is possible to extend the functionality of Jupyter Notebook with extensions. After looking at some of the more useful keyboard shortcuts, we will go through a few of these extensions.

Useful keyboard shortcuts

First, I would like to go through a few of the most useful keyboard shortcuts. The general approach to keyboard shortcuts in Jupyter Notebook is very simple. It has *two* main modes: *command* and *edit* mode. As you might have suspected, edit mode is when you edit text in a cell and command mode is when you run commands in your notebook. The available keyboard shortcuts are of course reflected in what mode you are in. However, in both modes, *Shift + Enter* will run the current cell and *Ctrl + S* will save the notebook (and create a checkpoint).

Command mode shortcuts

Once in command mode, either by pressing *Ctrl + M* or *Esc*, the following keyboard shortcuts are available:

- *B/A*: This creates a new cell, *B* below or *A* above the current cell.
- *X/C/V*: This cuts, copies, and pastes the cell, just like you are used to in other programs. Pasting the cell here will paste it below the current cell.
- *D, D*: This deletes a cell.
- *Z*: This undoes the deletion.
- *L*: This shows line numbers. This is especially useful when getting error messages with a reference to a line number in your code where it breaks.
- *M*: This converts the current cell to a Markdown cell.
- *Shift + M*: This merges the current cell with the cell below.
- *O*: This toggles to show/hide the output shown directly below the cell.
- *H*: This shows all the keyboard shortcuts.
- *Enter*: This enters edit mode of the selected cell.

Edit mode shortcuts

When you are in edit mode, by pressing *Enter* while selecting the cell you want to edit, you can do the following actions:

- *Tab*: Indent, or tab completion; that is, start typing a command, tab will list available commands/methods/objects/variables to complete with that are present in the name space.
- *Ctrl + Shift + –*: This splits a cell at the current line
- *Ctrl + A*: This selects all content in a cell
- *Ctrl + Z*: This is for undo
- *Ctrl + Shift + Z*: This is for redo
- *Esc*: This enters command mode

As mentioned, these are some of the keyboard shortcuts available. These are the ones that are the most useful in my opinion. If you want to look at *all* of them, enter command mode and press *H*.

Markdown cells

In a Markdown cell that is created by selecting an existing cell and pressing *M*, you can perform the following functions:

- Create headings by preceding the text by a hash and space, "# ".
- Type normal text, just like in any text editor. You can style the text as follows:

  - *Italics* by surrounding the text with stars, that is, *text*
  - **Bold** by surrounding the text with two stars, that is, **text**

- Make bullet lists by preceding each bullet item with a star, as follows:

```
*  Item1
*  Item 2
   *  Sub-item1
```

- Include a URL by typing [your link text](http://your-url.com).
- Include an image with ![image text](url_or_path_to_image.png).
- Make a numbered list by preceding each item in the list with a number.

If you convert a cell to Markdown text, but want to convert it back to a code cell, you simply press *Ctrl* + *M* or *Esc* to enter command mode and then *Y* to convert the selected cell.

Markdown syntax is very extensive and Jupyter Notebook follows much of the same syntax as that used at GitHub; thus, for more information on what can be done, see `https://help.github.com/articles/basic-writing-and-formatting-syntax/`. Some of the possibilities are also shown in the accompanying notebook of this appendix.

Notebook Python extensions

Jupyter's functionality can be extended with extensions. Some of the extensions rely only on Jupyter, while others rely on external libraries and software. A few of them are inspired by plugins or functions of the CodeMirror online JavaScript editor (`https://codemirror.net`). A collection of Python-specific extensions can be installed from the IPython-contrib repository on GitHub. The URL for the collection is `https://github.com/ipython-contrib/IPython-notebook-extensions`. In this appendix, we will cover some of these extensions.

Installing the extensions

To install the collection of extensions along with the extension manager from the Anaconda repository, follow these steps:

1. Start an Anaconda command prompt and run the following:

    ```
    conda install -c https://conda.binstar.org/juhasch nbextensions
    ```

2. To activate some of the extensions that we want to use, start Jupyter Notebook.
3. Open a new browser tab and go to `http://localhost:8888/nbextensions` (where `8888` is the port that Jupyter listens to).
4. The page that you are presented with should look something like the following screenshot. The page is basically a list of the available extensions with checkboxes to activate them. If you click on the name of an extension, the page will load details about that extension:

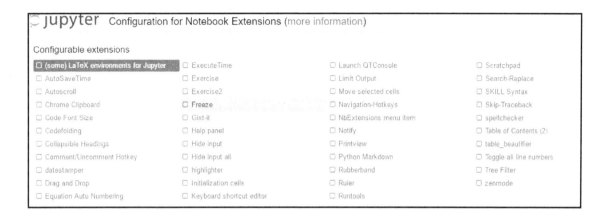

5. Now, by clicking on the checkbox next to the names, activate the following extensions that we will go through (alphabetical order):

- **Codefolding**
- **Collapsible Headings**
- **Help panel**
- **Initialization cells**
- **NbExtensions menu item**
- **Ruler**
- **Skip-Traceback**
- **Table of Contents (2)**

When you have done these things, each extension will have the checkbox next to it marked, as shown in the following screenshot:

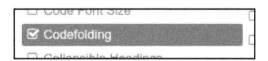

 To install the latest version from GitHub instead of that in the Anaconda repository (that is, the previous step 2), you can run the following:
pip install https://github.com/ipython-contrib/ IPython-notebook-extensions/archive/master.zip --user

In my experience, the click response is a bit buggy, so make sure that they are all marked. After selecting all the specified extensions to be activated, you can also configure some of them. We will look at each of them separately, but the general layout revealed by clicking on the name of each extension is as follows:

- The name of the extension
- A short description
- Which versions of Jupyter Notebook it is compatible with
- An activation/deactivation button
- An image to the right, showing roughly what it does
- Possible parameters/settings for the extension

After this, the interface will grab and output the readme file, which is in Markdown syntax. In this file, the author of the extension puts any additional information that might be useful. In the coming sections, we will go through the extensions one by one.

Codefolding

The codefolding extension is a simple yet very useful extension. It will fold the indented lines of code, for example, functions or classes can be folded. Furthermore, it will also give you the option of folding at comments. The top of the information pane for this extension is shown here:

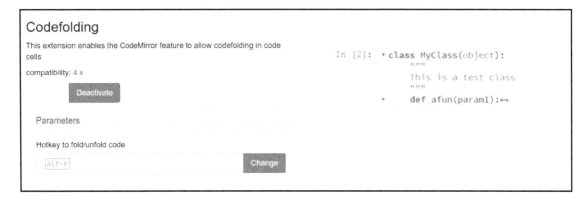

As an example of what you see in the readme file, I'll show you the top of the codefolding extension readme that Jupyter Notebook outputs here:

/nbextensions/usability/codefolding/readme.md?v=20160501205159

This extension adds codefolding functionality from CodeMirror to a codecell.

After clicking on the gutter (left margin of codecell) or typing `Alt+F` , the code gets folded. See the examples below. The folding status is saved in the cell metadata of the notebook, so reloading of a notebook will restore the folding view.

Supported modes

Three different folding modes are supported:

The readme is simply a more extensive description with figures and external links. With the codefolding extension, it is possible to hide long code snippets and functions within a cell. This is shown in the following example. The first image shows an arbitrary function in the way it looks in Jupyter Notebook:

```
def function_one(p1,p2):
    sel = [p1, p2][np.random.randint(2)]
    return sel
```

Clicking on the small arrow in the left margin will collapse the code into one line. It will then look like this:

```
def function_one(p1,p2):↔
```

As you can see in the first image of this section showing the parameters for this extension, the keyboard shortcut *Alt* + *F* will toggle the folding. Folding will also work on nested functions and statements; for each indentation level, you can fold the code. You can collapse code cells with comments as the first line as well:

```
# it is possible to use comments
# to hide code as well
function_one(10,30)
```

Once again by clicking on the arrow, you will collapse the rest of the code in the whole cell below it:

```
▸ # it is possible to use comments ↔
```

This is a very useful extension when you tend to write long functions or code, perhaps a plot with many different components, or if you have help functions written in the notebook.

Collapsible headings

With the collapsible heading extension, it is possible to group whole sections of cells by creating Markdown cells and defining headings. Normally, this would only display the text as a heading. The extension makes the heading and all cells below it collapsible—it will collapse everything below it until a heading of equal or greater level is encountered. The available parameters in the settings page are shown here:

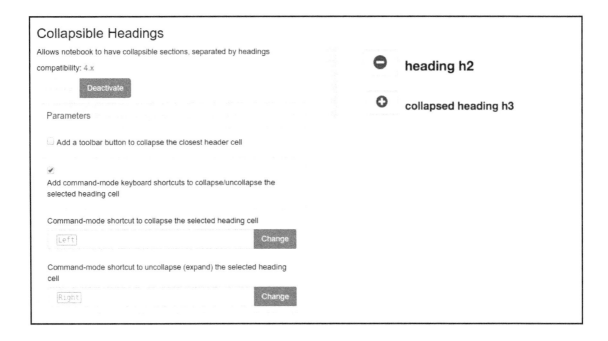

You can set the keyboard shortcuts to (un)collapse a selected heading, add a toolbar button, and toggle the use of keyboard shortcuts. An example of what the results of using the extension are shown here:

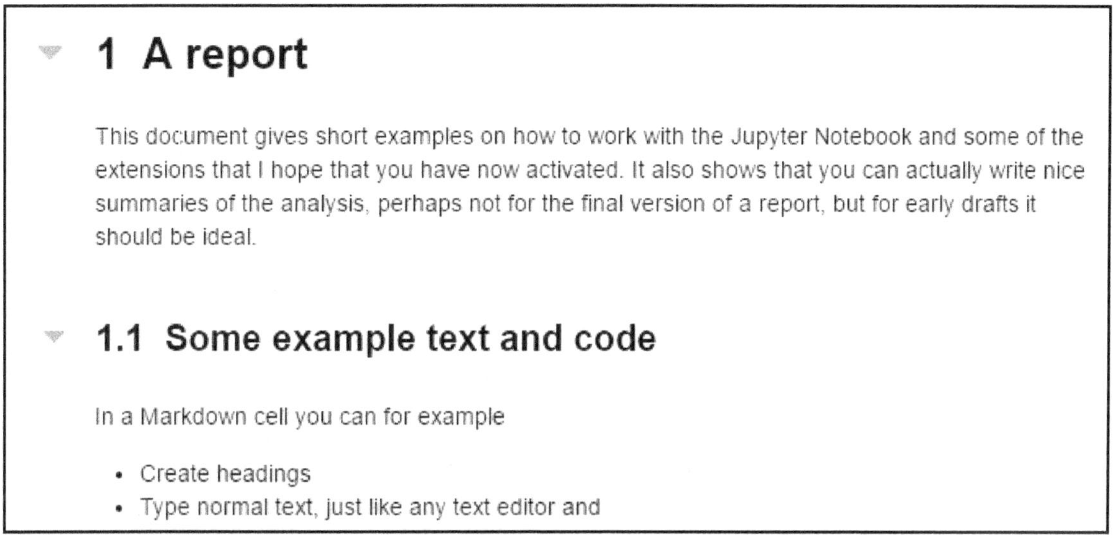

▼ **1 A report**

> This document gives short examples on how to work with the Jupyter Notebook and some of the
> extensions that I hope that you have now activated. It also shows that you can actually write nice
> summaries of the analysis, perhaps not for the final version of a report, but for early drafts it
> should be ideal.

▼ **1.1 Some example text and code**

> In a Markdown cell you can for example
>
> - Create headings
> - Type normal text, just like any text editor and

Clicking on the little arrow to the left of the heading will collapse the heading and everything below it under the same section. It will then look like the following image:

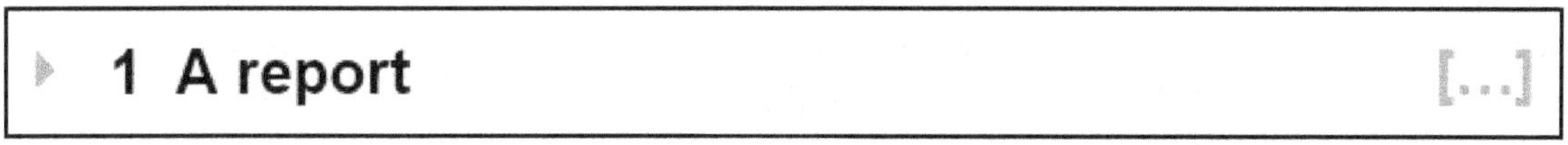

▷ **1 A report**   [...]

This is very helpful when you are doing multiple analyses of similar or the same data. Try opening up one of the chapters that we worked on in the book with the extension active, and you will see the usefulness of this.

Help panel

The help panel is useful when you start out writing your own code in Jupyter Notebook, as it has the possibility of displaying all the keyboard shortcuts in a panel alongside your notebook. The top of the details page for the extension looks as follows:

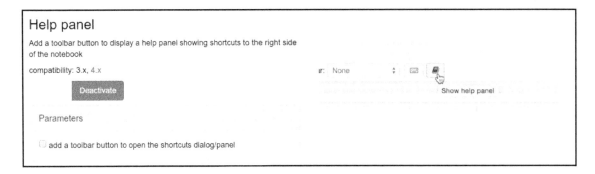

Here, you can check the box for **add a toolbar button to open the shortcuts dialog/panel**. Then you will have a button, as is shown to the right in the preceding image.

Initialization cells

Much of the code in the beginning of an analysis session is something that you want to run every time it is opened. The initialization cells extension alleviates this by adding two things—a cell toolbar that allows you to mark initialization cells and a button to rerun all these marked initialization cells. The following image shows the details page of the extension, and to the right is the button to trigger the rerunning of the initialization cells:

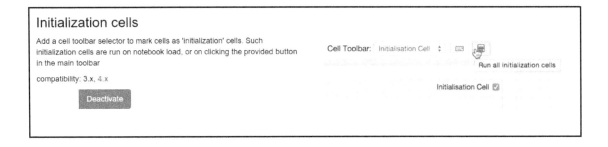

To use this extension, perform the following steps:

1. When activated, go and open a notebook and create the cells you want to have for starters. The accompanying example notebook has some initialization cells in it.
2. To change cells into initialization cells, you navigate to **View | Cell Toolbar | Initialization Cell**. When you have clicked this, each cell will get a toolbar (that is, cell toolbar) with a checkbox in the upper right corner, as shown in the following image:

3. Click on the checkbox for the cells that you want to run automatically when you open the notebook, for example, cells with imports, data reading, and data cleaning.
4. Now, close the notebook, open it again, and watch the checked cells run automatically. You can also trigger this by clicking on the button that looks like a calculator; see the first image of this section.

This extension is very useful because sometimes we have to restart our kernel or notebook and when this happens, it is not that much fun to have to rerun all the cells that simply import modules and load data.

NbExtensions menu item

The NbExtensions menu item extension is very simple; it adds a menu item to open the extensions settings page where you can activate/deactivate extensions. The menu item can be found under the **Edit** item. The following is a screenshot from the extension details page showing the menu item to the left:

Ruler

The ruler is a simple extension and is for aesthetics so that you know when to wrap your code for it to follow standards. The available parameters are the column width and the color of the ruler and its line style, as shown in the following image:

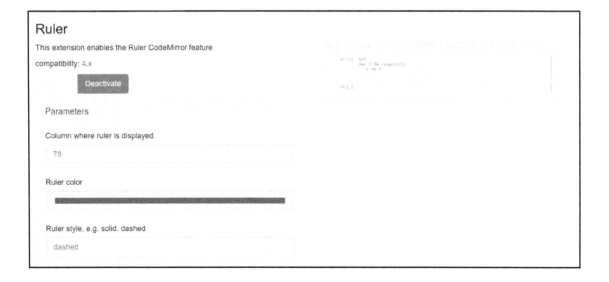

The extension will draw a vertical line in each cell at the column width given in the parameters. The following image shows what it looks like:

```
%matplotlib inline
import numpy as np
import pandas as pd
import matplotlib.pyplot as plt
```

Skip-traceback

Sometimes there is an exception raised in the code that you run in a cell. When the stack trace to the exception is long, Jupyter Notebook will still display the whole trace. It can be a bit tedious to scroll to the bottom of the cell output to get to what caused the exception. There are no parameters to set for this extension. To give you a good example of this, I found a filed bug in the current version of NumPy giving a long trace. You can read about the bug at https://github.com/numpy/numpy/issues/7547. To test the skip-traceback extension, follow these instructions:

1. After the standard imports (with the extension activated as we described before), run the following:

```
values = (1+np.array([0, 1.e-15]))*1.e27
plt.plot(values)
```

2. You should now see something like the following screenshot:

3. The trace is really long; you have to scroll through a long list of pointers and files. Now, click on the button on the toolbar that shows a triangle and an exclamation mark (see the preceding and following images); it toggles the hiding of the traceback.

4. Run the code again and you get the following:

```
In [34]:   values = (1+np.array([0, 1.e-15]))*1.e27
           plt.plot(values)

Out[34]:   [<matplotlib.lines.Line2D at 0x2910e536128>]

           Error in callback <function install_repl_displayhook.<locals>.post_execute at 0
           x00000291040B30D0> (for post_execute):

           AttributeError: 'float' object has no attribute 'rint'

           AttributeError: 'float' object has no attribute 'rint'

           <matplotlib.figure.Figure at 0x2910e405828>
```

This is much better and less confusing and shows why skipping traceback is very useful sometimes. There are of course situations when viewing the full trace is useful, for example, when you want to report a bug.

Table of contents

The collapsible headings extension is good when working with long notebooks with multiple sections. The table of contents is useful when navigating around in such notebooks. The plugin only has a few parameters. You can let it number sections, choose to what depth the table of contents go to, and toggle if it should show a floating window or a table at the top of the notebook. Some of these can be set in the floating window as well:

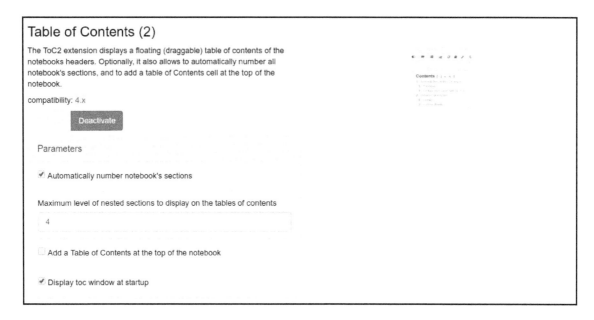

In the notebook, you can toggle the floating window with the table of contents by pressing the button. This is shown in the following image:

Once you have pressed the button, the floating window will appear to the right. For the example notebook of this appendix, it will look like the following:

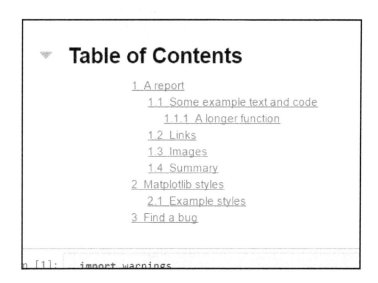

Here, you have four buttons next to **Contents**, except for the clickable headings of the table. Clicking on the headings will take you to that part of the notebook. The first button, **[-]**, will simply collapse the table of contents, and the button next to it will reload it; **n** will toggle the section numbering in the notebook; lastly, the **t** will toggle a table of contents at the top of the notebook in a separate cell. The output of clicking on the last button is shown here:

Other Jupyter Notebook tips

Here, I will give you some extra tips on using Jupyter Notebook. There are many things you can use it for and that is what makes it so good.

External connections

Starting Jupyter Notebook with the extra flag `-ip *`, or an actual IP instead of `*`, will allow external connections, that is, on the same network as your computer (or the Internet if you are connected directly). It will allow others to edit the notebook and actually run code on your computer, so be very careful with this. The full call would look as follows:

```
jupyter notebook -ip *
```

It can be useful in educational settings where you want people to be able to focus on coding and not installing things or if they do not have the right version of a certain package.

Export

All the notebooks can be exported to PDF, HTML, and other formats. To reach this, navigate to **File** | **Download as** in the menu. If you export in PDF, then you might want to put the following in a cell at the beginning of your notebook. It will try to make PDF versions of your figures first, which will be vector-based graphics and thus lossless when you resize them and eventually be of better quality when incorporated into the PDF:

```
ip = get_ipython()
ibe = ip.configurables[-1]
ibe.figure_formats = { 'pdf', 'png'}
print(ibe.figure_formats)
```

To export to PDF, you need other external software—a Latex distribution (`https://www.latex-project.org`) and Pandoc (`http://pandoc.org`). Once installed, you should be able to export your notebook to PDF; any Latex compilation errors should show up in the terminal that you started Jupyter Notebook from.

Additional file types

It is also possible to edit any other text file with Jupyter. In the Jupyter dashboard, that is, the main page that is opened when you start it, you can create new files that are not notebooks:

To give you an idea, I have included additional files in the appendix data files—one text file in Markdown format (ending with .md) and a file called `helpfunctions.py` with the `despine()` function that we created in previous chapters. In addition to these two, you also have the `mystyle.mplstyle` file to edit. In the editor, you can choose what format the file is in, and you will get highlighting for it.

Matplotlib styles

Throughout the book, we have worked with our custom style file, `mystyle.mplstyle`. As covered before, in matplotlib, there are numerous style files already included. To print out the styles available in your distribution, simply open a Jupyter Notebook and run the following:

```
import matplotlib.pyplot as plt
print(plt.style.available())
```

I am running matplotlib 1.5, and so I will get the following output:

```
['seaborn-deep', 'grayscale', 'dark_background', 'seaborn-whitegrid',
'seaborn-talk', 'seaborn-dark-palette', 'seaborn-colorblind', 'seaborn-
notebook', 'seaborn-dark', 'seaborn-paper', 'seaborn-muted', 'seaborn-
white', 'seaborn-ticks', 'bmh', 'fivethirtyeight', 'seaborn-pastel',
'ggplot', 'seaborn-poster', 'seaborn-bright', 'seaborn-darkgrid',
'classic']
```

To get an idea of how a few of these styles look like, let's create a test plot function:

```
def test_plot():
        x = np.arange(-10,10,1)
        p3 = np.poly1d([-5,2,3])
        p4 = np.poly1d([1,2,3,4])
        plt.figure(figsize=(7,6))
        plt.plot(x,p3(x)+300, label='x$^{-5}$+x$^2$+x$^3$+300')
        plt.plot(x,p4(x)-100, label='x+x$^2$+x$^3$+x$^4$-100')
        plt.plot(x,np.sin(x)+x**3+100, label='sin(x)+x$^{3}$+100')
        plt.plot(x,-50*x, label='-50x')
        plt.legend(loc=2)
        plt.ylabel('Arbitrary y-value')
        plt.title('Some polynomials and friends',
                fontsize='large')
        plt.margins(x=0.15, y=0.15)
        plt.tight_layout()
        return plt.gca()
```

It will plot a few different polynomials and a trigonometric function. With this, we can create plots with different styles applied and compare them directly. If you do not do anything special and just call it, that is, `test_plot()`, you will get something that looks like the following image:

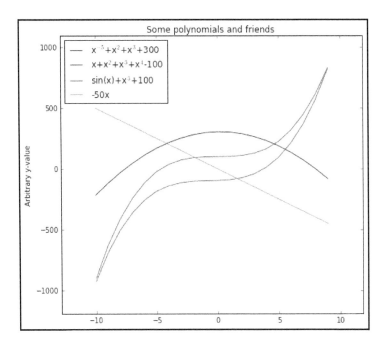

This is the default style in matplotlib 1.5; now we want to test some of the different styles from the preceding list. As the Jupyter Notebook *inline* graphics display uses the style parameters differently (that is, `rcParams`), we cannot reset the parameters that each style sets as we could if we were running a normal Python prompt. Thus, we cannot plot different styles in a row without keeping some parameters from the old style if they are not set in the new. What we can do is the following, where we call the plot function with the `'fivethirtyeight'` style set:

```
with plt.style.context('fivethirtyeight'):
    test_plot()
```

By putting in the `with` statement, we confine whatever we set in that statement, thus, not changing any of the overall parameters:

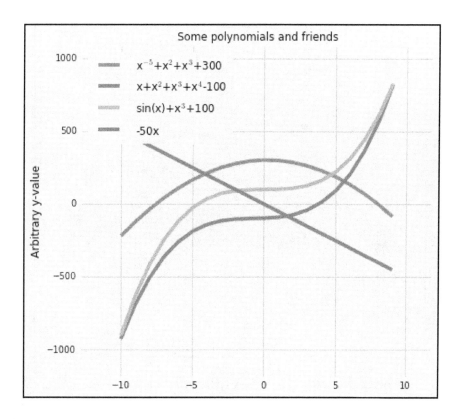

This is what the 'fivethirtyeight' style looks like, a gray background with thick colored lines. It is inspired by the statistics site, http://fivethirtyeight.com. To spare you a bunch of figures showcasing several different styles, I suggest you run some on your own. One interesting thing is the 'dark-background' style, which can be used if you, for example, usually run presentations with a dark background. I will quickly show you what the with statement lets us do as well. Take our mystyle.mplstyle file and plot it as follows:

```
import os
stylepath = os.path.join(os.getcwd(), 'mystyle.mplstyle')
with plt.style.context(stylepath):
    test_plot()
```

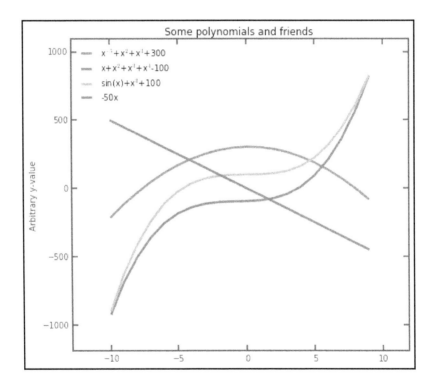

You might not always be completely satisfied with what the figure looks like—the fonts are too small and the big frame around the plot is unnecessary. To make some changes, we can still just call functions to fix things as usual within the with statement:

```
from helpfunctions import despine
plt.rcParams['font.size'] = 15
with plt.style.context(stylepath):
```

```
plt.rcParams['legend.fontsize'] ='Small'
ax = test_plot()
despine(ax)
ax.spines['right'].set_visible(False)
ax.spines['top'].set_visible(False)
ax.spines['left'].set_color('w')
ax.spines['bottom'].set_color('w')
plt.minorticks_on()
```

The output will be something as follows:

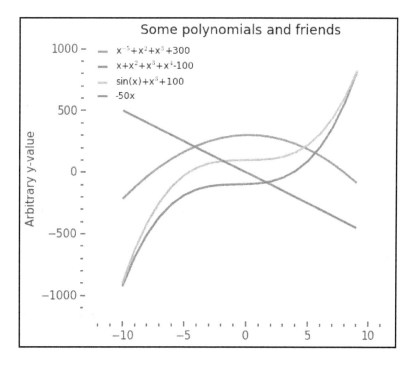

This looks much better and clearer. Could you incorporate some of these extra changes into the mystyle.mplstyle file directly? Try to do this—much of it is possible—and in the end, you have a nice style file that you can use.

One last important remark about style files. It is possible to chain several in a row. This means that you can create one style that changes the size of things (axis, lines, and so on) and another, the colors. In this way, you can adapt the one changing sizes if you are using the figure in a presentation or written report.

Useful resources

There are a vast number of resources on the topic of data analysis online, focused especially on Python. I have tried to compile a few here and hope that it will be of use to you. You will find a few sections under which I have listed resources, a short description, and a link where you can find more information.

General resources

General links to Python-related resources:

Continuum Analytics

`https://www.continuum.io`

Makers of Anaconda Python distribution. On their web page, you can find documentation and support.

Python and IPython

`https://python.org` and `http://ipython.org`

There's really no need for an explanation. We thank much in the world for these two projects.

Jupyter Notebook

`https://jupyter.org`

The Jupyter Notebook project web page where you can find more information, documentation, and help.

Python weekly newsletter

`http://www.pythonweekly.com`

A weekly (e-mail) newsletter to make it easier to keep up to date on what is going on in the world of Python.

Stack Overflow

`http://stackoverflow.com`

A question and answer page for basically everything. If you search online for any kind of Python programming problem, chances are high that you will land on one of their web pages. Register and ask or answer a question!

Enthought

https://www.enthought.com

Makers of Enthought Canopy that is, just like an Anaconda distribution, a full Python distribution. Enthought also has lots of courses and training for anyone interested.

PyPI

https://pypi.python.org/pypi

A repository of most Python packages and the first place that `pip` looks for packages.

Scipy-toolkits

https://www.scipy.org/scikits.html

The portal for the Scipy Toolkits (Scikits), affiliated packages for SciPy. The `scikit-learn` is a Scikit package.

GitHub

https://github.com

A repository for code that uses the famous Git versioning system to keep track of changes to the code. You can register and upload your own code for free as long as you make the code public. The code can be in Python or any other programming language.

Packages

This is a list of useful Python packages. Most of them can be installed via the `conda` or `pip` packaging systems.

PyMC

https://pymc-devs.github.io/pymc/

Alternatively, https://github.com/pymc-devs/pymc

A package for Bayesian inference/modeling analysis in Python; used in `Chapter 6`, *Bayesian Methods*, in this book.

emcee

`http://dan.iel.fm/emcee/`

An alternative to PyMC, an MCMC package for Bayesian inference.

scikit-learn

`http://scikit-learn.org`

A tool for machine learning data analysis with Python; used in `Chapter 7`, *Supervised and Unsupervised Learning*, of this book.

AstroML

`http://www.astroml.org/`

A package for machine learning, focusing on astronomical applications.

OpenAI Gym

`https://gym.openai.com/`

An open and publicly released toolkit to develop and test reinforcement learning algorithms.

Quandl

`https://www.quandl.com/`

A hub to access financial and economic data—they have a Python API that you can install and access large amounts of data with.

Seaborn

`https://stanford.edu/~mwaskom/software/seaborn/`

A package for statistical data visualization with Python. It has a few unique plotting functions that have not yet made it into the matplotlib package.

Data repositories

Here, I list some of the data repositories that are available online.

UCI Machine Learning Repository

http://archive.ics.uci.edu/ml

The University of California Irvine, Center for Machine Learning and Intelligent Systems repository of datasets, which is targeted at machine learning problems.

WHO – Global Health Observatory data repository

http://apps.who.int/gho/data/node.home

A large database of key health-related data from the whole world.

Eurostat

http://ec.europa.eu/eurostat

A database for various key statistics on all the countries in the European Union.

NTSB

http://www.ntsb.gov

The National Transportation Safety Board web page, which is a statistics database on automotive, rail, aviation, and marine accidents in USA.

OpenData by Socrata

https://opendata.socrata.com

A big database of various datasets (for example, airline accidents statistics for the whole world) that are easy to explore and find data.

General Social Survey (USA)

http://gss.norc.org

Yearly surveys in USA, with open and downloadable datasets and an online data exploration tool.

CDC

`http://www.cdc.gov/datastatistics/`

Centers for Disease Control and Prevention (CDC) have a lot of public data available on various diseases and health-related statistics.

Open Data Inception (+2500 sources)

`http://opendatainception.io`

A map showing the location and links to open data resources.

Data.gov.in

`https://data.gov.in`

The Indian government public data portal. It contains a rich and broad set of publicly available data to practice your data analysis skills.

Census.gov

`http://www.census.gov`

The United States census bureau has conducted surveys and collected data on various topics in USA.

Data.europa

`https://data.europa.eu/euodp`

The European Union Open Data Portal provides a single point of access to data from all the EU countries.

Visualization of data

The following is a list of some resources that are useful for visualization (overlapping here is Seaborn, which has been listed previously).

Fivethirtyeight

`http://fivethirtyeight.com/`

A great inspiration when it comes to the visualization of data. The site presents statistical analysis and presentation of data from around the world.

Plotly

https://plot.ly

Data analysis and visualization done online. Their tool for Python is now open source and free to use when self-hosted.

mpld3

http://mpld3.github.io/

Create interactive Python plots and export to the browser for others to explore.

Summary

In this appendix, we covered several things that are useful when doing data analysis and working in Jupyter Notebook. Hopefully, you will find great use of these resources and knowledge. There is so much data out there from so many different parts of the society just waiting to be analyzed. Given the increase in the amount of data that is produced and stored, we need more people who can analyze and present the data in an understandable way.

Index

exponential distribution 57

F

feature-rich emcee package
URL 141

G

General Social Survey (GSS)
about 20
data, downloading 20
data, obtaining 20
data, reading 21, 22
URL 265
GitHub
URL 263
gross domestic product (GDP)
about 91
versus absolute latitude 117, 119, 120, 121

H

Heliocentric distance 124
hierarchical cluster algorithm 133, 135, 136, 138
hierarchical clustering analysis
about 123
agglomerative clustering 123
data, reading in 123, 132
data, reducing 123, 128
divisive clustering 123
Hierarchical Data Format (HDF) 99
histogram 23, 26, 27

I

imports 10
indexing
and slicing 210, 212
intercept 72
International Organization for Standardization
(ISO) 82
IPython library
URL 8
IPython notebook 7
about 9

J

John Snow
on cholera 111, 112, 113, 114, 115
Jupyter library
URL 8
Jupyter Notebook
about 9, 239
command mode shortcuts 240
edit mode shortcuts 241
keyboard shortcuts 240
markdown cells 241
URL 262
Jupyter
URL 9

K

K-means clustering 117
K-Nearest Neighbor 201
Kernel Density Estimation (KDE) 29
keyboard shortcuts 240

L

Law Dome
URL 165
Least Absolute Shrinkage and Selection Operator
(LASSO) 177
libraries 8
linear analysis
Bayesian analysis and OLS, checking with 182,
183, 184
linear regression
about 71, 72, 73, 177
climate data 177, 179, 180, 182
dataset, getting 73, 74, 75, 76, 78, 80
testing with 81, 82, 83, 84, 86, 87, 89, 91
logistic regression 100, 103, 104

M

machine learning
supervised 175, 176
unsupervised 175, 176
Markov Chain Monte Carlo (MCMC) 141
matplotlib library
URL 8, 28

CPSIA information can be obtained
at www.ICGtesting.com
Printed in the USA
LVHW062343080919
630372LV00003B/33/P